PRESIDENCY IN THE UNITED STATES

PRESIDENTIAL LIBRARIES: ELEMENTS AND CONSIDERATIONS

PRESIDENCY IN THE UNITED STATES

Additional books in this series can be found on Nova's website
under the Series tab.

Additional E-books in this series can be found on Nova's website
under the E-books tab.

PRESIDENCY IN THE UNITED STATES

PRESIDENTIAL LIBRARIES: ELEMENTS AND CONSIDERATIONS

JAMIE D. REYNOLDS
EDITOR

Nova Science Publishers, Inc.
New York

Copyright ©2011 by Nova Science Publishers, Inc.

All rights reserved. No part of this book may be reproduced, stored in a retrieval system or transmitted in any form or by any means: electronic, electrostatic, magnetic, tape, mechanical photocopying, recording or otherwise without the written permission of the Publisher.

For permission to use material from this book please contact us:
Telephone 631-231-7269; Fax 631-231-8175
Web Site: http://www.novapublishers.com

NOTICE TO THE READER

The Publisher has taken reasonable care in the preparation of this book, but makes no expressed or implied warranty of any kind and assumes no responsibility for any errors or omissions. No liability is assumed for incidental or consequential damages in connection with or arising out of information contained in this book. The Publisher shall not be liable for any special, consequential, or exemplary damages resulting, in whole or in part, from the readers' use of, or reliance upon, this material. Any parts of this book based on government reports are so indicated and copyright is claimed for those parts to the extent applicable to compilations of such works.

Independent verification should be sought for any data, advice or recommendations contained in this book. In addition, no responsibility is assumed by the publisher for any injury and/or damage to persons or property arising from any methods, products, instructions, ideas or otherwise contained in this publication.

This publication is designed to provide accurate and authoritative information with regard to the subject matter covered herein. It is sold with the clear understanding that the Publisher is not engaged in rendering legal or any other professional services. If legal or any other expert assistance is required, the services of a competent person should be sought. FROM A DECLARATION OF PARTICIPANTS JOINTLY ADOPTED BY A COMMITTEE OF THE AMERICAN BAR ASSOCIATION AND A COMMITTEE OF PUBLISHERS.

Additional color graphics may be available in the e-book version of this book.

Library of Congress Cataloging-in-Publication Data

Presidential libraries : elements and considerations / editor, Jamie D. Reynolds.
     p. cm.
  Includes index.
  ISBN 978-1-61324-581-1 (hardcover)
  1. Presidential libraries--United States. I. Reynolds, Jamie D.
  CD3029.82.P74 2011
  973.09'9--dc22
                              2011014550

Published by Nova Science Publishers, Inc. † New York

CONTENTS

Preface		vii
Chapter 1	The Presidential Libraries Act and the Establishment of Presidential Libraries *Wendy R. Ginsberg and Erika K. Lunder*	1
Chapter 2	Fundraising for Presidential Libraries: Recent Legislative and Policy Issues for Congress *R. Sam Garrett*	27
Chapter 3	Presidential Libraries: The Federal System and Related Legislation *Wendy R. Ginsberg*	35
Chapter 4	Presidential Records: Issues for the 111th Congress *Wendy R. Ginsberg*	43
Chapter 5	Framework Governing Use of Presidential Library Facilities and Staff *United States Government Accountability Office*	51
Chapter 6	Report on Alternative Models for Presidential Libraries, Issued in Response to the Requirements of PL 110-404 *National Archives and Records Administration*	65
Chapter 7	Statement of Senator Lieberman on the Presidential Records Act	143
Chapter Sources		147
Index		149

PREFACE

Through the National Archives and Records Administration (NARA), the federal government currently operates and maintains 13 presidential libraries, and it may soon assume responsibility for a new facility for the records of former President George W. Bush. The libraries, which primarily serve as archival repositories and museums in which the records and memorabilia of the former Presidents are held and made available to researchers, are privately constructed on behalf of former Presidents. This book details the legislative history of the Presidential Libraries Act and provides information on existing library facilities and their locations, as well as analyzing legislative options for the act, including increasing endowment requirements for the library foundations and clearly delineating the relationship between NARA and the libraries' supporting organizations.

Chapter 1- The Presidential Libraries Act (P.L. 84-373; 69 Stat. 695), as originally enacted in 1955, sought to create a system of government "preservation and administration ... of papers and other historical materials of any President or former President of the United States." Pursuant to the law, the General Services Administration's (GSA's) Administrator could, among other actions, accept ... the papers and other historical materials of any President or former President of the United States, or of any other official or former official of the Government, and other papers relating to and contemporary with any President or former President of the United States. (P.L. 84-373)

Chapter 2- In recent Congresses, some Members have expressed concern about the lack of information surrounding private fundraising for presidential libraries. Those calling for additional regulation argue that more transparency could reduce potential conflicts of interest surrounding library contributions. Contributions from foreign sources have also been the subject of debate.

Federal law and regulation are largely silent on contributions to presidential libraries. Contributions to library fundraising organizations may be unlimited and can come from any otherwise lawful source. In addition, although certain aspects of library contributions are similar to campaign contributions, library contributions are not considered to be campaign contributions and are not subject to limits on amounts and funding sources specified in the Federal Election Campaign Act (FECA). In one of the few relatively recent regulatory changes affecting library contributions, the Honest Leadership and Open Government Act (HLOGA), enacted in the 110th Congress, requires registered lobbyists to report their contributions to presidential libraries. However, non-lobbyists are not required to report their library contributions. Library fundraising organizations must report certain information to the Internal Revenue Service, but those organizations are not required to publicize information about individual donors.

Chapter 3- Through the National Archives and Records Administration (NARA), the federal government currently manages and maintains 12 presidential libraries. Inaugurated with the Presidential Libraries Act of 1955, these entities are privately constructed on behalf of former Presidents and, upon completion, are deeded to the federal government. Deposited within these edifices are the official records and papers of the former President, as well as documentary materials of his family and, often, his political associates. These holdings are made available for public examination in accordance with prevailing law concerning custody, official secrecy, personal privacy, and other similar restrictions. This report provides a brief overview of the federal presidential libraries system, and discusses three pieces of related legislation introduced the 111th Congress (H.R. 35, H.R. 36, and H.R. 1387).

Chapter 4- Most records of recent former Presidents and former Vice Presidents are required by statute to be turned over to the National Archives and Records Administration at the end of each administration. These records are then disclosed to the public, unless the Archivist of the United States, the incumbent President, or the appropriate former President claims the records should be kept private.

On his first full day in office, President Barack Obama issued an executive order (E.O. 13489), rescinding E.O. 13233, changing substantially the presidential record preservation policies promulgated by the George W. Bush Administration. E.O. 13489 grants the incumbent President and the relevant former Presidents 30 days to review records prior to their being released to the public. Under the policies of the Bush Administration, the incumbent President, former Presidents, former Vice Presidents, and their designees were granted broad authority to deny access to presidential documents or to delay their release indefinitely. Moreover, former Presidents had 90 days to review whether requested documents should be released.

Chapter 5- The National Archives and Records Administration (NARA) operates presidential libraries for all of the former U.S. presidents since Herbert Hoover. These libraries received over 2.4 million visits in 2009, including researchers, public program attendees, and museum visitors. Each library is associated with a private foundation, which raised the funds to build the library and then turned the library facility over to the federal government. These foundations typically have ongoing relationships with the libraries they built, and some of these library–foundation relationships involve sharing of staff and facilities.

Per your request, this report describes the principal laws, regulations, and NARA policies that govern library–foundation relationships and the appropriate use of library facilities and staff.

GAO reviewed specific laws governing presidential libraries, and NARA regulations and policies. We also reviewed applicable laws and regulations governing activities held on government property and acceptable activities of federal employees. Further, we interviewed relevant NARA officials.

NARA reviewed a draft of this report and had no substantive comments. NARA made technical suggestions which we incorporated as appropriate. GAO is not making any recommendations in this report.

Chapter 6- In preparing this report, NARA explored a range of issues relating to Presidential Libraries. This report will provide an overview of the history of the Library system and the statutory and other legal frameworks which govern Presidential Library operations. This context will inform the discussion of proposed alternative models for a Presidential Library that might reduce the financial burden to the Government and improve preservation and public access to Presidential records. In addressing the requirements of the Act, it should be noted that there is a tension among the three charges. Alternative models for a Presidential Library that reduce the Government's financial burden may not necessarily result in better preservation or quicker public access to Presidential records. Likewise, improvements in both of these areas could result in increased costs to the Federal Government. The models proposed in the report have tried to consider and balance this tension.

Chapter 7- Mr. President, recently the Obama Administration asked the National Archives to speed up its already planned release of Supreme Court nominee Elena Kagan's records from her time in the Clinton Administration.

I applaud the Administration's openness. But this speedy release of documents is not required by the current Presidential Records Act and might have been impossible under an executive order issued by former President George W. Bush. That order allowed former presidents, vice presidents, and their heirs to withhold the release of documents indefinitely by claiming executive privilege.

On his first day in office, President Obama repealed the Bush executive order, but a future President could just as easily change it back or add new impediments to the timely release of an Administration's records.

In: Presidential Libraries: Elements and Considerations
Editor: Jamie D. Reynolds

ISBN: 978-1-61324-581-1
© 2011 Nova Science Publishers, Inc.

Chapter 1

THE PRESIDENTIAL LIBRARIES ACT AND THE ESTABLISHMENT OF PRESIDENTIAL LIBRARIES

Wendy R. Ginsberg and Erika K. Lunder

SUMMARY

The Presidential Libraries Act (P.L. 84-373; 69 Stat. 695), as originally enacted in 1955, sought to create a system of government "preservation and administration ... of papers and other historical materials of any President or former President of the United States." Pursuant to the law, the General Services Administration's (GSA's) Administrator could, among other actions,

> accept ... the papers and other historical materials of any President or former President of the United States, or of any other official or former official of the Government, and other papers relating to and contemporary with any President or former President of the United States. (P.L. 84-373)

Amid concerns about growing costs of the libraries, the act was substantially amended in 1986 (P.L. 99-323; 100 Stat. 495) to "shift the burden of on-going building operations costs of future libraries from the taxpayer to endowment funds."

Through the National Archives and Records Administration (NARA), the federal government currently operates and maintains 13 presidential libraries, and it may soon assume responsibility for a new facility for the records of former President George W. Bush. The libraries, which primarily serve as archival repositories and museums in which the records and memorabilia of the former Presidents are held and made available to researchers, are privately constructed on behalf of former Presidents. Upon completion, and with approval from both the Archivist of the United States and Congress, the land, buildings, and sometimes other amenities for the library may be deeded to or otherwise placed under the control of the federal government.

Among some concerns associated with the construction and maintenance of presidential libraries is the role of the private organizations that build and, sometimes, continue to inhabit the buildings. The private organizations, commonly referred to as presidential library foundations, support the construction of the libraries and sometimes provide funding for the exhibitions displayed within the library or its museum. Each library and foundation has a unique partnership. Such a relationship, however, may also lead to difficulties over which exhibits are displayed at the libraries as well as concerns over which spaces are publicly owned and which are privately owned.

Moreover, some presidential library scholars have raised concerns over whether library exhibits, which are often funded by the library foundations, present a balanced version of each President's administration or if they tend to portray the President in an inaccurate or, at least, more favorable, light.

This report details the legislative history of the Presidential Libraries Act. The report then provides information on existing library facilities and their locations. It also analyzes legislative options for the act, including increasing endowment requirements for the library foundations and clearly delineating the relationship between NARA and the libraries' supporting organizations. Congress, for example, might consider consolidating the libraries into one centralized location or could attempt to create standards for the historical exhibits at the libraries.

INTRODUCTION

The Presidential Libraries Act (P.L. 84-373; 69 Stat. 695),[1] as originally enacted in 1955, sought to create a system of government "preservation and administration ... of papers and other historical materials of any President or former President of the United States." Pursuant to the law, the General Services Administration's (GSA's) Administrator could, among other actions,

> accept ... the papers and other historical materials of any President or former President of the United States, or of any other official or former official of the Government, and other papers relating to and contemporary with any President or former President of the United States. (P.L. 84-373)

As the presidential library system continued to grow after the 1955 act, funding and construction issues became a policy concern. Amid the concerns about growing costs of the libraries, the act was substantially amended in 1986 (P.L. 99-323; 100 Stat. 495) to "shift the burden of on-going building operations costs of future libraries from the taxpayer to endowment funds."[2]

Today, presidential libraries are funded through a combination of congressional appropriations and private sources.[3] In general, funds for archiving and management of a President's papers are appropriated to the National Archives and Records Administration (NARA), while funds raised by private organizations support facility construction, programming, and other activities related to a President's legacy. Under the act, the Archivist of the United States has the authority to accept and take title to land, facilities, and equipment for a library—or to enter into an agreement with certain public or private entities to use their land, facilities, and equipment.[4] Prior to accepting title to the property or entering into the agreement, the Archivist must submit a report to Congress that includes, among other information, estimates of the costs and funding requirements of the proposed library. Congress then has 60 days of continuous session to disapprove of the acquisition or agreement. If Congress does not act, NARA may take title to the property or enter into the agreement for use of the property, so long as the statutorily required endowment for maintenance and similar costs contains sufficient funding.[5] Congress most recently updated funding requirements in 2008.

Through NARA, the federal government currently operates and maintains 13 presidential libraries, and may soon assume responsibility for a new facility for the records of former President George W. Bush. Table 1 includes all of the current NARA presidential library facilities. The libraries, which primarily serve as archival depositories for presidential records and memorabilia, are privately constructed on behalf of former Presidents. Upon completion, the land, buildings, and sometimes other library amenities are deeded to or otherwise placed under the control of the federal government.

Table 1. Presidential Library Facilities and Locations

Facility Name	Location
Herbert Hoover Presidential Library and Museum	West Branch, Iowa
Franklin D. Roosevelt Presidential Library and Museum	Hyde Park, New York
Harry S. Truman Library and Museum	Independence, Missouri
Dwight D. Eisenhower Presidential Library and Museum	Abilene, Kansas
John F. Kennedy Presidential Library and Museum	Boston, Massachusetts
Lyndon Baines Johnson Library and Museum	Austin, Texas
Nixon Presidential Library and Museum	Yorba Linda, California
Gerald R. Ford Presidential Library and Museum	Ann Arbor, Michigan
Jimmy Carter Library and Museum	Atlanta, Georgia
Ronald Reagan Presidential Library and Museum	Simi Valley, California
George Bush Presidential Library and Museum	College Station, Texas
William J. Clinton Presidential Library and Museum	Little Rock, Arkansas
George W. Bush Presidential Library[6]	Lewisville, Texas

Source: Hebert Hoover Presidential Library and Museum, http://www.hoover.archives.gov/; Franklin D. Roosevelt Presidential Library and Museum, http://www.fdrlibrary.marist.edu/; Harry S. Truman Library and Museum, http://www.trumanlibrary.org/; Dwight D. Eisenhower Presidential Library and Museum, http://www.eisenhower.archives.gov/; John F. Kennedy Presidential Library and Museum, http://www.jfklibrary.org/JFK+Library+and+Museum/General+Information/Visit+Directions+and+Public+Accessibility.htm; Lyndon Baines Johnson Library and Museum, http://www.lbjlibrary.org/; Nixon Presidential Library and Museum, http://www.nixonlibrary.gov/index.php; Gerald R. Ford Presidential Library and Museum, http://www.fordlibrarymuseum.gov/; Jimmy Carter Library and Museum, http://www.jimmycarterlibrary.gov/; Ronald Reagan Presidential Library and Museum, http://www.reagan.utexas.edu/; George Bush Presidential Library and Museum, http://bushlibrary.tamu.edu/; William J. Clinton Presidential Library and Museum, http://www.clintonlibrary.gov/; and George W. Bush Presidential Library, http://www.georgewbushlibrary.gov/.

Among some concerns associated with the construction and maintenance of presidential libraries is the role of the private organizations that build and, sometimes, continue to inhabit the library buildings. The private organizations, commonly referred to as presidential library foundations, support the construction of the libraries and sometimes the exhibitions displayed within the library or its museum. This close association with the library may create an amicable public- private partnership at library facilities. Such a relationship, however, may also render unclear which portions of the library and its exhibitions are funded by government appropriations and which portions are not.

Moreover, some presidential library scholars have raised concerns over whether library exhibits present a balanced version of each President's administration or if they tend to portray the President in an inaccurate or, at least, more favorable, light. The concerns of these scholars have grown as presidential libraries began to share their materials with K- 12 schools as educational programming.[7]

Although there have not been recent modifications to the Presidential Libraries Act, there is legislation pending in the 111th Congress that seeks to make library foundation fundraising more transparent. For example, H.R. 36 would require library fundraising organizations to file quarterly reports itemizing contributions totaling at least $200.[8] Under the bill, the reports would be filed with NARA, the House Committee on Oversight and Government Reform, and the Senate Committee on Homeland Security and Governmental Affairs.[9] The House passed the Presidential Library Donation Act of 2009 (H.R. 36) on January 7, 2009. On January 8, 2009, H.R. 36 was referred to the Senate Committee on Homeland Security and Governmental Affairs. No further action has been taken on this bill. The bill is substantially similar to H.R. 1254, which was passed by the House during the 110th Congress. The Senate Committee on Homeland Security and Governmental Affairs reported an amended version of H.R. 1254, but the measure did not receive floor consideration.

This report details the legislative history of the Presidential Libraries Act. It then provides information on existing library facilities and their locations. The report also discusses the private organizations that financially support their construction and, sometimes, their exhibitions. It then analyzes legislative options for the act, including changing endowment requirements; creating a single, centralized presidential library; or more clearly identifying the role of the libraries' supporting foundations. This report does not address the laws governing the collection, processing, and archiving of presidential records.[10]

LIBRARY FACILITIES AND LOCATION

Although there are 13 distinct presidential libraries, some traditions and patterns have emerged in their location and operation. For example, the first four presidential libraries— Roosevelt, Truman, Hoover, and Eisenhower—established two patterns: the facilities were located at what was considered to be the particular former President's hometown (birthplace or principal residence) and the libraries' buildings, grounds, and holdings were deeded to the federal government.

Change in this practice first occurred with the Lyndon Baines Johnson Presidential Library, which was located on the campus of the University of Texas at Austin. The university could not legally deed its land to the federal government, so another provision of the PLA was relied upon to effect federal supervision of the facility. Rather than taking title to the presidential archival facility, the Archivist of the United States relied upon his authority to

> make agreements, upon terms and conditions he considers proper, with a State, political subdivision, university, institution of higher learning, institute, or foundation to use as a Presidential archival depository land, buildings, and equipment of the State, subdivision, university or other organization, to be made available by it without transfer of title to the United States, and maintain, operate and protect the depository as a part of the national archives system.[11]

Pursuant to this authority, an agreement or memorandum of understanding was executed regarding the federal supervision of the Johnson Presidential Library. The Gerald R. Ford Presidential Library was similarly not deeded to the federal government because of its location on the Ann Arbor campus of the University of Michigan. A separate Ford museum is located in the former President's hometown of Grand Rapids, Michigan. The museum, which shares the same director as the Ford library, is part of the NARA presidential library system.

The John Fitzgerald Kennedy, Jimmy Carter, Ronald Reagan, and William J. Clinton presidential libraries, while deeded to the federal government—in part or in whole[12]—are located in major cities in close proximity to respective presidential hometowns. The George W. Bush library is currently under construction on the campus of Southern Methodist University, the alma mater of his wife, Laura Bush.

In addition to funding the 13 "official" presidential libraries, Congress has occasionally provided specific funding for private facilities honoring former presidents. These libraries, which hold the documents of former Presidents who served prior to Franklin D. Roosevelt, may receive a direct line item in the annual appropriations process. For example, Congress appropriated $1 million in 1996 for the Calvin Coolidge Memorial Foundation,[13] $500,000 in 1997 for the Rutherford B. Hayes home,[14] $3 million in 1999 for the Abraham Lincoln library,[15] and $365,000 in 2000 for the Ulysses S. Grant boyhood home.[16] Such funds have been used to support construction, maintenance, or other projects. Because they are not part of the federal library system, however, facilities such as these are beyond the scope of this report.

All of the presidential libraries have also adapted to the Internet. A large number of the records available at the various libraries around the nation are now available online or in other electronic formats. The presidential libraries and their support foundations use the Internet for more than just giving researchers access to records: many libraries now offer virtual tours of their facilities online.[17] Use of these electronic resources can make presidential records available to researchers anywhere in the country, rather than requiring researchers to visit the library facilities.

HISTORY OF THE PRESIDENTIAL LIBRARY

Starting with President George Washington and going through the first century and a half of the American republic, the papers of the President were regarded as personal property to be taken with a President when he left office.[18] In many cases, records were given to the Library of Congress for archiving, but the Library did not have the staff or funding to "service these collected papers adequately and make them easy for the general researcher to use."[19] In other cases, the records were "burned, lost, purloined or destroyed. Impecunious heirs sought to sell them to the [g]overnment, and in the course of some of these transactions, some parts of the collections were withheld or separated out and passed on to relatives or sold to collectors."[20] According to one scholar, the records of the Presidents are "a whole epoch of American history as seen from the office of the Chief Executive," that may include "letters and memos ... on which great decisions and official acts were based."[21] As scholars, the general public, and Presidents themselves began to understand the value of these records, interest grew in creating standards for their preservation.

Franklin D. Roosevelt

After Franklin D. Roosevelt established the Executive Office of the President (EOP) in 1939, the maintenance and archiving of presidential records became a more pertinent issue to him. President Roosevelt sought to return presidential papers to the public realm and create a "rich deposit of historical source materials for his particular era in American history"[22] through a new type of institution: the presidential library. When President Roosevelt advanced the concept of the presidential library in 1938,[23] two prototype libraries were already in existence—the Rutherford B. Hayes Memorial Library and the Hoover Institution on War, Revolution, and Peace.

In 1916, the state of Ohio completed the Hayes Memorial in Fremont, Ohio.[24] At that time, the library was maintained jointly by the state of Ohio and the Rutherford B. Hayes-Lucy Webb Hayes Foundation.[25] Today the repository, still run by Ohio and the foundation, is known as the Rutherford B. Hayes Library. In 1919, Herbert Hoover pledged $50,000 to Stanford University in Palo Alto, California, to establish an institution that would serve as a repository of records of both Hoover's military and political careers, and would later hold President Hoover's personal materials.[26] The record-keeping repository and research institution was completed for $600,000, and was named the Hoover Library on War, Revolution, and Peace.[27]

President Roosevelt built upon these two models and developed the concept of a privately built, publicly maintained presidential library. In December 1938, he organized an executive committee to create a presidential library for his records and recruited Waldo Gifford Leland, a distinguished historian and leader in the archiving field, to be chairman of the committee.[28] Prior to the committee's first meeting, Mr. Leland outlined a roster of issues that would need to be addressed, including the following:

- Determining the functions and responsibilities of the executive committee
- Outlining the relationship of the proposed archive to the federal government
- Investigating the possible creation of new legislation to authorize federal participation or acquisition of the project
- Determining the types of and quantities of materials that should be kept in the future repository

- Determining space requirements in both architectural and structural terms for the repository
- Calculating the cost of the building and its equipment[29]

At the initial organizational meeting on December 17, 1938, the seven-member committee determined its role should be strictly advisory, and should not involve raising funds for the construction or operation of the repository.[30] The members also concluded that "new legislation would have to be enacted ... to enable the [g]overnment to accept the gifts of collections, land, and building and to provide for their administration." The executive committee then decided to create a larger 30-member National Advisory Committee, consisting of historians and scholars to help determine what should be included in the repository.[31] In addition, the executive committee formalized the creation of a so-called Committee on Ways and Means—a group of 63 underwriters for the repository project. The Committee on Ways and Means made a collective guarantee of $450,000 for the project.[32] Finally, the executive committee created a corporation, the Franklin D. Roosevelt Library, Inc., which had the "power to solicit, accept, borrow, invest, and expend money, to transfer property to the United States provided that adequate legislation should have been enacted for the acceptance of such property and for its permanent care and maintenance."[33]

In 1939, Congress enacted chartering legislation for the Roosevelt library.[34] The Archivist of the United States, acting on behalf of the federal government, accepted the completed library edifice on July 4, 1940. The museum portion of the facility was opened to the public approximately a year later. Visitors to the museum were charged a quarter.[35] Library materials were available for research use by the public in the spring of 1946.

Harry S. Truman[36]

President Harry S. Truman also had concerns about the preservation of his records. In the aftermath of his 1948 election, Truman—following the Franklin D. Roosevelt Presidential Library model—oversaw the creation of a Missouri corporation in 1950 to collect donations and establish a presidential library on his behalf.[37] While the Truman Library Corporation was endeavoring to raise funding for the construction of the archival edifice, however, Congress enacted the Presidential Libraries Act of 1955.

LEGISLATIVE HISTORY OF THE PRESIDENTIAL LIBRARIES ACT

The Presidential Libraries Act (P.L. 84-373; 69 Stat. 695), as originally enacted in 1955, sought to create a system of government "preservation and administration ... of papers and other historical materials of any President or former President of the United States."[38] Amid concerns about growing costs of the libraries, the act was substantially amended in 1986 (P.L. 99-323; 100 Stat. 495) to "shift the burden of on-going building operations costs of future libraries from the taxpayer to endowment funds."[39]

These two laws, in addition to several other amendments, currently shape how and where presidential records are collected, preserved, and administered. The following sections of the report detail the legislative history of the PLA.

The Presidential Libraries Act of 1955

On June 2, 1955, Representative Edward Herbert Rees of Kansas introduced H.J. Res 330 "To provide for the acceptance and maintenance of Presidential libraries and for other purposes." On June 29, 1955, the House Committee on Government Operations favorably reported the bill with amendments.[40] According to the report, H.J. Res 330 sought to give the Administrator of the General Services Administration (GSA)[41] the authority to accept for preservation the "papers and materials" of a President or former President of the United States, as well as papers relating to and contemporary with any President or former President of the United States, and of any other official or former official of the United States."[42]

The committee report detailed the need for a presidential library system, saying that the lack of a systematic arrangement for such documents "has resulted in irreparable loss or dispersion of important bodies of Presidential documents during the 166 years of our Nation's existence."[43] In addition, the report said the new law

> would enable our Presidents and former Presidents to plan for the preservation of their papers at the place of their choice with the knowledge that the Government has made provisions to receive them in the archives of the Nation with adequate provisions for their preservation, with proper safeguards for their administration, and with restrictions on their use that recognize and protect the President's rights.[44]

The report also noted the bill's goal of "housing within one establishment ... all types of materials that help to explain the history of a President and his period." It also mentioned the bill's requirement to decentralize the collections, permitting each President or former President to decide where in the United States his records would be located, which the report said would be a "highly desirable objective at any time, particularly in this atomic age."[45]

On July 5, 1955, the bill passed the House. On July 7, 1955, the bill was referred to the Senate Committee on Government Operations. The committee favorably reported the bill on July 28, 1955.[46] On August 2, the Senate passed H.J. Res 330 with technical amendments. That same day, the House agreed to the Senate amendments. On August 12, 1955, President Dwight D. Eisenhower signed the Presidential Libraries Act (PLA) into law (P.L. 84-373).

Pursuant to the new statute, the GSA Administrator could

- accept the papers and other historical materials of any President or former President of the United States, or of any other official or former official of the government, and other papers relating to and contemporary with any President or former President of the United States;[47]
- accept and take title to, for and in the name of the United States, after a detailed report to Congress in each instance, land buildings, and equipment offered as a gift to the United States to be utilized as a presidential archival depository;

- enter into agreements, after a detailed report to Congress in each instance, with any state, political subdivision, university, institution of higher learning, institute, or foundation, to utilize as a presidential archival depository land, building, and equipment of any such state, subdivision, institution, or organization to be made available by it without transfer of title to the United States;[48]
- maintain, operate, and protect such presidential archival depositories as part of the national archives system; and
- accept gifts or bequests of money or other property for the purpose of maintaining, operating, protecting, or improving any presidential archival depository.[49]

The authorities granted to the GSA Administrator were subject to strict congressional approval and oversight. Prior to entering into any agreement to accept an archival depository for presidential materials, the administrator was required to write a report to Congress about the agreement that included cost estimates for "maintaining, operating, and protecting" the depository.[50] The descriptive report was also to include any terms or conditions placed on the materials to be deposited in the archive.[51]

Once the administrator submitted the report, he would have to wait for the expiration of "sixty calendar days of continuous session of the Congress" before he could accept the title of any land or depository. The 60 days of continuous session were to provide Congress with "an opportunity to review proposals ... and to take action within 60 days disapproving any such proposal."[52]

The enactment of the PLA did not eliminate continued disagreements between the executive and legislative branches over the size of, the costs associated with, and the records to be included in presidential records depositories.

The Case of the Herbert Hoover Presidential Library

The acquisition of the Herbert Hoover Presidential Library involved unique context. Herbert Hoover preceded Franklin D. Roosevelt as President. No law governing the future of Hoover's records or legacy, however, existed when Hoover left office. As noted earlier, however, in 1919, Hoover established the Hoover Library on War, Revolution, and Peace at Stanford University.[53] In 1960, former President Hoover took advantage of the Presidential Records Act and created the Herbert Hoover Presidential Library in West Branch, Iowa.

Interest in Revamping the PLA

In the 1980s, as the size and maintenance costs of presidential libraries increased, so, too, did congressional interest in finding non-federal funding sources that could supplement appropriated funds. According to a Senate report on the Presidential Libraries Act, the annual cost of maintaining the presidential library system had grown from $63,745 in 1955 to $15,734,000 in 1985.[54]

In the 96th and 97th Congresses, legislators introduced bills[55] that attempted to stop the construction of presidential libraries, and, instead, to create one, central location to serve as a depository for the records of all Presidents.

On March 24, 1981 (97th Congress), Senator Lawton Chiles introduced S. 1325, a bill that would have required the GSA Administrator and the Archivist of the United States to promulgate architecture and design standards for presidential archive depositories. These standards were to include limits on the size of a depository that was to be donated to the federal government. The Senate Committee on Governmental Affairs held a hearing and a markup on the bill. The bill, however, was not reported from committee. Senator Chiles introduced a bill identical to S. 1325 in the 98th Congress (S. 563). A companion bill (H.R. 5478) was introduced in the House on April 12, 1984. The Committee on Governmental Affairs favorably reported S. 563 on September 27, 1984. No further action was taken on S. 563. H.R. 5478 was not reported from committee.[56]

On April 24, 1984 (98th Congress), Senator David L. Boren introduced legislation (H.R. 2567) that sought to authorize the GSA Administrator to create separate accounts within the National Archives Trust Fund.[57] These new accounts could be used to pay exclusively for the "maintenance of depository land, buildings, and equipment." The bill would have allowed donors to the trust fund to limit the use of their donations for maintenance and utility costs. H.R. 2567 would have also prohibited the GSA Administrator from accepting any land or building donated as a presidential library unless the donation included an endowment large enough to cover maintenance and utility costs for the entity. The bill was not reported from committee.[58]

Although many bills related to presidential record depositories were introduced in the 98th Congress, only one was enacted: S. 905, the National Archives and Records Administration Act of 1984. On October 19, 1984, Congress enacted S. 905 (P.L. 98-497), which gave the Archivist of the United States many of the responsibilities formerly assigned to the GSA Administrator. Included in this transition of duties were those delineated in the Presidential Libraries Act.

The Presidential Libraries Act of 1986 and Changes to the Endowment Formula

Like the 98th Congress, the 99th Congress included the introduction of several bills related to presidential libraries. Only the Presidential Libraries Act of 1986 (P.L. 99-323) was enacted.[59] The Presidential Libraries Act of 1986 was prompted by congressional concerns about the escalating "taxpayer costs associated with Presidential libraries" as well as a desire to "strengthen the role to be played by the Archivist of the United States in preserving, protecting and sharing our nation's heritage."[60]

Introduced on February 28, 1985, by Representative Glenn English, the Presidential Libraries Act was favorably reported by the House Committee on Government Operations on May 15, 1985. In the House Report (H.Rept. 99-125), the committee wrote that the bill would "shift the burden of on-going building operations costs of future libraries from the taxpayer to endowment funds required to be provided by the same private parties who build and donate the library buildings."[61] The report continued:

> Without bowing to any illusions, the Committee hopes that this requirement will act as somewhat of a brake on grandiose plans which have caused some to refer to some existing Presidential libraries as "pyramids."[62]

The bill passed the House on June 6, 1985, and was then sent to the Senate Committee on Government Operations. The Senate committee reported the bill on March 7, 1986.

On March 21, 1986, the Senate passed the bill with one substantive amendment, which limited library facilities to 70,000 square feet "unless additional endowment requirements" were met.[63] On May 13, 1986, the House agreed to the Senate's amendments. On May 27, 1986, President Ronald Reagan signed the bill into law. The act applies to "any Presidential archival depository created as a depository for the papers, documents, and other historical materials and Federal records pertaining to any President who takes the oath of office as President for the first time on or after January 20, 1985."[64]

Among a variety of changes to the 1955 act, the 1986 amendments required that the Archivist could not accept and take title to, or enter into an agreement to use, any land, facility, or equipment for a library unless he or she determined the library's endowment is sufficient to cover at least 20% of the total costs of acquiring, constructing, and installing the facility and its equipment, plus either (1) 20% of the total costs of acquiring the land (or another measure of the land's value that is mutually agreed upon by the Archivist and donor) if the United States is taking title to the land, or (2) 20% of the total costs to the donor of any improvements to the land if the government is not taking title to it.[65] Similarly, the act required the endowment to have sufficient funding before changes or additions could be made to a library if they would result in increased operational costs. These requirements applied only to presidential depositories built for Presidents who took the oath of office for the first time after January 20, 1985.[66] Congress subsequently increased the 20% requirement to first 40% and then 60% for presidential depositories built for Presidents who take the oath of office for the first time after July 1, 2002, as discussed below.

In addition, the 1986 PLA also placed additional endowment requirements on facilities larger than 70,000 square feet.[67] Under the law, foundations may construct facilities larger than 70,000 square feet, but the endowment requirements for the library increases with each square foot the edifice is in excess of 70,000 square feet.[68] Specifically, the additional amount is equal to the total costs multiplied by the percentage determined by dividing the number of square feet that the library exceeds 70,000 by 70,000.[69]

It is important to note that foundations may maintain control of certain portions of the library for their own use, and therefore a foundation and NARA, in some cases, concurrently occupy office space in a single presidential archival depository. The endowment percentages have historically been applied only to the portions of the library that were "NARA program space or usable space and was not applied to support space," which excluded foundation-controlled space from the calculation.[70]

While pursuing avenues for private funds in some circumstances during consideration of the 1986 PLA, Congress also drew a distinction between how different funding sources reflect different responsibilities. Although appropriated funds would still be largely responsible for archiving of materials, endowment funds would be relied on to support operations, maintenance, and programming. As the House Committee on Government Operations noted in 1985 while considering the legislation, endowment income "is intended to offset ... building operations costs and reduce ... the amount of appropriations required for building operations."[71] The Senate Governmental Affairs Committee concurred, noting that "income from the endowments is to be applied to functions beyond the 'core' archival responsibilities [which would be covered by appropriated funds]. The basic responsibility to preserve and care for Presidential records is a government responsibility."

In addition, the law required the Archivist, the Secretary of the Smithsonian Institution, and the National Capital Planning Commission to study "the demand for, and the cost, and space and program requirements of" creating a museum of the Presidents.[72] Specifically, the ad hoc coalition was to examine ways to create a museum of the Presidents without using federal funds. The 1986 NARA annual report included the coalition's findings, which stated "there would be serious difficulties in establishing a full-scale museum with permanent collection for research and exhibition."[73] The report did find "[m]ore optimism ... for a modest exhibition program as part of a White House visitors center."[74] Unless a full museum were created, however, the report said it would not be appropriate for the Smithsonian Institution or the National Archives to "administer the center."[75] Such a museum has not been constructed.[76]

Subsequent Amendments to the Endowment Requirement

There have been two significant amendments to the endowment requirement since the 1986 act. First, in 2003, Congress increased the endowment funding requirement from 20% of the total costs to 40% of such costs for libraries of Presidents who take the oath of office after July 1, 2002.[77] The 2003 act also gives the Archivist the authority to reduce the endowment funding requirement if he or she determines that the proposed library will have construction features or equipment that are expected to result in quantifiable long-term savings in operational costs to the U.S. government. The funding reduction cannot exceed 20% of the amount that would have otherwise been required. A similar reduction may be provided for endowment funding required for changes or additions to an existing library.[78]

The second major amendment occurred in 2008, when Congress increased the 40% endowment threshold to 60%.[79] This requirement will apply to libraries for Presidents who take the oath of office after July 1, 2002. The 2008 act also required, among other things, the Archivist to report to Congress on alternative models for presidential libraries that would reduce costs to the government, improve record preservation, and reduce delays in public access to presidential records.[80] The report was produced in 2009.[81]

PRESIDENTIAL LIBRARY FOUNDATIONS

Private organizations typically raise funds to support facility construction, programming, and other activities related to a President's legacy. These entities are commonly referred to as presidential library foundations, and they play key roles in raising private funds to support the endowments necessary for NARA to take possession of a library facility.

The library foundations are separate legal entities from the libraries. It appears that all of the currently operating presidential library foundations are structured as tax-exempt public charities[82] described in § 501 (c)(3) of the Internal Revenue Code (IRC).[83] As such, they are subject to regulation under the federal tax laws. Among other things, § 501(c)(3) status requires that the earnings of library foundations not be used to benefit any person having a personal and private interest in the organizations' activities, and they are limited in the amount and types of political activities they may engage in.[84] Additionally, federal law may impose other requirements or restrictions on their activities. For example, the tax laws look disfavorably upon transactions of § 501(c)(3) organizations that provide an economic benefit to a disqualified person (e.g., certain organizational insiders or related individuals), and if such a transaction occurs, the disqualified person and organization managers may be subject to a penalty tax.[85]

Certain information about the library foundations' income and expenses is publicly available, although the identities of their donors generally do not have to be publicly disclosed. As § 501(c)(3) organizations, the library foundations are required to file with the IRS an annual information return (Form 990) that discloses information relating to the organizations' finances and operations. These returns are open to public inspection, along with the library foundations' application for exempt status and, if applicable, unrelated business income tax return.[86] However, while the organization must disclose donors who have contributed at least $5,000 during the year to the IRS,[87] no identifying information about these donors is subject to public disclosure.

While contributor information generally does not have to be disclosed, there are limited exceptions. In particular, under the Honest Leadership and Open Government Act of 2007 (HLOGA), registered lobbyists who contribute $200 or more to library foundations (in the aggregate and over six-month reporting periods) must disclose the contributions in reports filed with the Clerk of the House and Secretary of the Senate.[88] These requirements also apply to organizations employing registered lobbyists and political action committees (PACs) maintained or controlled by lobbyists. It should also be noted that libraries may choose to publicize additional information about contributions.[89]

SCHOLARSHIP ON PRESIDENTIAL LIBRARIES

This section of the report reviews scholarship on the presidential libraries. Among the issues that scholars discuss in their work is the accuracy of the history presented in exhibitions at the presidential libraries, the wisdom of maintaining a federated system, and the costs and benefits of the close relationship between the presidential foundations and the federal libraries.

Library Exhibitions

As noted earlier in this report, private foundations often pay for the exhibits that are displayed in the presidential libraries and their accompanying museums. Private funding, therefore, supports the research and design of the exhibits that may inhabit areas that are owned and run by the federal government.

In 2002, one scholar wrote of an internal tension in the design of presidential libraries, which have become both archival depositories and history museums.[90] The scholar wrote,

> While the libraries were built originally for housing the records, it is the museums today that seem to get the most attention, with more than one and a half million visitors annually walking through the exhibitions....[91]

> It is difficult to ascertain the effectiveness of these libraries as tourist attraction, cultural

center, and educational institution, but it is not difficult to understand that these rationales are a bit of an afterthought to their original purposes of creation—as repositories for the protection of the papers and their use by researchers and the public.[92]

He continued by saying that the libraries had become "a system that is more useful for tourism, the local economy, and unbridled hero worship than any useful role in keeping Presidents accountable to Congress and the American people."[93] The presidential libraries, therefore, can become "a system not providing sufficient oversight and impartial decisions."[94]

Another scholar wrote that the Reagan and Kennedy libraries, "as well as some other libraries in the system," fail to meet the ethical standards of the National Council on Public History, which require "the historical truth insofar as it can be determined from the available sources."[95] That same scholar argued that the libraries have become like temples that shape public memory.[96] The scholar also suggested that the libraries tend to morph presidential history into presidential myth.[97]

In 2006, *The Public Historian*, a scholarly journal that focuses on public history, published an issue that focused on presidential libraries. Within the issue, several scholars—including a representative from NARA—expressed concerns about the practices at presidential libraries.

In the issue, scholar Benjamin Hufbauer, for example, described the dual nature of presidential libraries as follows:

> Because federal presidential libraries are built and their operations are then partially supported by private foundations created by a president and his supporters, but are run by the federal government's National Archives and Records Administration (NARA), the museum's exhibits display a tension between history and "heritage." The heritage industry, as Michael Kammen has written, advances "an impulse to remember what is attractive and flattering and to ignore all the rest."[98]

Mr. Hufbauer noted, for example, that the Reagan library's "museum displays do not have 'any coverage' at all of the [Iran-Contra] scandal."[99] The JFK Library Museum, he noted, "does not address in detail JFK's numerous health problems and extramarital affairs, even though they have been thoroughly documented."[100] The Nixon library does not mention that Gerald Ford pardoned President Nixon for his participation in the Watergate cover up.[101]

Also in *The Public Historian,* Sharon K. Fawcett, who currently serves as NARA's Assistant Archivist at the Office of Presidential Libraries, cited a handbook on presidential libraries that required "exhibits in Presidential libraries ... be consistent with the dignity of the presidency and ... present historically accurate and balanced interpretations of the former President and major events."[102] Ms. Fawcett continued:

> The manual, now largely obsolete, offers no suggestions for achieving this important goal other than a requirement, not strictly enforced when funding for new exhibits shifted from the government to the foundations or other non-appropriated revenue sources, that exhibit plans be submitted to the assistant archivist for approval.[103]

Ms. Fawcett, however, said that in all cases, "the library and the supporting foundation often work seamlessly together to provide a wide variety of public programming."[104]

Scholar Larry J. Hackman argued in *The Public Historian*, that the Office of Presidential Libraries within NARA has not instituted "significant policies or guidelines" for the establishment of educational and public programs at the libraries, and the programs that are on display "do not appear to have received meaningful evaluation."[105] Mr. Hackman suggested that this lack of policy may be the result of NARA feeling that "it should not be held fully accountable if it cannot fund, or adequately control, the development of this major museum component of each library. Most of all, the Archives may fear that a more formal and extensive policy on exhibits would create high tension with influential individuals interested in such exhibits, especially in new libraries and those of living presidents."[106] Hackman argued for centralized policies and procedures for vetting permanent exhibits within the libraries.

Ms. Fawcett pointed out, however, that the supporting foundations could choose not to fund any exhibits that contain content with which they do not agree.[107] Later in the article Ms. Fawcett said NARA and, specifically, the Office of Presidential Libraries can offer "to those who view the exhibit a better understanding of what they are seeing by explaining that the exhibit is donated to the government by the president's foundation."[108]

Although foundation-sponsored exhibits may prompt some concern, some libraries have partnered with their supporting foundation to create what Ms. Fawcett called "a remarkable program of temporary exhibits, scholarly conferences, and other public programs."[109]

The Federated System

As discussed earlier in this report, the presidential library system is federated—not centralized— with each library in a different physical location. The reasons for this separation of libraries were varied. In a 1955 scholarly article on presidential papers and presidential libraries, one observer argued that keeping presidential libraries in the hometowns of the Presidents allows researchers to understand "first-hand, that Independence, Missouri or Abilene, Kansas does not leave the same mark upon the personality of a man as Hyde Park, New York or Fremont, Ohio."[110] And, as stated in the House report that accompanied the PLA, having such important records dispersed in various locations is a "highly desirable objective at any time, particularly in this atomic age."[111]

Since the 1955 enactment of the PLA, Members of Congress and scholars have debated whether the federated system is the most practical system for the presidential libraries. During the congressional debate surrounding the enactment of the PLA of 1986, for example, Senator Lawton Chiles feared the increasing size of the newer presidential libraries and thought that a single centralized library would prevent any attempts to build ever grander edifices.

At the same time, other Members of Congress argued that the architectural limitations on the library buildings penalized two-term presidents because "the final act that passed provided for no such distinctions" between one- and two-term presidents, "thereby essentially penalizing a two-term president whose records would require substantially more storage space."[112] For example, Ms. Fawcett wrote in *The Public Historian* in 2006 that the William J. Clinton Presidential Library "has almost no space for the growth of collections through donations or to house all the papers expected from President Clinton's active postpresidential life."[113] She continued: "Any substantial growth of the collections will require using off-site storage space."

In the same 2006 edition of *The Public Historian*, Mr. Hackman argued that the federated system inhibits collaborative efforts among the presidential libraries—"beyond lending documents and artifacts."[114] Mr. Hackman stated that such collaboration "would make possible exhibits on important issues that cut across some or all presidencies, as most of them do, as well as offer an exhibit quality not ordinarily possible by a single library."[115] According to Mr. Hackman, the exhibits would then be more balanced because they would offer a wider variety of perspectives on the topic or event. Creating a centralized presidential library, therefore, could mitigate any concerns about the balance of historical views in creating museum and library exhibits.

Clarifying the Relationship between the Foundation and the Federal Government

As noted earlier, most presidential libraries currently have a partnership with a nonprofit foundation that supported construction of the library building and may continue to support the library through such activities as funding exhibitions.[116] The relationship between the foundation and the library is different at each facility. Some foundations have relationships that Mr. Hackman said "appear tense, even volatile at times," while others are "smooth and settled."[117] Ms. Fawcett also noted that some foundations "support other institutions including associated schools of public affairs, policy, or service, and charitable causes of the former president."[118] Some libraries' supporting foundations also maintain control of portions of the actual library facility and, in fact, inhabit the facility. According to Ms. Fawcett, for example, "[t]he foundation-operated portions of the libraries have increased to include many public spaces once operated by the government, especially event venue space that can generate revenue for the foundation."[119]

> Most major public and private museums now rely heavily on income from corporate and private use of event spaces. At the George H.W. Bush Library, the rotunda/lobby and museum store spaces are operated by the Bush Foundation. The Clinton Foundation owns the Great Hall, the off-site museum store, the café, and the verandas surrounding the Clinton Library. Libraries built before the amendments have also been reshaped by this new model. The Reagan Foundation owns the Air Force One Pavilion, which houses the plane that flew five presidents, and the museum store. The Nixon Foundation owns a stunning reproduction of the White House East Room. These public spaces were built to be available for a fee as event venues. Library foundations need these revenue sources to pay construction loans, to meet their commitments to provide continuing support for library programs, and in some cases, to support their other charitable endeavors.[120]

Additionally, Fawcett added, "[w]ithout government support for their public programs and exhibits, the libraries are now much more dependent on their foundations for support."[121]

In some cases, the library director, which is a government position, has concurrently served as the chief executive officer of the supporting foundation.[122] Ms. Fawcett argued that this dual role "helps to align foundation and government goals for the library."[123] On the other hand, Mr. Hackman argued that "little information is made available about these organizations [t]he foundations—or even requested about them by the National Archives."[124]

Mr. Hackman argued that the relationships between the foundations and the libraries should be made more transparent—"to make certain that they operate effectively in the public's interest."[125] Moreover, Mr. Hackman noted that NARA's Office of Presidential Libraries has historically "not gathered ... lists of the boards of directors of these organizations or their annual reports or the reports they are required to file under federal statutes."[126] Mr. Hackman said it is in the interest of NARA to obtain and "report to the public information about the plans, activities, methods, and support of these organizations."[127] To clarify the relationship between the foundations and NARA, Mr. Hackman outlined a series of desired characteristics for the partnership:

- Clarity in roles, goals, and priorities; responsibility; and authority in order to minimize friction and maximize success in the relationship between the presidential library and its nonprofit partners
- Collaboration in annual and long-term planning, resource development, and budgeting so that all resources are used to achieve maximum impact
- Dedication of financial support from the nonprofit partner to programs that address library priorities and that are highly unlikely to be supported from federal operations or library earned revenue
- Library coordination of programs supported by the partner where these programs related to basic library functions including exhibitions, education, and, when possible, other programs for the public
- Library participation in the planning and decision making of the nonprofit partner, ordinarily by having the library director serve as a member of the board of the nonprofit and as its coordinator of library-related programs[128]

ANALYSIS[129]

The National Archives and Records Administration currently oversees 13 separate presidential libraries, which serve as repositories for presidential archival materials. Since enacted in 1955, the Presidential Libraries Act has provided for the preservation and administration of the historical materials of an outgoing President by authorizing the federal government to accept land, buildings, and other materials. A private nonprofit organization funded the construction of each presidential repository and provided the required endowment. Almost every library is associated with that nonprofit, which often supports library and presidential museum exhibitions. As this report has noted, the Presidential Libraries Act has placed various requirements on both libraries and foundations to assist in the preservation of presidential legacies. Congress has the authority to legislate the mission and operation of all of the presidential libraries. Congress may choose to clarify the best method of preserving a President's legacy—by creating accurate and balanced exhibits on the presidency and each administration or by providing a user-friendly repository of each president's records.

Congress may determine that the current operation of presidential libraries should continue, and that foundations should continue to fund and oversee the creation of public museum exhibits. NARA has final approval of all exhibit content, but the foundations, in many cases, have assumed control of creating the public exhibit portions of the libraries. Congress, however, may determine that NARA should play a more active role in the creation and display of library exhibitions. With greater control, NARA could coordinate exhibits among the 13 current libraries and, possibly, offer a more thorough and balanced treatment of the presidency as an institution as well as the historical context of each individual presidential administration.

Congress may also reconsider having a disparate collection of presidential libraries around the country. Congress could determine that having all historical presidential materials in one location is a less expensive and more accessible option than operating 13 or more distinct libraries. Congress would have to determine what to do with library buildings they currently own that would no longer be used as repositories.[130] Congress would also have to appropriate funding for the construction and use of a single facility. Moving all materials into a single facility could make the total collection of presidential materials more accessible to researchers. Such a change, however, could make materials from individual former Presidents less accessible to other researchers.

If a new single archive for presidential materials were constructed in Washington, D.C., then researchers living in California who had interest in materials on Richard Nixon may have to travel across the country instead of to Yorba Linda (the current location of the Richard Nixon Library) to access them—or a scholar living in Kansas may have to leave the Midwest to learn more about Dwight D. Eisenhower.

Moreover, keeping the presidential libraries in the hometowns of the presidents may, arguably, help scholars better understand the environmental and social factors that shaped a President's earlier years and influenced his decisions. If the libraries of former Presidents are no longer constructed in the hometowns of the Presidents themselves, as will occur with the future repository for George W. Bush, this argument is rendered invalid. Congress, therefore, may have an interest in requiring the construction of future presidential libraries in the hometown of the President. On the other hand, the location of presidential materials may become increasingly irrelevant as the records of earlier former Presidents are put online and a majority of the records of more recent Presidents are electronic, making all presidential records more accessible to researchers no matter their location.

One centralized presidential archive could eliminate the need to replicate certain resources that are essential to a records repository. For example, moving all presidential records into one facility run exclusively by NARA would eliminate the need for each individual presidential library to have a specialized facility to protect classified presidential documents.[131] Currently, each presidential library has had to construct and maintain facilities for such sensitive materials. Other services that may currently be required in each library are technology services and security personnel. Moving the materials into a central library, however, could render them susceptible to destruction by a single fire, flood, or other disaster. Additionally, construction of a centralized library could influence the type of research that scholars conduct. Research may focus on the institution of the presidency, as a whole, rather than on the individual Presidents.

Congress may also be concerned about the relationship between the presidential libraries and the library foundations that provide financial support.[132] Congress, of course, has the authority to legislate whether one person can or should concurrently hold a position in the federal government and an unpaid position within the supporting organization. Such an arrangement may make certain that the foundation and NARA have similar missions and ideas about the future of the entities. On the other hand, Congress may determine that one person holding a position in both the foundation and NARA may present a conflict of interest in which the person could advance private sector preferences over the interests of the federal government.

To reduce the public costs associated with presidential libraries, Congress has the authority to legislate the percentage of the required endowment to accompany the deeding of any presidential library facility. Congress may determine that the current required endowment to accompany the deeding over of a presidential library to the federal government (60%) should be raised, lowered, or maintained at its current level.

As this report has suggested, the federal presidential libraries and their private funding sources typically fulfill different roles. Because of the varied and unique relationships between the libraries and foundations, however, the precise division of labor and property is sometimes unclear. In addition, as noted previously, relatively little information about private funding sources must be publicly disclosed. If the various funding relationships among public and private sources are a concern, Congress could mandate public disclosure of additional information about funding, division of duties, or office space. H.R. 36 would require library fundraising organizations to file quarterly reports itemizing contributions totaling at least $200. Under the bill, the reports would be filed with NARA, the House Committee on Oversight and Government Reform, and the Senate Committee on Homeland Security and Governmental Affairs. As noted earlier, H.R. 36 passed the House in January 2009 and was referred to the Senate Homeland Security and Governmental Affairs Committee. No further action has been taken on the bill.

NARA, in its report on presidential libraries, suggested a possible alternative to the current libraries system that would require foundations to provide the government with a library-only building and "no museum component."[133] Any museum associated with the corresponding President could be placed "in the same general vicinity," but the facility would be separate and distinct from the library.[134] Removing the foundation from the library facility could clarify to visitors what is privately owned space and what is publicly owned.

Finally, the presidential libraries and museums often charge visitors an admission fee. In some cases, this fee is then divided between the federal government and the foundation. This fee division, however, is not always made clear to visitors. In fact, in some libraries, the foundations pay the federal government for access to federal government-owned portions of the library facility. At the Reagan and Clinton libraries, for example, each foundation pays the federal government a per person fee after it holds events at which attendees are given free access to the library's museum. In addition to collecting fees from foundations in certain circumstances, Congress has the authority to require NARA to clearly identify to visitors what portion of their fees go to the federal government and what portion does not. Congress also has the authority to enact legislation that would allow visitors to pay only for access to the areas of the library or museum that interest them. Regardless of ownership of that portion of the facility, the visitor would pay only for those parts of the facility he or she visited. Congress could, therefore, require visitors to pay separate fees for access to federal property and non-federal property.

Acknowledgments

Historical portions of this report are based on CRS Report 95-3 89 *Federal Presidential Libraries* by Harold Relyea, who has retired from CRS. R. Sam Garrett, Analyst in American National Government, contributed to this report.

End Notes

[1] The act is currently codified at 44 U.S.C. § 2112.

[2] U.S. Congress, House Committee on Government Operations, *Reduction of Costs of Presidential Libraries*, to accompany H.R. 1349, 99th Cong., 1st sess., May 15, 1985, H.Rept. 99-125 (Washington: GPO, 1985), pp. 1-2.

[3] For additional information on presidential libraries and presidential records, see CRS Report R40238, *Presidential Records: Issues for the 111th Congress*, by Wendy R. Ginsberg; and CRS Report R40209, *Fundraising for Presidential Libraries: Legislative and Policy Issues in the 111th Congress*, by R. Sam Garrett.

[4] 44 U.S.C. § 2112(a).

[5] 44 U.S.C. § 2112(g).

[6] The repository for the George W. Bush materials is under construction at Southern Methodist University in Dallas, Texas. The presidential papers of former President George W. Bush are currently stored at a NARA facility in Lewisville, Texas. The Lewisville facility is included as one of the 13 presidential libraries maintained by NARA. See George W. Bush Presidential Library, http://www.georgewbushlibrary.gov/. This facility will be replaced by the one that is under construction as part of the George W. Bush Presidential Center on the Southern Methodist University Campus. For more information on the George W. Bush Presidential Center, see Southern Methodist University, "SMU: Home of the George W. Bush Presidential Center," http://smu.edu/bushlibrary/index.asp.

[7] Sharon K. Fawcett, "Presidential Libraries: A View from the Center," *The Public Historian*, vol. 28, no. 3 (Summer 2006), p. 25.

[8] For more information on H.R. 36 see CRS Report R40209, *Fundraising for Presidential Libraries: Legislative and Policy Issues in the 111th Congress*, by R. Sam Garrett.

[9] The bill refers to reports being filed with "the Administration." Although the bill does not define that term, H.R. 36 would amend 44 U.S.C. § 2112, which defines "the Administration" as NARA.

[10] For information on presidential records, see CRS Report R40238, *Presidential Records: Issues for the 111th Congress*, by Wendy R. Ginsberg.

[11] See 44 U.S.C. § 2112(a) (1982); and 44 U.S.C. § 21 12(a)(1)(B)(i) (1988).

[12] The Ronald Reagan Presidential Library and the William J. Clinton Presidential Library each have more square footage than the federal government can accept without having to raise the endowment requirement for the buildings. Any square footage over 70,000 square feet statutorily requires a higher endowment percentage rate. Pursuant to statute, the endowment percentage increases with each square foot the edifice is in excess of the 70,000 cap. Parts of these libraries, therefore, are deeded to the federal government while other parts of the buildings are owned by the organizations that supported the buildings' construction. The foundations do not have to pay additional endowment fees if they maintain control of the additional square footage. The endowment calculations will be discussed in greater length later in this report.

[13] See 110 Stat. 3 009-258 for appropriations language and 110 Stat. 3868 for authorizing language.

[14] 111 Stat. 1550.

[15] 113 Stat. 1501A-143.

[16] 114 Stat. 930.

[17] The Lyndon Baines Johnson Library and Museum, for example, has an online photo archive available on its website that allows users to enter a search term and find a variety of archived presidential photographs. See Lyndon Baines Johnson Library and Museum, "Online Photo Archive Search," http://www.lbjlibrary.org/collections/photoarchive.html. The Ronald Reagan Presidential Foundation hosts a virtual online tour of the Ronald Reagan Library and Museum on its website. See The Ronald Reagan Presidential Foundation and Library, "Reagan Library Video Tour," http://www.reaganfoundation.org/reagan-library-video-tour.aspx.

[18] See Waldo Gifford Leland, "The Creation of the Franklin D. Roosevelt Library: A Personal Narrative," *American Archivist*, vol. 18 (January 1955), p. 13. Certain papers from the presidencies of George Washington, Thomas Jefferson, and Andrew Jackson were maintained at the Library of Congress, but no laws existed that required outgoing Presidents to maintain these records.

[19] David Demarest Lloyd, "Presidential Papers and Presidential Libraries," *Manuscripts*, vol. 8 (Fall 1955), p. 5.

[20] *Id.*

[21] *Id.*, p. 4.

[22] *Id.*

[23] On December 10, 1938, Franklin D. Roosevelt told 18 people assembled at a luncheon his plans to donate to the federal government a plot of his mother's land five miles north of Poughkeepsie on which to store his documents, books, correspondence, pamphlets, pictures and other objects of both personal and historical interest. See Waldo Gifford Leland, "The Creation of the Franklin D. Roosevelt Library: A Personal Narrative," *American Archivist*, vol. 18 (January 1955), p. 11.

[24] Thomas A. Smith, "Before Hyde Park: The Rutherford B. Hayes Library," *The American Archivist*, vol. 43, no. 4 (Fall 1980), p. 485.The Rutherford B. Hayes Presidential Library is part of the Rutherford B. Hayes Presidential Center. The library holds more than 70,000 books that include volumes on a variety of topics that go beyond the former President's administration records. Included in this collection are volumes on genealogy and local history of Fremont, Ohio. For more information about the center and the library, see Rutherford B. Hayes Presidential Center, "About the Library," http://www.rbhayes.org/hayes/library/.

[25] Thomas A. Smith, "Before Hyde Park: The Rutherford B. Hayes Library," *American Archivist*, vol. 43 (Fall 1980), pp. 485.

[26] Hoover Institution, Stanford University, "Library and Archives: History," http://www.hoover.org/library-and-archives/history

[27] David Demarest Lloyd, "Presidential Papers and Presidential Libraries," *Manuscripts*, vol. 8 (Fall 1955), p. 15; President Hoover's presidential records were transferred to the Herbert Hoover Presidential Library in West Branch, Iowa, when that facility was completed and turned over to the government in 1964.

[28] Waldo Gifford Leland, "The Creation of the Franklin D. Roosevelt Library: A Personal Narrative," *American Archivist*, vol. 18 (January 1955), pp. 11-29. See also Donald R. McCoy, "The Beginning of the Franklin D. Roosevelt Library," *Prologue*, vol. 7 (Fall 1975), pp. 137-150.

[29] Waldo Gifford Leland, "The Creation of the Franklin D. Roosevelt Library: A Personal Narrative," *American Archivist*, vol. 18 (January 1955), p. 14.

[30] *Id.*, p. 15. The advisory committee itself was funded through a grant of $1,500 provided by the Carnegie Corporation. Leland wrote that nearly $800 of the $1,500 grant was later refunded to the Carnegie Corporation because it was not used by the committee.

[31] *Id.*, p. 16.

[32] *Id.*

[33] *Id.*, p. 17-18. According to Leland, creating the corporation also provided a "hedge" if Congress did not enact legislation that would have allowed for the acquisition of the repository. If such legislation were not enacted, "the corporation would have been obliged to seek endowment or other permanent funding for the perpetual maintenance of the establishment." More than 28,000 people contributed a total of $400,000 to the library (p. 25). Construction costs totaled $367,000 (p. 23).

[34] 53 Stat. 1052.

[35] *Id.*, p. 21. President Roosevelt was adamant that a variety of objects and gadgets associated with his life be displayed in the museum, despite Leland's concern that too much space was allotted to the museum functions of the library. According to Leland, President Roosevelt responded by saying, "Well, you know, if people have to pay a quarter to get into the library they want to see something interesting inside."

[36] Some editors argue that there is no period after the "S" in Harry S. Truman. This report follows the recommendation of the Harry S. Truman Library and Museum, which states that "S." is correct. See Harry S. Truman Library and Museum, "Use of the Period After the 'S' in Harry S. Truman's Name," http://www.trumanlibrary.org/speriod.htm.

[37] Background information on the establishment of the Truman Presidential Library was provided by NARA. See also David D. Lloyd, "The Harry S. Truman Library," *American Archivist*, vol. 18 (April 1955), pp. 107-110; and Philip C. Brooks, "The Harry S. Truman Library—Plans and Reality," *American Archivist*, vol. 25 (January 1962), pp. 25-3 7.

[38] U.S. Congress, House Committee on Government Operations, *Presidential Libraries*, report to accompany H.J. Res. 330, 84th Cong., 1st sess., June 29, 1955, H.Rept. 84-998 (Washington: GPO, 1955), pp. 1-2. This report details the legislative creation of the presidential library system.

[39] U.S. Congress, House Committee on Government Operations, *Reduction of costs of Presidential Libraries*, to accompany H.R. 1349, 99th Cong., 1st sess., May 15, 1985, H.Rept. 99-125 (Washington: GPO, 1985), pp. 1-2.

[40] U.S. Congress, House Committee on Government Operations, *Presidential Libraries*, report to accompany H.J. Res. 330, 84th Cong., 1st sess., June 29, 1955, H.Rept. 84-998 (Washington: GPO, 1955).

[41] At the time the H.J. Res. 330 was being debated in Congress, the National Archives was under the aegis of the General Services Administration.

[42] U.S. Congress, House Committee on Government Operations, *Presidential Libraries*, report to accompany H.J. Res. 330, 84th Cong., 1st sess., June 29, 1955, H.Rept. 84-998 (Washington: GPO, 1955), p. 2.

[43] *Id.*

[44] *Id.*

[45] Id.
[46] U.S. Congress, Senate Committee on Government Operations, *Providing for the Acceptance and Maintenance of Presidential Libraries*, report to accompany H.J.Res. 330, 84th Cong., 1st sess., July 28, 1955, S.Rept. 84-1189 (Washington: GPO, 1955).
[47] The law stated that the Administrator should "accept for deposit ... documents, including motion-picture films, still pictures, and sound recordings, from private sources that are appropriate for preservation by the government as evidence of its organization, functions, policies, decisions, procedures, and transactions." 69 Stat. 695.
[48] This authority was transferred to the Archivist in the NARA Act. P.L. 98-497. Under it, the Archivist may "make agreements [with a foundation or other entity], upon terms and conditions the Archivist considers proper ...." 44 U.S.C. § 21 12(a)(1)(B)(i). Thus, the Archivist may agree to use restrictions imposed by, for example, a foundation.
[49] 69 Stat. 695; P.L. 84-3 73. The authority to solicit and accept gifts or bequests was transferred to the Archivist in the NARA Act. P.L. 98-497. The trigger for the Archivist's authority to solicit and accept gifts or bequests is that he or she "considers it to be in the public interest." 44 U.S.C. § 21 12(g)(1). This section seems to expressly authorize the Archivist to accept gifts on a continuing basis since it does not appear to have any temporal limitation and speaks to ongoing, post-construction actions taken in connection with a library.
[50] 69 Stat. 695; P.L. 84-3 73.
[51] Id.
[52] U.S. Congress, House Committee on Government Operations, *Presidential Libraries*, report to accompany H.J. Res. 330, 84th Cong., 1st sess., June 29, 1955, H.Rept. 84-998 (Washington: GPO, 1955), p. 5.
[53] Hoover Institution, Stanford University, "Library and Archives: History," http://www.hoover.org/library-and-archives/history
[54] Id. According to a 1982 Government Operations Committee Report (H.Rept. 97-732), much of the increasing costs for presidential libraries was "artificial—the result of the imposition of inappropriate space rental and unduly large service charges on the Archives by its parent agency, the General Services Administration." For more information, see U.S. Congress, House Committee on Government Operations, *Presidential Libraries: Unexplored Funding Alternatives*, 97th Cong., 2nd sess., August 12, 1982, H.Rept. 97-732 (Washington: GPO, 1982), p. 2.
[55] In the 96th Congress, see S. 2408; H.R. 7224; H.R. 7713. In the 97th Congress, see H.R. 3904 and H.R. 4671.
[56] Additional bills that included restrictions similar to those in S. 563 and H.R. 5478 were also introduced in the 97th Congress, including H.R. 2446; H.R. 5843; and H.R. 6335.
[57] The 1955 Presidential Libraries Act (84-3 73) also authorized the GSA Administrator to collect certain fees and deposit them in a National Archives Trust Fund to help defray each library's operating costs. H.R. 2567 referred to the trust fund as the Presidential Library Trust Fund.
[58] H.R. 3138, introduced by Representative Glenn English, was similar to H.R. 2567. H.R. 3138 was modified and later incorporated into H.R. 5798, which passed both the House and Senate as different versions. After the bill went to conference, however, only the House agreed to the conference report. No further action was taken on the bill. Other bills that were introduced and not enacted in the 98th Congress included H.R. 3987; H.R. 4017; H.R. 4786; H.R. 5584; and S. 2490.
[59] The bills not enacted were H.R. 1236, H.R. 2113; H.R. 4320; H.R. 4890; S. 1047.
[60] U.S. Congress, Senate Committee on Governmental Affairs, *Presidential Library Act of 1985*, report to accompany H.R. 1349, 99th Cong., 2nd sess., March 7, 1986, S.Rept. 99-257 (Washington: GPO, 1986), p. 2.
[61] U.S. Congress, House Committee on Government Operations, *Reduction of Costs of Presidential Libraries*, report to accompany H.R. 1349, 99th Cong., 1st sess., May 15, 1985, H.Rept. 99-125 (Washington: GPO, 1985), pp. 1-2.
[62] Id. p. 12.
[63] U.S. Congress, Senate Committee on Governmental Affairs, *Presidential Library Act of 1985*, report to accompany H.R. 1349, 99th Cong., 2nd sess., March 7, 1986, S.Rept. 99-257 (Washington: GPO, 1986), p. 4.
[64] P.L. 99-323; 100 Stat. 498.
[65] 100 Stat. 497; codified at 44 U.S.C. § 2112(g). The 20% (or other relevant amount) funding is deposited in a National Archives Trust Fund account. See 44 U.S.C. § 21 12(g)(1). As later discussed, Congress increased the threshold to first 40% and then 60% for libraries built for Presidents who take the oath of office for the first time after July 1, 2002.
[66] P.L. 99-323, Sec. 4; 100 Stat. 498. The statute did not, therefore, apply to then-President Reagan. It currently applies to the presidential depository libraries of former Presidents George H.W. Bush and William J. Clinton—as well as the depository under construction for former President George W. Bush.
[67] The Senate Committee on Governmental Affairs explained, during consideration of the act, that "The purpose of the additional endowment requirement is effectively to eliminate added taxpayer costs that would be associated with the operation and maintenance of space exceeding 70,000 square feet. A facility of 70,000 square feet is adequate for a Presidential library. While larger facilities are not precluded, an additional

endowment would be necessary." U.S. Congress, Senate Committee on Governmental Affairs, 99th Cong., 2nd Sess., March 7, 1986, Rpt. 99-257 (Washington: GPO, 1986), pp. 2-3.

[68] According to NARA, no current presidential library facility has more than 70,000 square feet under federal government control or ownership.

[69] For example, assume a library is built for a President who first takes the oath of office before July 1, 2002, and, therefore, the relevant endowment percentage is 20%. The library is 100,000 square feet in area and the total relevant costs of the creating the library are $200 million. The total endowment required for this library would be $125.8 million. The first step in computing this amount is multiplying the total cost of the library's creation ($200 million) by 20%, which equals $40 million. Next, the total cost of $200 million is multiplied by 42.9% (which is determined by dividing 30,000—the number of square feet the building is more than the 70,000 cap—by 70,000), which equals $85.8 million. These two amounts are then combined for an endowment requirement of $125.8 million.

[70] National Archives and Records Administration, *Report on Alternative Models for Presidential Libraries Issued in Response to the Requirements of P.L. 110-404*, September 25, 2009, p. 34, http://www.archives.gov/presidentiallibraries/reports/report-for-congress

[71] U.S. Congress, House Committee on Government Operations, *Reduction of Costs of Presidential Libraries*, report to accompany H.R. 1349, 99th Cong., 1st sess., May 15, 1985, H.Rept. 99-125 (Washington: GPO, 1985), p. 15.

[72] P.L. 99-323 Sec. 5; 100 Stat. 499.

[73] National Archives and Records Administration, *Annual Report for the Year Ended September 30, 1986*, (Washington: GPO, 1986), p. 37.

[74] *Id.*

[75] *Id.*

[76] The Smithsonian Institution's National Museum of American History—located on the National Mall in Washington, D.C.—contains a permanent exhibition entitled "The American Presidency: A Glorious Burden," which "explores the personal, public, ceremonial and executive actions of the 43 men" who have served as President. The exhibit contains "[m]ore than 900 objects, including [items] from the Smithsonian's vast presidential collections." Smithsonian National Museum of American History, "The American Presidency: A Glorious Burden," http://americanhistory.si.edu/ exhibitions/exhibition.cfm?key=38&exkey=87. An online version of the exhibition is available on the Smithsonian's website at http://americanhistory.si.edu/presidency

[77] Consolidated Appropriations Resolution, 2003, P.L. 108-7, Div. J, Title V, § 513, 117 Stat. 462.

[78] *Id.*, codified at 44 U.S.C. § 21 12(g)(5)(C),(D).

[79] Presidential Historical Records Preservation Act of 2008, P.L. 110-404, § 6, *codified at* 44 U.S.C. § 21 12(g)(5)(B).

[80] *See id.*

[81] National Archives and Records Administration, *Report on Alternative Models for Presidential Libraries Issued in Response to the Requirements of P.L. 110-404*, Washington, DC, September 25, 2009, available at http://www.archives.gov/presidential-libraries/reports/report-for-congress

[82] Presidential library foundations, despite being referred to as foundations, are public charities, and not private foundations, under the tax laws. Public charities receive broad public support, while private foundations have a small number of donors, who often have significant control over the organization. Due to fears of abuse, private foundations are subject to additional regulation that would not be applicable to the presidential library foundations.

[83] IRC § 501(c)(3) describes organizations "organized and operated exclusively for religious, charitable, scientific, testing for public safety, literary, or educational purposes, or to foster national or international amateur sports competition ... or for the prevention of cruelty to children or animals, no part of the net earnings of which inures to the benefit of any private shareholder or individual, no substantial part of the activities of which is carrying on propaganda, or otherwise attempting, to influence legislation ... and which does not participate in, or intervene in (including the publishing or distributing of statements), any political campaign on behalf of (or in opposition to) any candidate for public office."

[84] IRC § 501(c)(3). For more information, see CRS Report 96-264, *Frequently Asked Questions About Tax-Exempt Organizations*, by Erika K. Lunder; CRS Report RL33377, *Tax-Exempt Organizations: Political Activity Restrictions and Disclosure Requirements*, by Erika K. Lunder; and CRS Report 96-809, *Lobbying Regulations on Non-Profit Organizations*, by Jack Maskell.

[85] IRC § 4958.

[86] IRC § 6104, *see also* IRC § 6652 (imposing penalties on an organization for failing to disclose).

[87] IRC § 6033; *see also* IRC § 6652 (imposing penalties on the failure to file).

[88] 121 Stat. 743. HLOGA is devoted primarily to other lobbying and ethics issues. For additional discussion, see CRS Report RL34166, *Lobbying Law and Ethics Rules Changes in the 110th Congress*, by Jack Maskell; and CRS Report RL34377, *Honest Leadership and Open Government Act of 2007: The Role of the Clerk of the House and the Secretary of the Senate*, by Jacob R. Straus On campaign finance provisions in HLOGA, see CRS Report RL34324, *Campaign Finance: Legislative Developments and Policy Issues in the 110th Congress*,

by R. Sam Garrett and CRS Report R40091, *Campaign Finance: Potential Legislative and Policy Issues for the 111th Congress*, by R. Sam Garrett.

[89] A recent and prominent example concerns the William J. Clinton Foundation, which supports the William J. Clinton presidential library, among other activities. In December 2008, amid concerns about potential conflicts of interest surrounding then-Senator Hillary Rodham Clinton's nomination as Secretary of State, the foundation agreed to voluntarily disclose names and donation ranges of its contributors. On the relationship between the library and the foundation, and the disclosure agreement between the foundation and the Obama Presidential Transition Foundation, see William J. Clinton Foundation and Obama Presidential Transition Foundation, Memorandum of Understanding, December 12, 2008. A copy of the Memorandum of Understanding is available at http://www.washingtonpost.com/wpsrv/politics

[90] Richard Cox, "America's Pyramids: Presidents and Their Libraries," *Government Information Quarterly*, vol. 199 (2002), http://arizona.openrepository.com/arizona/bitstream/10150/106274/1/AmericasPyramids.pdf.

[91] *Id.*, p. 46

[92] *Id.*, p. 57.

[93] *Id.*, p. 61.

[94] *Id.*

[95] Benjamin Hufbauer, *Presidential Temples: How Memorials and Libraries Shape Public Memory* (Lawrence, KS: University Press of Kansas, 2005), p. 124.

[96] *Id.*

[97] *Id.*, p. 8.

[98] Benjamin Hufbauer, "Spotlights and Shadows: Presidents and Their Administrations in Presidential Museum Exhibits," *The Public Historian*, vol. 28, no. 3 (Summer 2006), p. 118.

[99] *Id.*, p. 124.

[100] *Id.*

[101] *Id.* Ms. Sharon K. Fawcett noted that NARA has requested changes to proposed exhibits to offer a more balanced history, but NARA does not "expect an exhibit in a presidential library to denigrate the president's legacy." Sharon K. Fawcett, "Presidential Libraries: A View from the Center," *The Public Historian*, vol. 28, no. 3 (Summer 2006), p. 31.

[102] Sharon K. Fawcett, "Presidential Libraries: A View from the Center," *The Public Historian*, vol. 28, no. 3 (Summer 2006), p. 18. Ms. Fawcett's position at the NARA was noted in the article, but it is unclear whether she was writing as an official representative of the Archives.

[103] *Id.*

[104] *Id.*, p. 17.

[105] Larry J. Hackman, "Better Policies and Practices for Presidential Libraries," *The Public Historian*, vol. 28, no. 3 (Summer 2006), p. 172.

[106] *Id.*, p. 174.

[107] Sharon K. Fawcett, "Presidential Libraries: A View from the Center," *The Public Historian*, vol. 28, no. 3 (Summer 2006), p. 25.

[108] *Id.*, p. 31.

[109] *Id.*, p. 26. The National Archives also has the right to refuse any exhibit proposed or created by the foundation, but Ms. Fawcett notes that NARA has never rejected any exhibit. Ibid., p. 30.

[110] David Demarest Lloyd, "Presidential Papers and Presidential Libraries," *Manuscripts*, vol. 8 (Fall 1955), p. 8.

[111] U.S. Congress, House Committee on Government Operations, *Presidential Libraries*, report to accompany H.J. Res. 330, 84th Cong., 1st sess., June 29, 1955, H.Rept. 84-998 (Washington: GPO, 1955), p. 2.

[112] Sharon K. Fawcett, Assistant Archivist at the Office of Presidential Libraries in NARA, "Presidential Libraries: A View from the Center," *The Public Historian*, vol. 28, no. 3 (Summer 2006), p. 23.

[113] *Id.*

[114] Larry J. Hackman, "Better Policies and Practices for Presidential Libraries," *The Public Historian*, vol. 28, no. 3 (Summer 2006), p. 176.

[115] *Id.*

[116] The Carter library is the only library that does not have a foundation that directly support its initiatives. The Carter library, however, does have a working relationship with the Carter Center, an educational research center at Emory University that is dedicated to working on human rights issues.

[117] Larry J. Hackman, "Better Policies and Practices for Presidential Libraries," *The Public Historian*, vol. 28, no. 3 (Summer 2006), p. 179.

[118] Sharon K. Fawcett, "Presidential Libraries: A View from the Center," *The Public Historian*, vol. 28, no. 3 (Summer 2006), p. 24.

[119] *Id.*

[120] *Id.*

[121] *Id.*

[122] Larry J. Hackman, "Better Policies and Practices for Presidential Libraries," *The Public Historian*, vol. 28, no. 3 (Summer 2006), p. 176, and Sharon K. Fawcett, "Presidential Libraries: A View from the Center," *The Public*

Historian, vol. 28, no. 3 (Summer 2006), p. 21. Fawcett noted that the CEO positions, in these cases, were unpaid. The libraries in which this dual position was held were the Reagan and Truman libraries.

[123] Sharon K. Fawcett, "Presidential Libraries: A View from the Center," *The Public Historian*, vol. 28, no. 3 (Summer 2006), p. 21.

[124] Larry J. Hackman, "Better Policies and Practices for Presidential Libraries," *The Public Historian*, vol. 28, no. 3 (Summer 2006), p. 170.

[125] *Id.*, p. 180.

[126] *Id.*, p. 181.

[127] *Id.*, p. 182.

[128] *Id.*

[129] This report does not consider possible legal issues that might arise from changing the location of the Presidential libraries or their relationships with their foundations.

[130] This is just one possible model for the presidential library system outlined in the following report: National Archives and Records Administration, *Report on Alternative Models for Presidential Libraries Issued in Response to the Requirements of P.L. 110-404*, Washington, DC, September 25, 2009, p. 43, http://www.archives.gov/presidentiallibraries/reports/report-for-congress. Other models included requiring smaller presidential library facilities as records become increasingly electronic and require less storage space, prohibiting presidential libraries and museums from existing in the same building, or creating a presidential museum that could accompany a single, centralized presidential records archive.

[131] This is just one possible model for the presidential library system outlined in the following report: National Archives and Records Administration, *Report on Alternative Models for Presidential Libraries Issued in Response to the Requirements of P.L. 110-404*, Washington, DC, September 25, 2009, p. 43.

[132] For example, a 2009 NARA report on presidential libraries noted that the goals of the foundations "are not always aligned with NARA's view of our stewardship responsibilities." The report suggested that prior to accepting control of any new presidential library facilities, "a clearer understanding between the [f]oundation and the [g]overnment should be memorialized in agreement." Ibid., p. 33.

[133] Ibid., 40.

[134] Ibid.

In: Presidential Libraries: Elements and Considerations
Editor: Jamie D. Reynolds

ISBN: 978-1-61324-581-1
© 2011 Nova Science Publishers, Inc.

Chapter 2

FUNDRAISING FOR PRESIDENTIAL LIBRARIES: RECENT LEGISLATIVE AND POLICY ISSUES FOR CONGRESS

R. Sam Garrett

SUMMARY

In recent Congresses, some Members have expressed concern about the lack of information surrounding private fundraising for presidential libraries. Those calling for additional regulation argue that more transparency could reduce potential conflicts of interest surrounding library contributions. Contributions from foreign sources have also been the subject of debate.

Federal law and regulation are largely silent on contributions to presidential libraries. Contributions to library fundraising organizations may be unlimited and can come from any otherwise lawful source. In addition, although certain aspects of library contributions are similar to campaign contributions, library contributions are not considered to be campaign contributions and are not subject to limits on amounts and funding sources specified in the Federal Election Campaign Act (FECA). In one of the few relatively recent regulatory changes affecting library contributions, the Honest Leadership and Open Government Act (HLOGA), enacted in the 110th Congress, requires registered lobbyists to report their contributions to presidential libraries. However, non-lobbyists are not required to report their library contributions. Library fundraising organizations must report certain information to the Internal Revenue Service, but those organizations are not required to publicize information about individual donors.

Library-fundraising issues emerged during Senate consideration of Hillary Clinton's nomination as Secretary of State, amid concerns about fundraising for former President Clinton's library and other initiatives. Calls for additional disclosure, however, are not new. During the 110th Congress, the House passed H.R. 1254 (Waxman), which would have required library fundraising organizations to file quarterly reports itemizing contributions of at least $200 and identifying donors. The Senate Committee on Homeland Security and

Governmental Affairs reported an amended version of the bill, but the measure did not receive Senate floor consideration. In the 111th Congress, the House passed H.R. 36 (Towns) in January 2009; that measure was virtually identical to the House-passed version of H.R. 1254 from the 110th Congress. It did not advance in the Senate. An additional disclosure measure, H.R. 775 (Duncan), which would also require reporting of donations of at least $200, was introduced in the 112th Congress, in February 2011. If Congress wishes to pursue broader regulation of library fundraising, aspects of campaign finance policy may be a useful model. However, certain aspects of a campaign-finance disclosure model may invite controversy.

This report provides an overview of recent policy issues and legislation surrounding library fundraising.

INTRODUCTION

Presidential libraries serve not only as repositories of official papers, but also as museums and monuments to the nation's leaders.[1] In response to these varied missions, two sources provide funds to construct and maintain presidential libraries. First, private funds raised by non-profit foundations typically cover library construction and programming costs. Second, funds appropriated to the National Archives and Records Administration (NARA) cover the cost of archiving and managing presidential papers housed at the libraries.

Through agreements negotiated by the Archives and foundations[2] affiliated with each facility, NARA eventually takes control of most presidential libraries. The NARA system currently includes the libraries of 12 former Presidents: (1) George H.W. Bush (College Station, Texas); (2) Jimmy Carter (Atlanta, Georgia); (3) William J. Clinton (Little Rock, Arkansas); (4) Dwight D. Eisenhower (Abilene, Kansas); (5) Gerald R. Ford (Ann Arbor, Michigan); (6) Herbert Hoover (West Branch, Iowa); (7) Lyndon B. Johnson (Austin, Texas); (8) John F. Kennedy (Boston, Massachusetts); (9) Richard M. Nixon (Yorba Linda, California); (10) Ronald Reagan (Simi Valley, California); (11) Franklin D. Roosevelt (Hyde Park, New York); and (12) Harry S. Truman (Independence, Missouri).[3] Foundations affiliated with these libraries typically continue operations to support library programming, exhibits, or other events sustaining a President's legacy.

Private fundraising supporting library foundations has emerged as a matter of concern in recent Congresses largely because private fundraising is not subject to public disclosure. Some Members of Congress have expressed concern that the lack of public disclosure—or private fundraising altogether—invites potential conflicts of interest from those wishing to influence sitting or former Presidents through library contributions. Contributions from foreign sources have also been a concern, including during Senate consideration of Hillary Clinton's nomination as Secretary of State.[4] In December 2008, the William J. Clinton Foundation[5] agreed to voluntarily disclose names and donation ranges of its contributors, but this practice would not necessarily extend to other presidential-library foundations. Apparently unrelated to the Clinton nomination, the House passed H.R. 36 (Towns) on early in the 111th Congress. That bill would have required library fundraising organizations to publicly disclose contributions of at least $200, along with the names and occupations of donors. In February 2011, in the 112th Congress, Representative Duncan introduced a similar bill, H.R. 775 (discussed later in this report).

This report provides an overview of recent legislation regarding presidential library fundraising. It also discusses policy issues and options. Requiring additional disclosure surrounding library fundraising could increase transparency and potentially discourage conflicts of interest. Disclosure alone, however, is unlikely to change fundraising practices. Amounts and sources of library fundraising would continue to be unlimited.

HOW PRESIDENTIAL LIBRARIES ARE FUNDED

Presidential libraries are funded through a combination of public and private sources. In general, funds for archiving and management of a President's papers are appropriated to NARA, while funds raised by foundations associated with the library support facility construction, programming, and other activities related to a President's legacy. The first step in funding presidential libraries typically occurs when a President's supporters or family members establish a 501(c)(3) foundation to raise money for acquiring land (if necessary) and constructing the library. After the library is constructed and per agreements negotiated between NARA and the foundation, the Archives typically takes control of the facility, land, and the foundation's operating endowment. As the House Committee on Government Operations noted in 1985, endowment income "is intended to offset ... building operations costs and reduce ... the amount of appropriations required for building operations."[6] Even after NARA takes control of a library, the foundation may continue to operate to support specific programming or exhibits.

Private fundraising has generated greater legislative concern than has public funding. The public nature of appropriated funds, and accompanying congressional oversight, ensures transparency about where federal funds originate and how they are spent. Appropriated funds, therefore, have not been the subject of substantial legislative activity in recent Congresses. By contrast, and as discussed below, public information about private fundraising is limited. Library foundations are not required to publicly disclose detailed information about their fundraising activities.

In addition to funding "official" presidential libraries, Congress has occasionally provided specific funding for private facilities honoring former presidents. For example, Congress appropriated $1 million in 1996 for the Calvin Coolidge Memorial Foundation,[7] $500,000 in 1997 for the Rutherford B. Hayes home,[8] $3 million in 1999 for the Abraham Lincoln library,[9] and $365,000 in 2000 for the Ulysses S. Grant boyhood home.[10] Such funds have been used to support construction, maintenance, or other projects.

RECENT FUNDRAISING POLICY ISSUES

Disclosure

The major current policy issue surrounding library fundraising is whether private contributions are sufficiently transparent. Library foundations typically do not publicize identifying information about their contributions, nor are they required to do so under federal law. Library foundations are typically established as tax-exempt organizations under section

501 (c)(3) of the Internal Revenue Code (IRC).[11] Although those organizations must report certain information to the Internal Revenue Service (IRS), they are not required to publicly disclose identifying information about their donors. Contributions to libraries are also not subject to disclosure requirements or limitations contained in the Federal Election Campaign Act (FECA), which governs campaign financing.[12]

In recent Congresses, some Members have expressed concern about the lack of information surrounding private fundraising for library foundations. These Members, and some media organizations and interest groups, argue that additional disclosure could help make transparent and reduce potential conflicts of interest from donors who may wish to curry favor with current or former Presidents, their administrations or the U.S. government generally.

In response to these and related concerns, the 110th Congress placed additional reporting requirements on library contributions from lobbyists and lobbying organizations. Under the Honest Leadership and Open Government Act of 2007 (HLOGA), registered lobbyists who contribute $200 or more to library foundations (in the aggregate and over six-month reporting periods) must disclose the contributions in reports filed with the Clerk of the House or Secretary of the Senate.[13] These requirements also apply to organizations employing registered lobbyists and political action committees (PACs) maintained or controlled by lobbyists. Overall, HLOGA requires that lobbyists' contributions to library foundations be publicly reported, but the act does not address contributions from non-lobbyists.

Financial Viability

A second, but currently less prominent, policy issue surrounding library fundraising concerns costs to the federal government. Congress requires library organizations to demonstrate financial viability before NARA takes over the facility. Amid size and maintenance-cost concerns (particularly during the 1980s), Congress established architectural and design requirements in the Presidential Libraries Act of 1986.[14] The act also established an endowment requirement for libraries deeded over to NARA. Before taking possession of a library facility, the Archivist of the United States must determine that the endowment is sufficient to cover at least 40% of the cost of constructing or acquiring the facility.[15] President Barack Obama's library would be the first that must adhere to the 40% requirement, which applies only to Presidents taking office for the first time after July 1, 2002.

LIBRARY FUNDRAISING: LEGISLATION IN THE 112TH CONGRESS

On February 17, 2011, Representative Duncan introduced H.R. 775, a bill to require additional fundraising disclosure surrounding presidential libraries and related organizations. Like H.R. 36 from the 111th Congress, H.R. 775 would require additional disclosure of all contributions aggregating $200 or more to library fundraising organizations. Also like its predecessor, the Duncan bill would require disclosure to NARA, the House Committee on Oversight and Government Reform, and the Senate Committee on Homeland Security and

Governmental Affairs. However, H.R. 775 would require annual rather than quarterly reporting.

The bill applies to fundraising activities by library organizations affiliated with current presidents rather than all such facilities. Proposed disclosure requirements would also apply to facilities not administered by NARA or for which NARA has entered into an agreement to take over the facility.[16] These provisions suggest that H.R. 775's primary emphasis is on documenting library fundraising for current presidents or, perhaps, those who have recently left office but for whom agreements with NARA have not yet been finalized. It is possible, however, that the bill is also intended to apply to any fundraising organization that has not entered into an agreement with NARA, such as private facilities that NARA has chosen not to administer (the fundraising arms of presidential homes, for example) or that have chosen not to seek NARA administration. If necessary, the language could be clarified through amendments or rulemakings.

LIBRARY FUNDRAISING: LEGISLATION IN THE 111TH CONGRESS

In one of its first acts of legislative business, and with minimal debate, the House passed the Presidential Library Donation Act of 2009 (H.R. 36; Towns) on January 7, 2009. The measure passed under suspension of the rules by a 388-31 vote. The bill was referred to the Senate Committee on Homeland Security and Governmental Affairs. As the House vote suggests, H.R. 36 generally received broad, bipartisan support.

Generally similar to H.R. 775 introduced in the 112th Congress, H.R. 36 would have required library fundraising organizations to file quarterly reports itemizing contributions totaling at least $200. Under the bill, the reports would have been filed with NARA, the House Committee on Oversight and Government Reform, and the Senate Committee on Homeland Security and Governmental Affairs.[17] The bill would have required continued filing until the later of: (1) the Archivist of the United States took control of the library facility or entered into an agreement to do so; or (2) the President, whose archive is in question, had been out of office for at least four years.

Despite generally broad support for the bill, one provision generated some controversy during House floor debate. Civil and criminal penalties specified in H.R. 36 could have applied to those filing false disclosure reports. While voicing overall support for the bill, Representative Gohmert expressed concern that the criminal-penalty provisions had not been considered by the Judiciary Committee and could be used to imprison those who had made simple reporting mistakes.[18] Representative Towns expressed willingness to reexamine parts of the legislation, although the bill was not amended before passage.[19]

LIBRARY FUNDRAISING: LEGISLATION IN THE 110TH CONGRESS

H.R. 36 in the 111th Congress was virtually identical to the version of H.R. 1254 (Waxman) passed by the House during the 110th Congress.[20] The Senate Committee on Homeland Security and Governmental Affairs (HSGAC) favorably reported an amended version of H.R. 1254, but the measure did not receive floor consideration. Under the version of H.R. 1254 reported by HSGAC, reporting thresholds would have varied depending on whether NARA had already taken control of (or agreed to take control of) the library. For those facilities that were not yet under NARA control, the reporting threshold would have been $200, compared with $1,250 for those already under NARA control. Unlike the version of the bill passed by the House, the HSGACreported version of H.R. 1254 also would have required reporting to continue throughout the President's lifetime.

ANALYSIS AND CONCLUDING COMMENTS

The debate over library fundraising suggests tension between the relatively narrow policy goal of making presidential papers publicly accessible on one hand, and in constructing what can be elaborate research centers and museums to house those papers on the other. Appropriated funds typically address the former goal, while private funds cover the latter. As presidential libraries grow in number, scope, and size, interest in funding sources and alternatives is likely to continue. In the past, debate over those issues has centered around disclosure and financial viability. Currently, disclosure appears to be the major policy concern.

If Congress determines that fundraising for presidential libraries should remain essentially a private matter, it might choose not to enact legislation requiring additional disclosure and, in so doing, maintain the status quo. Under this option, private fundraising for presidential libraries would presumably continue unchanged. Additional information about funding sources and amounts would continue to be publicly unavailable, unless fundraising organizations chose to voluntarily disclose the information. This outcome could be objectionable to those who believe that public disclosure could enhance transparency or discourage conflicts of interest. On the other hand, those who believe that additional disclosure could be burdensome, could discourage private contributions, or who otherwise object to additional reporting may prefer to maintain the status quo.

If Congress favors additional disclosure, it could choose to enact measures requiring additional detail about contributions or fundraising practices. The disclosure provisions in H.R. 775 could ensure that additional information about contributions to library foundations is publicly available. Accordingly, although additional information about private funding sources would be required, the bill would not place new restrictions on how funds are raised, from whom, and in what amounts. The bill also would not require contributions from foreign sources to be specifically identified—a source of some controversy in recent debates surrounding library fundraising. Nonetheless, additional disclosure about contributions (regardless of source) could provide more public access to basic information about funding than is currently available. If flagging particular sources of contributions were important to Congress, additional reporting requirements could be placed on filers. Certain contribution sources could also be restricted or banned outright.[21]

If Congress wishes to pursue broader regulation of library fundraising, aspects of federal campaign finance policy may be a useful model, although certainly not the only model.[22] As noted previously, library contributions are not treated as campaign contributions, but some goals embodied in campaign finance regulation appear to be similar to those behind calls for additional library-fundraising disclosure. H.R. 775 already adopts certain aspects of campaign-finance disclosure found in FECA (e.g., reporting a contributor's name, address, and occupation,[23] the $200 reporting threshold,[24] and certain penalties). The bill does not, however, adopt FECA's restrictions on amounts and sources of contributions. In short, although H.R. 775 would require additional information about contributions, the bill would not affect the contributions themselves or, necessarily, fundraising practices.

Additional restrictions on amounts or sources of library contributions might be attractive to those who believe that disclosure alone will be insufficient to thwart potential conflicts of interest arising from private fundraising. Restricting contributions, however, suggest broader policy goals than are apparent in H.R. 775. As the debate over campaign finance suggests, regulating voluntary contributions can be far more contentious than the comparatively limited requirement of disclosure.

End Notes

[1] Parts of this report are adapted from CRS Report RS20825, *Presidential Libraries: The Federal System and Related Legislation*, by Wendy R. Ginsberg. Additional discussion about establishing presidential libraries and the presidential library system appears in CRS Report R415 13, *The Presidential Libraries Act and the Establishment of Presidential Libraries*, by Wendy R. Ginsberg and Erika K. Lunder; and CRS Report RS20825, *Presidential Libraries: The Federal System and Related Legislation*, by Wendy R. Ginsberg.

[2] Organizations that raise funds for presidential libraries are often referred to as "foundations," but they are not private foundations for tax purposes. See CRS Report 96-264, *Frequently Asked Questions About Tax-Exempt Organizations*, by Erika K. Lunder.

[3] The George W. Bush library is not yet complete. The facility eventually will be housed at Southern Methodist University in Dallas.

[4] See, for example, Kenneth P. Doyle, "House Overwhelmingly Approves Bill," *Daily Report for Executives*, January 8, 2009, p. A-7; and Susan Schmidt, Margaret Coker, and Jay Solomon, "Clinton Reveals Donors," *The Wall Street Journal*, December 19, 2008, p. A1, eastern edition.

[5] The Clinton Foundation raises funds for the former President's library and other causes. On the relationship between the library and the foundation, and the disclosure agreement between the foundation and the Obama Presidential Transition Foundation, see William J. Clinton Foundation and Obama Presidential Transition Foundation, Memorandum of Understanding, December 12, 2008, at http://msnbcmedia.msn.com/i/msnbc/sections/news/ understanding.pdf.

[6] U. S. Congress, House Committee on Government Operations, *Reduction of Costs of Presidential Libraries*, report to accompany H.R. 1349, 99th Cong., 1st sess., May 15, 1985, H.Rept. 99-125 (Washington: GPO, 1985), p. 15.

[7] See 110 Stat. 3 009-258 for appropriations language and 110 Stat. 3868 for authorizing language.

[8] 111 Stat. 1550.

[9] 13 Stat. 1501A-143.

[10] 114 Stat. 930.

[11] Details of IRC reporting requirements are beyond the scope of this report. For additional discussion, see CRS Report RL33377, *Tax-Exempt Organizations: Political Activity Restrictions and Disclosure Requirements*, by Erika K. Lunder.

[12] 2 U.S.C. § 431 et seq.

[13] 121 Stat. 743. HLOGA is devoted primarily to other lobbying and ethics issues. For additional discussion, see CRS Report RL34166, *Lobbying Law and Ethics Rules Changes in the 110th Congress*, by Jack Maskell; and CRS Report RL34377, *Honest Leadership and Open Government Act of 2007: The Role of the Clerk of the House and the Secretary of the Senate*, by Jacob R. Straus On campaign finance provisions in HLOGA, see CRS Report RL34324, *Campaign Finance: Legislative Developments and Policy Issues in the 110th Congress*, by R. Sam Garrett. For more recent discussion of campaign finance issues, see CRS Report R41542, *The State of Campaign Finance Policy: Recent Developments and Issues for Congress*, by R. Sam Garrett

[14] 100 Stat. 495, which primarily amended 44 U.S.C. § 2112(g).

[15] Larger endowments are required for libraries larger than 70,000 square feet. Congress established the 40% threshold in the FY2003 Consolidated Appropriations Act. See 117 Stat. 462, which amended 44 U.S.C. § 2112(g). The previous threshold was 20%. That amount was set in the Presidential Libraries Act of 1986 (100 Stat. 497, which also amended 44 U.S.C. § 2112(g)) and applies to the libraries of Presidents George H.W. Bush, William J. Clinton, and George W. Bush.

[16] H.R. 775, Sec. 1, proposed 44 U.S.C. 2112(h)(1).

[17] The bill refers to reports being filed with "the Administration." Although the bill does not define that term, H.R. 36 would amend 44 U.S.C. § 2112, which defines "the Administration" as NARA.

[18] Rep. Louie Gohmert, "Presidential Library Donation Reform Act of 2009," remarks in the House, *Congressional Record*, daily edition, vol. 155, part 2 (January 7, 2009), p. H46.

[19] Rep. Edolphus Towns, "Presidential Library Donation Reform Act of 2009," remarks in the House, *Congressional Record*, daily edition, vol. 155, part 2 (January 7, 2009), p. H46.

[20] On H.R. 1254, see CRS Report RS20825, *Presidential Libraries: The Federal System and Related Legislation*, by Wendy R. Ginsberg; U.S. Congress, House Committee on Oversight and Government Reform, report to accompany H.R. 1254, 110th Cong., 1st sess, March 9, 2007, H.Rept. 110-43 (Washington: GPO, 2007); and U.S. Congress, Senate Committee on Homeland Security and Governmental Affairs, report to accompany H.R. 1254, 1 10th Cong., 1st sess., October 22, 2007, S.Rept. 110-202 (Washington: GPO, 2007).

[21] Such a ban may raise constitutional questions, a topic that is beyond the scope of this report.

[22] For an overview of emerging and recent campaign finance issues, see CRS Report R41542, *The State of Campaign Finance Policy: Recent Developments and Issues for Congress*, by R. Sam Garrett.

[23] FECA also requires reporting employer information. On FECA reporting requirements for individual contributions, see 2 U.S.C. § 434(b)(3); 2 U.S.C. and 2 U.S.C. § 431(13) (on the "identification" definition in FECA).

[24] FECA requires reporting individual contributions *exceeding* $200 (2 U.S.C. § 434(b)(3)), whereas H.R. 36 would require reporting contributions of at least $200.

In: Presidential Libraries: Elements and Considerations
Editor: Jamie D. Reynolds

ISBN: 978-1-61324-581-1
© 2011 Nova Science Publishers, Inc.

Chapter 3

PRESIDENTIAL LIBRARIES: THE FEDERAL SYSTEM AND RELATED LEGISLATION

Wendy R. Ginsberg

SUMMARY

Through the National Archives and Records Administration (NARA), the federal government currently manages and maintains 12 presidential libraries. Inaugurated with the Presidential Libraries Act of 1955, these entities are privately constructed on behalf of former Presidents and, upon completion, are deeded to the federal government. Deposited within these edifices are the official records and papers of the former President, as well as documentary materials of his family and, often, his political associates. These holdings are made available for public examination in accordance with prevailing law concerning custody, official secrecy, personal privacy, and other similar restrictions. This report provides a brief overview of the federal presidential libraries system, and discusses three pieces of related legislation introduced the 111th Congress (H.R. 35, H.R. 36, and H.R. 1387).

During the first 150 years of government under the Constitution, the management and preservation of federal records was generally neglected.[1] Inattentiveness to the maintenance of official papers prevailed within both the infant bureaucracy and the White House. Although the Secretary of State bore responsibility for retaining copies of the most important government documents during these initial years, lesser papers without immediate administrative significance disappeared in a clutter, disintegrated, became otherwise lost, or were destroyed by design.

Within this atmosphere, departing Presidents had little choice with regard to the disposition of their records: there was no national archive to receive them, and, for reasons of etiquette, politics, or both, there was reluctance to leave them behind. Thus, the early Chief Executives carried away their documents of office, entrusting them to their families, estate executors, or often, to fate.[2] After several decades of private ownership, many collections of presidential records came to be established within the libraries of state and private universities, state historical societies, or at the Library of Congress. Wear and attrition, however, often levied a price on some caches of presidential documents before more reliable preservation efforts.

As the federal government grew, scholars, the public, and Congress realized increasing need to maintain a historical record of presidential decision-making and action. Questions arose as to the propriety and wisdom of neglecting the management and preservation of federal records, including the practice of regarding presidential papers as personal property to be taken away by the incumbent when he left office. By the 20th century, Congress and historians grew alarmed that such papers were accidently destroyed, lost, or sometimes only selectively released for research and edification.[3] Archivists and other scholars lamented omissions in the national governmental record created by the dearth of records.[4] Entire files were removed from the White House, and presidential correspondence could be taken from departmental files without review or recourse. As it applied to federal records, the concept of presidential papers was undefined. The situation became particularly acute with the creation of the Executive Office of the President in 1939. Franklin D. Roosevelt (FDR) established a panoply of emergency and wartime agencies within this domain, all of which served the President in immediate and direct capacities and all of which, therefore, could be considered producers of presidential records. These records were, therefore, not subject to preservation statutes and regulations. The potential loss of the documentary materials of these entities prompted records management, administrative continuity, and historical record concerns.

PRESIDENTIAL LIBRARIES

Addressing this situation, FDR sought to return presidential papers to the public realm through a new type of institution—the presidential library. When he advanced this concept in 1938, two prototype libraries were in existence. The Rutherford B. Hayes Memorial Library had been completed in Fremont, Ohio, in 1914.[5] Former President Herbert Hoover had placed his presidential records in a facility he had inaugurated in 1919 to house records deriving from his public service during World War I—the Hoover Library of War, Revolution, and Peace, located on the Stanford University campus.[6] Building upon these models, Roosevelt developed the concept of a federally maintained presidential library. Electing to locate his presidential library on the grounds of his family home in Hyde Park, NY, FDR approved the creation of a corporation to receive contributions and donations to pay for the construction of an archival edifice to house and preserve such historical materials as he might provide to the corporation or the United States. Chartering legislation for the Roosevelt presidential library was enacted in 1939.[7] The Archivist of the United States, acting on behalf of the federal government, accepted the completed library facility on July 4, 1940.[8]

FDR's successor, Harry S. Truman, was no less attentive to history and the preservation of his presidential papers for public examination. After his election, Truman saw the 1950 creation of a Missouri corporation to establish a presidential library on his behalf, following the FDR model.[9] While the Truman library corporation was endeavoring to raise funds for the construction of the archival edifice, Congress enacted the Presidential Libraries Act of 1955, which established the basic policy for the creation of all federally maintained presidential libraries.[10] These include the Franklin D. Roosevelt Library, Hyde Park, NY; Herbert Hoover Library, West Branch, IA; Harry S. Truman Library, Independence, MO; Dwight D.

Eisenhower Library, Abilene, KS; John F. Kennedy Library, Boston, MA; Lyndon Baines Johnson Library, Austin, TX; Richard M. Nixon Library, Yorba Linda, CA; Gerald R. Ford Library, Ann Arbor, MI; Jimmy Carter Library, Atlanta, GA; Ronald Reagan Library, Simi Valley, CA; George H. W. Bush Library, College Station, TX; and the William J. Clinton Library in Little Rock, AR.[11]

The George W. Bush Presidential Library is to be constructed on the campus of Southern Methodist University in Dallas, TX. Groundbreaking for the project is scheduled for late 2010.[12] The George W. Bush Presidential Center, which is to include the library, is scheduled to open in 2013.[13]

Library Records

As a consequence of the so-called Watergate incident—the June 17, 1972, burglary at the Democratic National Committee headquarters located in the Watergate office building in Washington, DC—the official papers and records of President Richard M. Nixon were placed under federal custody by the Presidential Recordings and Materials Preservation Act of 1974 (PRMPA) to assure their availability to federal prosecutors.[14] The statute required that these materials remain in Washington, DC, under the supervision of the Archivist. Thus, Nixon could neither take his presidential records with him when he left office, nor place them in a presidential library outside the nation's capital. Subsequently, a Nixon library was constructed at the former President's birthplace—Yorba Linda, CA. The completed facility was dedicated in July 1990, but remained under private operation for 17 years, housing Nixon's congressional and vice presidential records and a small collection of copies of his presidential papers.

A provision in the Consolidated Appropriations Act, 2004, amended the PRMPA to allow the Archivist, at a later time, to transfer the Nixon presidential materials to the Nixon library in the event NARA took over its administration. In the event of such a transfer, the federal government would retain custody of the records and materials and responsibility for their public availability.[15] Negotiations with the Nixon library resulted in its transfer to NARA on July 11, 2007. Concurrent with this assumption of Nixon library administration, NARA transferred and made publicly available 78,000 pages of previously restricted Nixon documents and more than 11 hours of taped conversations.[16]

Following the enactment of the PRMPA, Congress developed two other statutes affecting presidential libraries. The first of these, the Presidential Records Act of 1978, carefully defined "presidential records," and specified that all such materials created on or after January 20, 1981, were subject to its provisions.[17] The new law effectively made official presidential records federal property that was to remain under the custody and control of the Archivist when each incumbent President left the White House. Jimmy Carter was the last occupant of the Oval Office who could freely take away his records.

At about this same time, concern about the increasing cost of providing benefits to the nation's former Presidents was beginning to build in Congress, and was legislatively manifested initially in March 1980 in proposals to adjust the federal largesse bestowed upon former Presidents and their families. Federally maintained presidential libraries—particularly their physical size and continued maintenance—were among the perquisites seen to be contributing to the burden of the taxpayers.[18] The 99th Congress passed legislation addressing this single area of expense involving former Presidents. The Presidential Libraries Act of 1986 set certain reporting requirements, architectural and design conditions, and fiscal limitations regarding future presidential libraries, including requiring an operating endowment.[19] For example, prior to accepting any gift of land, a facility, or equipment to create a federally maintained presidential library or making any physical or material change in an existing one, the Archivist must submit a written report to Congress providing certain details, as specified in the statute, about the transaction. The endowment requirement for new presidential libraries—20% of assessed value—was made applicable "to any President who takes the oath of office as President *for the first time* on or after January 20, 1985."[20] George H. W. Bush's Presidential Library became the first such facility to be subject to this reform requirement. Subsequently, the Consolidated Appropriations Act for FY2003 increased the endowment requirement to 40% of assessed value and made it effective "to any President who takes the oath of office as President *for the first time* on or after July 1, 2002."[21]

Library Location

Federal experience with the first four presidential libraries—those of Roosevelt, Truman, Hoover, and Eisenhower—established two patterns: the facility was located at what was considered to be the particular President's hometown (birthplace or principal residence), and the library building(s), grounds, and holdings were deeded to the federal government for supervision.

Change in, or exception to, this practice occurred with the Johnson presidential library, which was located on the campus of the University of Texas at Austin. Because the university could not legally deed its land to the federal government, the Archivist, to take possession of the facility, relied upon his Presidential Libraries Act authority to "make agreements, upon terms and conditions he considers proper, with a State, political subdivision, university, institution of higher learning, institute, or foundation to use as a Presidential archival depository land, buildings, and equipment of the State, subdivision, university, or other organization, to be made available by it without transfer of title to the United States, and maintain, operate, and protect the depository as a part of the national archives system."[22] This innovation was used again in the case of the Ford library located on the Ann Arbor campus of the University of Michigan. A separate Ford museum is located in the former President's hometown of Grand Rapids, MI, but it is not a federally maintained presidential library.

The Kennedy, Carter, and Reagan presidential libraries are situated in locales in close proximity to respective presidential hometowns. The George H. W. Bush library is located in the former President's home state on the Texas A&M University campus. The George W. Bush Library is planned to be built at Southern Methodist University, the alma mater of former First Lady Laura Bush.[23]

Library Funding

In recent years, Congress occasionally has appropriated funds on a one-time basis for construction or other improvements at facilities honoring former Presidents that are not part of the presidential library program administered by the National Archives. These include $1 million in 1996 for the Calvin Coolidge Memorial Foundation,[24] $500,000 in 1997 for the Rutherford B. Hayes home,[25] $3 million in 1999 for the Abraham Lincoln library,[26] and $365,000 in 2000 for the Ulysses S. Grant boyhood home.[27] In his FY2010 budget request, President Barack Obama asked Congress to appropriate $22 million for construction and related costs for building an addition to the John F. Kennedy Presidential Library and Museum, $17.5 million for repair and renovation of the FDR library and museum, and $2 million "for the repair and restoration of the plaza that surrounds the Lyndon Baines Johnson Presidential Library and Museum."[28] House and Senate appropriators recommended $17.5 million for the FDR library.[29] Senate appropriators added that the FDR library "suffers from flooding," has an infrastructure that is "greatly deteriorated and outdated," and operates a variety of "systems [that] violate NARA's standards for preservation."[30] Senate appropriators also said the pending construction and oversight of the George W. Bush Library prompted them to increase NARA appropriations from the FY2009 level.[31]

ESTABLISHING A LIBRARY

To establish a federally maintained presidential library in compliance with prevailing law,[32] an incumbent President may informally enter into discussions with family members, close friends, and political associates regarding his wishes in this regard. Some combination of these individuals may create a foundation or other organization of private character to receive contributions and donations to obtain a site and construct an edifice for a presidential library. Because the President is not an official of this organization and because of the organization's private character, its activities are not necessarily subject to public scrutiny—nor is the President expressly subjected to any ethics law requirements as a consequence of its solicitation or receipt of contributions.

When the President leaves office, his official records remain in the custody of the federal government, under the supervision of the Archivist. It is expected that, once the Archivist accepts the archival edifice built in honor of the former President, the official records of the former President will be deposited there. Library staff are Archives employees and, as such, are compensated from funds appropriated for this purpose.

Upon completion of the presidential library facility, constructed in accordance with prescribed architectural and design conditions, arrangements are made by the former President's private foundation to deed it to the federal government, along with an operating endowment. Statutory law provides for the calculation of the amount of the endowment required,[33] and legislative history indicates that "the income to the endowments is intended to offset ... building operations costs and reduce, to the extent of the income, the amount of appropriations required for building operations."[34] Ceremonies for dedicating and deeding the facility are scheduled; the federal government takes possession; and an opening day is set. The former President may or may not maintain offices at his library, and his foundation may or may not sponsor or support activities at the library.

PRESIDENTIAL LIBRARIES AND THE 111TH CONGRESS

Preservation of Presidential Records

On January 21, 2009, President Barack Obama issued an executive order (E.O. 13489) that changed substantially the presidential record preservation policies promulgated by the George W. Bush Administration in E.O. 13233. President Obama's executive order grants the incumbent President and the relevant former Presidents 30 days to review records prior to their being released to the public. In contrast, under the Bush Administration executive order, the incumbent President, former Presidents, former Vice Presidents, and their designees were granted broad authority to deny access to presidential documents or to delay their release indefinitely. Moreover, former Presidents had 90 days to review whether requested documents should be released.

Prior to President Obama's issuance of E.O. 13489, legislation was introduced in the 111th Congress (H.R. 35) that would statutorily rescind the executive order (E.O. 13233) issued by former President George W. Bush. The Bush Administration's executive order allowed the incumbent President—as well as former Presidents whose records were affected—to withhold from public disclosure the records of former Presidents and Vice Presidents or to delay their release indefinitely under claims of executive privilege. In addition to statutorily overturning E.O. 13233, the House-passed version of H.R. 35 would reduce the time a President would have to review his records prior to their public release from 30 to 20 days.[35] On January 7, 2009, H.R. 35 passed the House under suspension of the rules. On May 19, 2009, the Senate Committee on Homeland Security and Governmental Affairs reported the bill with an amendment in the nature of a substitute. In its report, the Senate committee recommended that incumbent and former Presidents be given 60 days to review records prior to their release. A former or incumbent President could extend that review period by 30 additional days with approval from the Archivist.[36] The measure has not received Senate floor consideration.

Fundraising for Presidential Libraries

On January 6, 2009, Representative Edolphus Towns introduced the Presidential Library Donation Reform Act of 2009 (H.R. 36). H.R. 36 would require library fundraising organizations to file quarterly reports itemizing contributions of at least $200 and identify donors. The House passed the bill on January 7, 2009. The next day, the bill was referred to the Senate Committee on Homeland Security and Governmental Affairs.[37]

Electronic Record Preservation

On March 9, 2009, Representative Paul W. Hodes introduced the Electronic Message Preservation Act (H.R. 1387). The bill would require, among other things, the Archivist to report to Congress within a year of when a President left office on "the volume and format of Presidential records deposited into that President's Presidential archival depository," as well as whether the records satisfy the Presidential Records Act. On March 10, 2009, the House Committee on Oversight and Government Reform ordered the bill to be reported.

ACKNOWLEDGMENTS

This report originally was written by Harold C. Relyea, who has retired from CRS.

End Notes

[1] See H. G. Jones, *The Records of a Nation* (New York: Atheneum, 1969), pp. 3-23.

[2] Nancy Kegan Smith and Gary M. Stern, "A Historical Review of Access to Records in Presidential Libraries," *The Public Historian*, vol. 28, no. 3 (Summer 2006), pp. 8 1-82.

[3] U. S. Congress, House Committee on Government Operations, *To Provide for the Acceptance and Maintenance of Presidential Libraries, and for Other Purposes*, hearing on H.J.Res. 330, H.J.Res. 331, and H.J.Res. 332, 84th Cong., 1st sess., June 13, 1955, S. Hrg. 84-0014 (Washington: GPO, 1955).

[4] Ibid., pp. 50-64.

[5] The Hayes library is currently maintained jointly by the Hayes family foundation and the State of Ohio; see Thomas A. Smith, "Before Hyde Park: The Rutherford B. Hayes Library," *American Archivist*, vol. 43, Fall 1980, pp. 485-488.

[6] Paul Dickson, *Think Tanks* (New York: Atheneum, 1971), p. 303; the Hoover presidential papers were subsequently transferred to the Hoover Presidential Library in West Branch, IA, when that facility came under federal operation in 1964.

[7] 53 Stat. 1062.

[8] Waldo Gifford Leland, "The Creation of the Franklin D. Roosevelt Library: A Personal Narrative," American Archivist, vol. 18, January 1955, pp. 11-29; Donald R. McCoy, "The Beginnings of the Franklin D. Roosevelt Library," *Prologue*, vol. 7, Fall 1975, pp. 137-150.

[9] Philip C. Brooks, "The Harry S. Truman Library—Plans and Reality," *American Archivist*, vol. 25, January 1962, pp. 25-37; David D. Lloyd, "The Harry S. Truman Library," *American Archivist*, vol. 18, April 1955, pp. 107-110.

[10] 69 Stat. 695.

[11] Access to the websites of any of these presidential libraries may be found at http://www.archives.gov/presidential-libraries/; addresses and telephone numbers for the libraries may also be found in the *Congressional Directory* at the National Archives entry.

[12] For more information on the library, see George W. Bush Presidential Center, "Library and Museum," at http://www.georgewbushlibrary.com/site/c.fqLOI5OAKlF/b.5011107/k.BC90/Library_and_Museum.htm.

[13] The George W. Bush Presidential Center, "Design and Construction," at http://www.georgewbushlibrary.com/site/c.fqLOI5OAKlF/b.5012059/k.5E3A/Design_amp_Construction.htm.

[14] 88 Stat. 1695.

[15] See Section 543 at 118 Stat. 346; George Lardner, Jr., "Nixon Data May Be Calif.-Bound," *Washington Post*, November 13, 2003, p. A12.

[16] Gillian Flaccus, "Federal Archivists Take Control of Nixon Library," *Washington Post*, July 12, 2007, p. C9; Jennifer Harper, "Nixon Papers Released: Presidential Library Opens With 'True Acceptance'," *Washington Times*, July 12, 2007, p. A8; Neil A. Lewis, "National Archives Release of 11 Hours of Nixon Tapes," *New York Times*, July 12, 2007, p. A15.

[17] 92 Stat. 2523.

[18] See U.S. Congress, House Committee on Government Operations, *Presidential Libraries: Unexplored Funding Alternatives*, 97th Cong., 2nd sess., H.Rept. 97-732 (Washington: GPO, 1982).

[19] 100 Stat. 495.

[20] 100 Stat. 498 (emphasis added).

[21] 117 Stat. 462 (emphasis added).

[22] See 44 U.S.C. 2112(a) (1982); 44 U.S.C. 2112(a)(1)(B)(i) (1996).

[23] Anna M. Tinsley and Eva-Marie Ayala, "Bush Library Panel Limits Negotiation to SMU," *Washington Post*, December 22, 2006, p. A12. See also Ariel Alexovich, "The Caucus: Bush Picks S.M.U. for Presidential Library," *The New York Times*, February 22, 2008, http://thecaucus.blogs.

[24] 110 Stat. 3009-258 (appropriation); 110 Stat. 3868 (authorization).

[25] 111 Stat. 1550.

[26] 13 Stat. 1501A-143.

[27] 114 Stat. 930.

[28] U.S. Office of Management and Budget, *Budget of the U.S. Government, FY2010: Appendix*, Washington, DC, May 7, 2009, p. 1249, http://www.whitehouse.gov/omb/budget/fy2010/assets

[29] U.S. Congress, House Committee on Appropriations, Subcommittee on Financial Services and General Government, *Financial Services and General Government Appropriation Bill, 2010*, report to accompany H.R. 3170, 111th Cong., 1st sess., July 10, 2009, H.Rept. 111-202 (Washington: GPO, 2009), p. 79; and U.S. Congress, Senate Committee on Appropriations, Subcommittee on Financial Services and General Government, *Financial Services and General Government Appropriations Bill, 2010*, report to accompany S. 1432, 111th Cong., 1st sess., July 9, 2009, S.Rept. 111- 43 (Washington: GPO, 2009), p. 105.

[30] U.S. Congress, Senate Committee on Appropriations, Subcommittee on Financial Services and General Government, *Financial Services and General Government Appropriations Bill, 2010*, report to accompany S. 1432, 111th Cong., 1st sess., July 9, 2009, S.Rept. 111-43 (Washington: GPO, 2009), p. 105.

[31] Ibid., p. 103.

[32] 44 U.S.C. § 2108. See also P.L. 99-323.

[33] See 44 U.S.C. 2112(g)(3).

[34] U. S. Congress, House Committee on Government Operations, *Reduction of Costs of Presidential Libraries*, report to accompany H.R. 1349, 99th Cong., 1st sess., S. 886 (Washington: GPO, 1985), p. 15.

[35] For more information on H.R. 35 and the Presidential Records Act, see CRS Report R40238, *Presidential Records: Issues for the 111th Congress*, by Wendy R. Ginsberg.

[36] U.S. Congress, Senate Committee on Homeland Security and Governmental Affairs, *Presidential Records Act Amendments of 2009*, report to accompany H.R. 35, 111th Cong., 1st sess., May 19, 2009, S.Rept. 111-21 (Washington: GPO, 2009).

[37] For more information on H.R. 36 and fundraising for presidential libraries, see CRS Report R40209, *Fundraising for Presidential Libraries: Legislative and Policy Issues in the 111th Congress*, by R. Sam Garrett.

In: Presidential Libraries: Elements and Considerations
Editor: Jamie D. Reynolds

ISBN: 978-1-61324-581-1
© 2011 Nova Science Publishers, Inc.

Chapter 4

PRESIDENTIAL RECORDS: ISSUES FOR THE 111TH CONGRESS

Wendy R. Ginsberg

SUMMARY

Most records of recent former Presidents and former Vice Presidents are required by statute to be turned over to the National Archives and Records Administration at the end of each administration. These records are then disclosed to the public, unless the Archivist of the United States, the incumbent President, or the appropriate former President claims the records should be kept private.

On his first full day in office, President Barack Obama issued an executive order (E.O. 13489), rescinding E.O. 13233, changing substantially the presidential record preservation policies promulgated by the George W. Bush Administration. E.O. 13489 grants the incumbent President and the relevant former Presidents 30 days to review records prior to their being released to the public. Under the policies of the Bush Administration, the incumbent President, former Presidents, former Vice Presidents, and their designees were granted broad authority to deny access to presidential documents or to delay their release indefinitely. Moreover, former Presidents had 90 days to review whether requested documents should be released.

Prior to President Obama's issuance of E.O. 13489, legislation was introduced in the 111th Congress (H.R. 35) that would statutorily rescind the executive order (E.O. 13233) issued by former President George W. Bush. E.O. 13233 allowed the incumbent President—as well as former Presidents whose records were affected—to withhold from public disclosure the records of former Presidents and Vice Presidents or to delay their release indefinitely under claims of executive privilege. In addition to statutorily overturning E.O. 13233, H.R. 35 would reduce the time a President would have review his records prior to their public release.

This report will analyze President Barack Obama's E.O. 13489, and discuss its departure from the policies of the previous administration. Additionally, this report will examine H.R. 35 and its possible legislative effects on the presidential records policies of the Obama Administration.

INTRODUCTION

Since 1955, the Presidential Libraries Act (44 U.S.C. § 2112) has governed the establishment of federally maintained presidential libraries. These libraries are created to serve as archives that return presidential papers and communications to the public realm. Currently, 12 presidential libraries are managed and maintained by the federal government through the National Archives and Records Administration (NARA).

In addition to the Presidential Libraries Act, presidential records are subject to the Presidential Records Act of 1978 (44 U.S.C. §§ 2201-2207; P.L. 95-591). The act details which records and materials are to be assumed by the National Archives at the end of a President's administration.[1] According to Chapter 22 of Title 44 of the U.S. Code, when a President leaves office, his official records remain in the custody of the federal government, under the supervision of the Archivist of the United States. Once a location for a presidential library has been determined, and the facility is deeded to the United States, the former President's records are to be deposited there.[2]

On November 1, 2001, President George W. Bush issued an executive order (E.O. 13233), which allowed the incumbent President—as well as former Presidents, former Vice Presidents, and their designees whose records are affected—to withhold from public disclosure the records of former Presidents and Vice Presidents or to delay their release indefinitely under claims of executive privilege.[3] On January 7, 2009, the House passed a bill (H.R. 35) that would statutorily revoke E.O. 13233. The bill would also allow the Archivist to reassume control of access to the records of former Presidents.

On January 21, 2009, President Barack Obama issued E.O. 1 3489[4] on his first full day in office. The new executive order explicitly rescinded E.O. 13233. Many of the aims of H.R. 35 are incorporated into President Obama's executive order. However, unlike H.R. 35, which would grant the Archivist final determination over record disclosure, President Obama's order allows the incumbent President to stop disclosure through claims of executive privilege. This report will discuss policy changes incorporated into E.O. 13489 and analyze the possible effects of H.R. 35.

THE POLICY QUESTION

Presidential records are a critical tool for understanding the powers and operations of the executive branch of the federal government. These presidential records, however, may include information that, if released to the public, could endanger national security, drastically affect the nation's economy, or result in an unwarranted invasion of personal privacy. The policy issue for Congress is to determine whether incumbent and former Presidents should be granted wide- ranging authority to assert claims of executive privilege—sometimes at the cost of government transparency and political scholarship. Presidential records are a critical piece of the nation's historical archive, yet some argue their public release is to be weighed against concerns for national security, privacy, and economic protection.

THE PRESIDENTIAL RECORDS ACT

Pursuant to Chapter 22 of Title 44 of the U.S. Code, upon leaving office, an outgoing President may restrict access to certain of his archived records for up to 12 years.[5] Certain presidential files and records may be excepted from public access if they qualify under any of the six criteria delineated in 44 U.S.C. § 2204. These criteria are

1. the information is specifically exempted by an executive order for the purpose of national security or foreign policy;
2. the information is related to federal office appointments;
3. the information is explicitly exempted from disclosure by statute;
4. the information includes trade secrets and commercial or financial information obtained from a person that is privileged or confidential;
5. the information is a confidential communication that requests or submits advice between the President and his advisers—or between the advisers themselves; or
6. the information is personnel or medical files, and their disclosure would amount to an unwarranted invasion of personal privacy.[6]

According to the act, the Archivist—or the courts—would have final determination over which records should be released to the public. The act also states that it is not to "be construed to confirm, limit, or expand any constitutionally-based privilege which may be available to an incumbent or former President."[7] The act does not define the parameters of this privilege.

EXECUTIVE ORDER 13233

President George W. Bush issued E.O. 13233 on November 1, 2001. The executive order gave the incumbent President, former Presidents, former Vice Presidents, and their designees broad authority to deny access to presidential documents or to delay their release indefinitely. Under the order, former Presidents had 90 days to review whether requested documents should be released (this is 60 days more than provided under earlier arrangements). Sitting Presidents had the authority to extend the review period indefinitely, and the Archivist had no recourse to challenge the status of materials that had been withheld or remained in review.[8]

The executive order also changed the procedure for the disclosure of presidential records. Under practices prior to E.O. 13233, presidential records would be released at the termination of the 12-year restriction period—unless the President, former President, or former Vice President asserted "constitutionally based privileges" to stop the disclosure.[9] E.O. 13233 required action by the

President, former President, or former Vice President for records to be released. If, therefore, none of the designated officers acted to release of presidential records, they may have remained undisclosed even if the 12-year restriction period lapsed. Moreover, the executive order permitted representatives of a former President or Vice President to challenge the release of presidential records. Formerly, all challenges to disclosure had to be made by the former President or former Vice President himself.

EXECUTIVE ORDER 13489

During his first full day in office, President Barack Obama issued an executive order (E.O. 13489) that explicitly revoked E.O. 13233. Under E.O. 13489, incumbent Presidents and former Presidents are granted 30 days to review presidential records to determine whether they should be released. If an incumbent President claims executive privilege for the records of a former President, the Counsel to the President is required to notify the Archivist, the appropriate former President, and the Attorney General of the action. The Archivist is then prohibited from releasing those records—unless instructed to do so by a court order.

In contrast to claims of executive privilege made by an incumbent President, claims of executive privilege made by a former President now require the Archivist to consult with the Attorney General, the Counsel to the President, or other appropriate officials to determine the validity of the request. According to the executive order, the incumbent President may instruct the Archivist whether to release the records of a former President, and the Archivist is to "abide by" the President's determination—unless directed otherwise by a court order. If the Archivist denies a former President's executive privilege claim and determines that records should be released, the incumbent President and appropriate former President are to be given 30 days notice of the records' release.

E.O. 13489 vests much of the records disclosure authority in the hands of the incumbent President. This broad authority to determine which records of a former President should be released to the public stands in contrast to the designs of the Presidential Records Act, which placed greater authority over records disclosure in the hands of the Archivist. The executive order does not define the boundaries of executive privilege, but it does define a "substantial question of executive privilege" as a situation in which "NARA's disclosure of Presidential records might impair national security (including the conduct of foreign relations), law enforcement, or the deliberative processes of the executive branch."

LEGISLATION IN THE 111TH CONGRESS

In the 111th Congress, Representative Edolphus Towns, with others, introduced The Presidential Records Act Amendments of 2009 (H.R. 35) on January 6, 2009. The bill passed the House under suspension of the rules on January 7, by a vote of 359-58. The bill was referred to the Senate Committee on Homeland Security and Governmental Affairs on January 9.

Among its changes to presidential recordkeeping, H.R. 35 would statutorily revoke E.O. 13233. In addition, the bill would limit the record review period for incumbent and former Presidents to 20 days (10 fewer days than President Obama's executive order mandates).[10] The bill would also require a former President or Vice President personally to request exemptions from records release.

H.R. 35 would modify a few practices mandated by President Obama's E.O. 13489—including granting the Archivist broader control over the disclosure of records of former Presidents. While E.O. 13489 grants the President vast authority to determine whether the records of a former President should be disclosed, H.R. 35 would vest that power in the Archivist. The bill does not attempt to define executive privilege or its boundaries.

LEGISLATION IN THE 110TH CONGRESS

The Presidential Records Act Amendments of 2009 (H.R. 35) is not Congress's first attempt to revoke E.O. 13233. In the 110th Congress, a similar bill (H.R. 1255) was passed under suspension of the rules in the House on March 14, 2007, by a vote of 333-93. A companion bill (S. 886) was introduced in the Senate on March 14. S. 886 was reported by the Committee on Homeland Security and Governmental Affairs without amendment on June 20 and placed on the legislative calendar that same day. No further action was taken on the bill.

Based on a review of the Legislative Information System, a database of congressional legislation, an additional eight bills related to presidential records were introduced in the 110th Congress. The only bill that was enacted (P.L. 110-404) authorized the Archivist to make grants available to help store and preserve the records of former Presidents who do not have an archival depository.

Among the other legislative initiatives was a bill that would have required the creation of guidelines for the preservation of electronic presidential records (H.R. 5811), and a few bills that would have provided funding or access to presidential archives that are not protected by the 1978 Act (H.R. 6872; H.R. 6669; S. 3350). The remaining pieces of legislation included a resolution that provided consideration for H.R. 5811 (H.Res. 1318), and two bills that would have authorized grants to establish a Woodrow Wilson Presidential Library (H.R. 1664; S. 1878).

ANALYSIS

Presidential documents provide a historical resource that can be used to better understand how the institution of the presidency functions and how individual Presidents have interpreted or modified the institution. Presidents, however, must be able to act quickly and deliberately on issues that are essential to national security, foreign policy, and other sensitive topics. Certain documents may need to be exempted from disclosure—for a period of time or in perpetuity—to protect security or for other reasons.

H.R. 35

H.R. 35 would reinstitute many of presidential records archiving policies that were in effect prior to George W. Bush's issuance of E.O. 13233. First, the bill seeks to shorten the record review period established by President Obama's executive order by 10 days (from 30 to 20 days). Second, it would also require personal requests from an incumbent President, former Presidents, or former Vice Presidents for exemption from the statute. Third, the bill would statutorily revoke Bush's executive order.[11]

If passed, H.R. 35 would reduce the amount of time required for presidential records to be disclosed. Under the proposed bill, an incumbent President, former Presidents, and former Vice Presidents would have to demonstrate why certain records should be afforded protected status for reasons of executive privilege. Under E.O. 13233, any person seeking to access records that had not been released had to demonstrate why these records should have been disclosed—without full knowledge of the information that the record may include. Under E.O. 13489, in contrast, incumbent and former Presidents must demonstrate why records should not be released. H.R. 35 would codify parts of President Obama's executive order. Passage of H.R. 35 would statutorily revoke E.O. 13233 and codify Congress's stance on the disclosure of presidential records. Such action could deter future Presidents from attempting to deny access to certain records or lengthen the records disclosure process because such a statute would delineate the legislative branch's disclosure requirements.

Some Members may believe, however, that H.R. 35 would remove a President's, former President's, or former Vice President's constitutionally legitimate claims of privilege for certain information or records. The legislation would statutorily mandate the time frame for the release of presidential documents and would require personal, explicit claims of executive privilege from incumbent or former Presidents. E.O. 13489 does not directly address whether designees of incumbent or former Presidents could assert claims of executive privilege. The executive order does mandate a 30-day record review period.

Congress may also choose not to act on H.R. 35. President Obama's executive order restores much of the Presidential Records Act. If the bill were not enacted, the incumbent President would have greater control over the disclosure of the records of incumbent and former Presidents under the provisions of E.O. 13489. Not enacting H.R. 35 could allow an incumbent President, former President, or former Vice President to keep from disclosure important historical documents for a longer period of time. Such action could increase public mistrust of the presidency, inhibit scholarship, or possibly permit abuses of executive power to go undetected.

Vice Presidential Records Controversy

Neither E.O. 13489 nor H.R. 35 directly addresses the controversy over whether an outgoing Vice President has the authority to determine which records should be handed over to NARA upon leaving office.[12] According to the Presidential Records Act, the incumbent President is the manager of his presidential records prior to leaving office. It is, therefore, his responsibility to maintain records responsibly and turn them over to the Archivist when he leaves office. Former Vice President Dick Cheney challenged a lawsuit filed by an organization that sought to preserve records that Mr. Cheney claims are subject to his control. In September 2008, a judge ordered Mr. Cheney to preserve all records until the case was decided, according to media reports.[13] Mr. Cheney's office submitted to the Federal District Court of Washington, D.C., a motion to dismiss the lawsuit on December 8, 2008, that claimed, "The vice president alone may determine what constitutes vice presidential records or personal records, how his records will be created, maintained, managed and disposed, and are all actions that are committed to his discretion by law."[14]

On January 19, 2009, a federal district court judge found that Citizens for Responsibility and Ethics in Washington (CREW), the organization seeking preservation of the records, could not demonstrate that the Vice President failed to comply with his obligations under the Presidential Records Act. The decision accepted Mr. Cheney's claim that he should have broad discretion over which of his records are to be preserved and released to the public.[15]

Presidential Records: Issues for the 111th Congress

The court also found that Vice Presidential records were, pursuant to 44 U.S.C. § 2207, to be preserved in the same manner as Presidential records.

End Notes

[1] As a consequence of the so-called Watergate incident, Congress passed the Presidential Recordings and Materials Preservation Act of 1974 (PRMPA; 44 U.S.C. § 2111) to assure that the presidential papers of Richard M. Nixon were placed under federal custody. Though this act, which directly addresses presidential records, was passed prior to the 1978 Presidential Records Act, it governed only documents associated with the Nixon presidency.

[2] CRS Report R40209, *Fundraising for Presidential Libraries: Legislative and Policy Issues in the 111th Congress*, by R. Sam Garrett.

[3] Executive privilege has never been defined definitively. The President, as the leader of the executive branch, is granted authority to determine which records should be afforded a privileged status that prevents their disclosure. This power is used to ensure that the power vested in the executive branch is not compromised in comparison to the two other branches of federal government: the legislature and the judiciary. The President may claim executive privilege over any record, and the claim does not need to coincide with any of the criteria in the Presidential Records Act that automatically exempt records from publication.

[4] Executive Order 13489, "Presidential Records," 74 *Federal Register* 4669, January 26, 2009. The executive order was issued on January 21, but not printed in the *Federal Register* until January 26.

[5] 44 U.S.C. § 2204(a). After 12 years have expired, Presidential records are subject to the Freedom of Information Act, which governs public access to agency records (5 U.S.C. § 552).

[6] Ibid.

[7] 44 U.S.C. § 2204.

[8] The executive order stated that "references in this order to a former President shall be deemed also to be references to the relevant former Vice President" (Sec. 11). A former Vice President, therefore, would have authority identical to a former President under E.O. 13233 to withhold certain records from disclosure.

[9] E.O. 13233 stated that the President could assert executive privilege for records that reflected "military, diplomatic, or national security secrets (the state secrets privilege); communications of the President or his advisors (the presidential communications privilege); legal advice or legal work (the attorney-client or attorney work product privileges); and the deliberative process of the President or his advisors (the deliberative process privilege)."

[10] According to the bill, the Archivist can extend the review period an additional 20 days if the incumbent President, former President, or Vice President claims the additional time is necessary to complete "an adequate review of the record."

[11] For more information on the power and limitations of executive orders, see CRS Report RS20846, *Executive Orders: Issuance and Revocation*, by T. J. Halstead.

[12] Defendants' Motion to Dismiss or, in the Alternative, for Summary Judgment, and Memorandum of Points and Authorities in Support of Defendants' Motion, *Citizens for Responsibility and Ethics in Washington et al. v. Cheney* (No. 08-1548) (D.D.C. filed Dec. 8, 2008). Neither the Presidential Records Act, nor subsequent executive orders, are explicit about an incumbent Vice President's authority and discretion over the preservation of his records.

[13] Christopher Lee, "Cheney Must Hold His Records," *The Los Angeles Times*, September 21, 2008, pp. A-28, available at http://articles.latimes.com/2008/sep/21/nation/na-cheney21.

[14] Defendants' Motion to Dismiss or, in the Alternative, for Summary Judgment, and Memorandum of Points and Authorities in Support of Defendants' Motion, *Citizens for Responsibility and Ethics in Washington et al. v. Cheney* (No. 08-1548) (D.D.C. filed Dec. 8, 2008). See also Pamela Hess, "Cheney Claims Power to Decide his Public Records," The Associated Press, December 18, 2008, available at http://www.wtop.com/?nid=116&sid=1474512.

[15] Citizens for Responsibility and Ethics in Washington v. Cheney, 2009 U.S. Dist. LEXIS 3113 (D.D.C. 2009).

In: Presidential Libraries: Elements and Considerations
Editor: Jamie D. Reynolds
ISBN: 978-1-61324-581-1
© 2011 Nova Science Publishers, Inc.

Chapter 5

FRAMEWORK GOVERNING USE OF PRESIDENTIAL LIBRARY FACILITIES AND STAFF

United States Government Accountability Office

WHY GAO DID THIS STUDY

The National Archives and Records Administration (NARA) operates presidential libraries for all of the former U.S. presidents since Herbert Hoover. These libraries received over 2.4 million visits in 2009, including researchers, public program attendees, and museum visitors. Each library is associated with a private foundation, which raised the funds to build the library and then turned the library facility over to the federal government. These foundations typically have ongoing relationships with the libraries they built, and some of these library–foundation relationships involve sharing of staff and facilities.

Per your request, this report describes the principal laws, regulations, and NARA policies that govern library–foundation relationships and the appropriate use of library facilities and staff.

GAO reviewed specific laws governing presidential libraries, and NARA regulations and policies. We also reviewed applicable laws and regulations governing activities held on government property and acceptable activities of federal employees. Further, we interviewed relevant NARA officials.

NARA reviewed a draft of this report and had no substantive comments. NARA made technical suggestions which we incorporated as appropriate. GAO is not making any recommendations in this report.

WHAT GAO FOUND

The federal laws specific to presidential libraries focus primarily on the design and construction of library facilities and, once constructed, the deeding of the library facilities, or the rights to use the facilities, to the federal government. NARA building-use regulations outline the permissible and prohibited uses of presidential library facilities by outside organizations. Prohibited uses include profit-making, commercial advertisement or sales, partisan political activities, or sectarian activities. Other laws and regulations govern what federal employees may and may not do in their official capacity. As federal employees, NARA library employees must follow these rules in their interactions with the foundation associated with the library. NARA's Office of Presidential Libraries has developed a policy manual and standards that address topics such as museum activities and records. This office also works with the NARA General Counsel to develop guidance governing the library–foundation relationship, such as those related to the foundations' use of library facilities and when and how library staff can support foundation activities. The libraries also have one or more written agreements with their associated foundation that govern different aspects of the relationship. These agreements differ in format; content; and the extent to which they address use of facilities, library and foundation staff relationships, and political activities.

ABBREVIATIONS

GSA   General Services Administration
NARA   National Archives and Records Administration
OSC   U.S. Office of Special Counsel

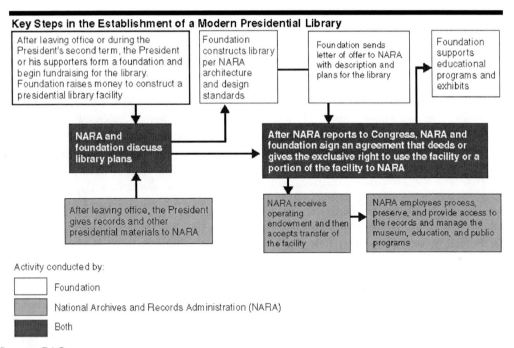

Source: GAO.
Note: Where the library is built on a university campus, the university is also involved in the various stages of library development.

The Honorable Danny K. Davis
Ranking Member
Subcommittee on Health Care, District of Columbia, Census and the National Archives
Committee on Oversight and Government Reform
House of Representatives

The Honorable William Lacy
Clay House of Representatives

The National Archives and Records Administration (NARA) operates presidential libraries for all of the former U.S. presidents since Herbert Hoover. These libraries received over 2.4 million visits in 2009, including researchers, public program attendees, and museum visitors. Each library is associated with a private foundation and some of these library–foundation relationships involve sharing of staff and facilities. Libraries are generally funded by appropriated funds, donations, museum store revenue, admission and other fees, endowments, and foundation funds. Some libraries are located on university campuses and also receive some support from the university. In some cases, state or local governments also contributed to library construction and provide ongoing support for some libraries. NARA manages its federal employees' activities and determines the appropriate use of federal facilities and federal funds at the presidential libraries based on an understanding of the applicable laws, regulations, and policies. On the basis of your request and subsequent discussions with your staff, this report describes the principal laws, regulations, and NARA policies that govern library–foundation relationships and the appropriate use of library facilities and staff.

We reviewed applicable laws and regulations governing activities held on government property and acceptable activities of federal employees. We also reviewed specific laws governing presidential libraries, and NARA regulations and policies. We interviewed NARA officials in the Office of Presidential Libraries, General Counsel, and Inspector General. To identify the principal laws, regulations, and NARA policies that govern library– foundation relationships, we reviewed 29 policy documents, laws, and regulations that related to presidential libraries. We identified 17 that were relevant to the library–foundation relationship for facilities use, staff, and political activities. We also reviewed an additional 30 documents that NARA described as agreements establishing the relationship between presidential libraries and private foundations.[1] We conducted our work from May 2010 through February 2011 in accordance with all sections of GAO's Quality Assurance Framework that are relevant to our objective. The framework requires that we plan and perform the engagement to obtain sufficient and appropriate evidence to meet our stated objectives and to discuss any limitations in our work. We believe that the information and data obtained, and the analysis conducted, provide a reasonable basis for the findings and conclusions in this product.

Table 1. Presidential Library Facts

Library name	Location	Year of transfer to the federal government[a]	Size of NARA-owned or controlled space (square feet)	Visits in 2009[b]
Herbert Hoover Presidential Library and Museum	West Branch, Iowa	1964	47,169	96,324
Franklin D. Roosevelt Presidential Library and Museum	Hyde Park, N.Y.	1940	108,750	144,332
Harry S. Truman Library and Museum	Independence, Mo.	1957	96,612	120,348
Dwight D. Eisenhower Presidential Library and Museum	Abilene, Kans	1964 (library) 1966 (museum)	109,254	207,367
John F. Kennedy Presidential Library and Museum	Boston, Mass.	1979	134,293[c]	329,766
Lyndon Baines Johnson Library & Museum	Austin, Tex.	1984	134,695	274,253
Nixon Presidential Library and Museum	Yorba Linda, Calif.	2007	55,373	82,906
Gerald R. Ford Presidential Library and Museum	Ann Arbor, Mich. (library) Grand Rapids, Mich. (museum)	1980-1982[d]	104,764[e]	134,276
Jimmy Carter Library and Museum	Atlanta, Ga.	1986	85,592	64,033
Ronald Reagan Presidential Library and Museum	Simi Valley, Calif.	1991	147,400	444,240
George Bush Presidential Library and Museum	College Station, Tex.	1997	69,049	228,209
William J. Clinton Presidential Library and Museum	Little Rock, Ark.	2004	68,698	321,430
George W. Bush Presidential Library	Dallas, Tex.[f]	NA	NA	NA

Source: GAO analysis of NARA and presidential library data.
Notes: NA=Not Applicable.

[a] The National Archives was created as an independent agency in 1934, but became a component of the General Services Administration (GSA) in 1950. In 1985, NARA again became an independent agency. As a result of these changes, some libraries were transferred to GSA and some were transferred to NARA, depending on whether NARA was an independent agency at the time of transfer. These dates indicate the year of transfer of title or legal control to the federal government.

[b] The number of visits includes researchers, public program attendees, and museum visitors. Researchers or others who return to the library on multiple days are counted once on each day they visit.

[c] An approximate 30,000 additional square feet of space is currently being constructed at the Kennedy Library.

[d] The museum is located in Grand Rapids, Michigan, and was transferred to the federal government in 1982. Although the dedication ceremony for the library in Ann Arbor was in 1981, according to NARA officials, staff moved into the library facility in 1980.

[e] The Gerald R. Ford Presidential Library and Museum is housed in two separate locations. This is the total square feet of both the museum and the library.

[f] The George W. Bush Library is temporarily located in Lewisville, Texas, while a permanent facility is under construction in Dallas.

BACKGROUND

Prior to 1940, U.S. presidents or their descendents typically retained ownership of papers documenting their terms of office. The fate of these papers was up to the former president or his descendents, and some were lost forever. In 1940, Franklin D. Roosevelt was the first president to arrange to have a library built using privately raised funds and to then transfer both the facility and his papers to the federal government. Through its Office of Presidential Libraries, NARA operates presidential libraries housing the papers of all subsequent presidents through George W. Bush,[2] as well as President Roosevelt's predecessor in the White House, Herbert Hoover. At the end of a president's term, NARA staff begin working with the president's official records and other materials. This work goes on during library construction and during the period between the dedication of the library facility and its transfer to the federal government. Table 1 provides facts about the 13 presidential libraries and museums operated by NARA.

For most of the libraries, as the president's term was coming to a close or after it ended, friends and supporters of the president created a private charitable foundation to collect donations to construct a library.[3] Under current law, NARA collaborates with each presidential library foundation on the construction of the library facility, and when the facility construction is complete, the foundation deeds or gives the right to use the library facility or a portion of the facility to NARA. The Presidential Libraries Act of 1986 also requires that the National Archives Trust Fund receive an operating endowment for each library before NARA can accept the transfer of the library.[4] These endowments fund some of the federal government's costs for the operation and maintenance of the presidential libraries.[5] Figure 1 captures key steps of the current process of establishing a presidential library. Some variations from this process may exist.

Each library is operated by a director who is a NARA employee, and other library staff who are also NARA employees. The staffs typically include an administrative officer, facility manager, education and exhibits specialists, archivists, archives technicians, and clerks, among other staff. The director of a presidential library is appointed by the Archivist of the United States, the head of NARA, who consults with the former president in selecting a candidate.[6]

The Office of Presidential Libraries is headed by the Assistant Archivist for Presidential Libraries. The Office of Presidential Libraries is responsible for overseeing the management of records at the libraries, the development of policies and procedures for the management and operation of presidential libraries, and the development and coordination of plans, programs, and resource allocations at presidential libraries. The Office of Presidential Libraries is also involved in the creation of new presidential libraries.

Funds appropriated by Congress support NARA's staffing, administration, security, maintenance, and renovation projects at the library. In fiscal year 2009, NARA spent more than $68 million in appropriations to operate the presidential libraries. In addition, for fiscal year 2009 NARA received $41.5 million in special appropriations for repairs and restoration to the John F. Kennedy Presidential Library and Museum ($22 million), the Franklin D. Roosevelt Presidential Library and Museum ($17.5 million), and the Lyndon Baines Johnson Library & Museum ($2 million).

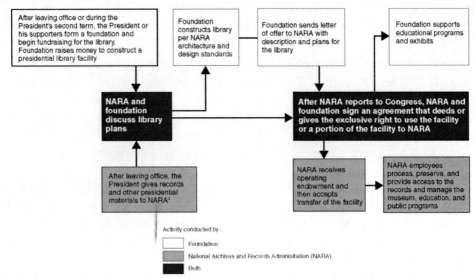

Source: GAO.

Notes: Where the library is built on a university campus, the university is also involved in the various stages of library development.

[a] Under the Presidential Records Act of 1978, 44 U.S.C. § 2201 et seq., the United States owns all presidential records from the moment of their creation or receipt by a President or his administration. The Archivist of the United States assumes custody and control of presidential records when the President leaves office.

Figure 1. Key Steps in the Establishment of a Modern Presidential Library.

Each private foundation is operated by a director, president, or CEO and other staff that may include a chief financial officer and director of communications, among other positions. Foundation support enables the libraries to expand their research and archival functions, as well as undertake additional projects such as public outreach efforts. The foundations' level of involvement in the activities at their associated library, such as collaboration on public and educational programs, varies from library to library. Foundations may also sponsor their own programs and activities, such as hosting a lecture series or academic discussion or producing a newsletter. NARA officials told us that, in most cases, these kinds of programs and activities are offered in conjunction with and supported by library staff. For example, a foundation may pay for a lecture series that is held in NARA-controlled space.

The foundations may also generally support their associated libraries with additional funding for new facilities and equipment and for updating permanent exhibits, adding program space, and giving the library the use of foundation staff time for library activities. Foundations provide these resources directly to their associated library. This process generally is handled at the library level based on the relationship between the library and the foundation. Each presidential library also has a trust fund that receives revenue from the sale of publications, museum shop sales, document reproductions, audio-visual reproductions, library admissions, public space rentals, educational conferences, and interest income. Trust-fund money helps the library cover the cost of museum shop inventory, personnel, operational and financial systems, equipment, and supplies. These funds may also support exhibit-related and public-programming expenses. In fiscal year 2009, the trust funds for presidential libraries had a total end-of-year balance of approximately $15 million. In addition to trust funds, presidential libraries also maintain funds from gifts donated to a library for general library support or for specific projects or programs.

FEDERAL LAWS AND REGULATIONS, NARA POLICIES, AND INDIVIDUAL LIBRARY AGREEMENTS PROVIDE GUIDANCE ON THE LIBRARY–FOUNDATION RELATIONSHIP

Federal Laws Govern Library Creation

The federal laws specific to presidential libraries focus primarily on the design and construction of library facilities and, once constructed, the deeding of the library facilities, or the rights to use the facilities, to the federal government. Congress has enacted three primary statutes[7] that provide the legal rules for the design, construction, and transfer of library facilities.

Table 2. Relevant Laws Governing Presidential Libraries

Law	Provisions
The Presidential Libraries Act of 1955 (Pub. L. No. 84-373)	Established the basic policy for the creation of federally maintained presidential libraries. Provided the policies for • accepting land and buildings for a presidential archival depository; • depositing presidential papers, documents, and other historical materials; • cooperating with organizations or individuals interested in studying/researching the historical materials; • entering into agreements with outside organizations, such as universities, institutes, or foundations, to use their land, facilities, or equipment for a presidential archival depository; and • charging fees for visiting the museum and exhibits and for accepting gifts or donations. This act, as amended by the statutes below, applies to all federally maintained presidential libraries.
The Presidential Libraries Act of 1986 (Pub. L. No. 99-323)	Established certain congressional reporting requirements, architectural and design requirements, and fiscal limitations for the constructing of presidential libraries. One of the main requirements was an operating endowment of 20 percent of the total cost of building and equipping the facility or the portion of the facility transferred to NARA control.[a] If the presidential library foundation constructs a facility that exceeds 70,000 square feet, the operating endowment increases with every square foot the facility is in excess of 70,000 square feet.[b] This act applies to those libraries starting with George H.W. Bush.
The Presidential Historical Records Preservation Act of 2008 (Pub. L. No. 110-404)	Increased the minimum endowment to 60 percent of the assessed value of the library facility.[c] This act applies to libraries whose presidents take the oath of office as President for the first time on or after July 1, 2002.

Source: GAO analysis of applicable legal statutes.

Notes: Other statutes relevant to presidential libraries, such as the Presidential Recordings and Materials Preservation Act of 1974 and the Presidential Records Act of 1978, discuss the ownership and management of presidential records.

[a] The foundation must offer the operating endowment by gift or bequest before the Archivist, the appointed head of NARA, may accept the library facility. NARA may only use income from the operating endowment to cover facility operation costs and may not use it for archival functions.

[b] The operating endowment requirement applies to the George Bush Presidential Library and Museum, the William J. Clinton Presidential Library and Museum, and all future libraries, including the George W. Bush Presidential Library.

[c] The act also established a grant program for "Presidential Centers of Historical Excellence." These grants are for eligible entities wishing to preserve and provide access to historical records of former Presidents that do not have a depository managed by the federal government.

Federal Regulations Govern the Use of Library Facilities by Outside Organizations

NARA's building-use regulations outline the permissible and prohibited uses of the presidential library facilities by other groups. According to the regulations, other groups may request the use of presidential library facilities when the activity is

- sponsored, cosponsored, or authorized by the library;
- conducted to further the library's interests; and
- does not interfere with the normal operation of the library.

The regulations prohibit the use of the facilities for profit-making, commercial advertisement or sales, partisan political activities, or sectarian activities.[8]

When NARA considers it to be in the public interest, NARA may allow for the occasional, nonofficial use of rooms and spaces in a presidential library and charge a reasonable fee for such use.[9] Additionally, the regulations require outside organizations to apply for the use of library space by writing to the library director and submitting an Application for Use of Space in Presidential Libraries.[10] Applying organizations must agree to review their event plans with library staff and that the plans will conform to library rules and procedures. The application also confirms that the organization will not charge admission fees, make indirect assessment fees for admission, or take collections for their events. Further, the application prohibits the organization from suggesting that the library endorses or sponsors the organization.

Federal Laws and Regulations Govern the Use of Staff

Federal laws and regulations specify for all federal employees—including federal employees working at presidential libraries—what they may and may not do in their official capacity. For example, federal employees may not engage in commercial or political activity associated with their federal positions. According to NARA's General Counsel, there are no special laws or regulations that apply only to how library employees interact with the foundation or, if applicable, university associated with their library, but the laws and regulations that apply throughout the federal government also apply to library employees.

The Hatch Act[11] provides the rules for the activities of library employees at events such as candidate debates or speeches by candidates that sometimes take place at the libraries. The Hatch Act, which is enforced by the U.S. Office of Special Counsel (OSC),[12] prohibits certain political activities for federal employees. At an event such as these (or at any other time) a library employee may not

- use official authority to interfere with an election;
- solicit, accept, or receive political contributions from any person;
- run for nomination or as a candidate for election to a partisan political office; or solicit or discourage the political activity of any person connected to the business of the employee's office.

NARA employees must also follow the Standards of Ethical Conduct for Employees of the Executive Branch issued by the Office of Government Ethics.[13] The standards emphasize that employees have a responsibility to the U.S. government and its citizens to place loyalty to the Constitution, laws, and ethical principles above private gain, and set forth 14 general principles. Among other things, the standards describe limitations on actions an employee may take while seeking other employment, and require that employees use the time they are serving in an official capacity in an honest effort to perform official duties.

The Office of Presidential Libraries Provides Further Guidance on Facilities' Use and Staff Activities

NARA's Office of Presidential Libraries oversees the 13 presidential libraries. That office has developed systemwide policies, including the Presidential Libraries Manual, which discusses museum activities and records topics, and the NARA/Office of Presidential Libraries Architecture and Design Standards for Presidential Libraries. The Office of Presidential Libraries also works with the NARA General Counsel on the development of policies governing the library–foundation relationship.

The NARA General Counsel has issued legal opinions on foundations' use of library facilities, when and how library staff can support foundation activities, and if library staff can fundraise for the foundations. Additionally, NARA officials explained that the NARA General Counsel and the Office of Presidential Libraries negotiate with the foundations on the agreements establishing the relationship between a new library and its associated foundation.

According to NARA officials, library directors at the individual libraries consult with the NARA General Counsel about activities that could have political undertones before allowing a program or event. For example, library directors have contacted NARA General Counsel to inquire about using libraries as polling places. NARA approved the use of libraries as polling places as long as certain requirements were met such as that no political solicitation occurs on library-controlled property. In another example, a local political party requested but was not allowed to hold a political forum at the library.

NARA officials told us that NARA does not have internal directives specifically regarding the supervision of library and foundation staff. They said that when library staff are concerned about supervision or other issues while working on a collaborative project with the foundations, they are expected to seek advice from the NARA General Counsel's ethics program staff. Table 3 provides a summary of NARA policies and NARA General Counsel opinions concerning library–foundation activities and other outside uses of the libraries.

Table 3. NARA Policies Relating to Library–Foundation Relationships

Library–foundation relationship scenarios/issues	Related NARA policies and General Counsel opinions addressing these situations
Use of library facilities by foundations or other organizations	• A library may provide office space at no charge to the foundation • Libraries and foundations may cosponsor events in public spaces • The public spaces can be used by foundations and other organizations for lectures, seminars, etc., when the activities are authorized by the Director. The events and activities must further the library's interests, not conflict with normal operations, relate to the mission and programs of the library, and be consistent with the perception of the library as a research and cultural institution. Religious services, partisan political, profit-making, or commercial events or events that are essentially social in nature are not permitted. The Director will ordinarily assess additional charges to reimburse the government for use of the space.
Employees working in support of foundation activities	• Library employees may engage in activities, including fundraising activities, involving the foundations as part of their official duties as long as NARA and the library are authorized to engage in the foundation-funded or sponsored activity and the agency/library expects to derive a direct benefit from the activity. • When working with the foundations, library employees cannot accept compensation from the foundations, lobby Congress, or represent the foundations before other federal agencies. • Employees are also subject to federal ethics statutes and regulations.
Candidate events (debates, forums, etc.)	• According to the NARA General Counsel, libraries can host candidate events, such as multicandidate debates and candidate speeches, because they further the libraries' mission of educating the public on matters of civic interest; the programs cannot endorse political views, policies, activities, or undertakings of any person or group. • Candidate events must be organized and sponsored by the foundation; a nonpartisan, nonprofit organization; or a media organization. A political party may sponsor a debate as long as a media organization or other nonpartisan group cosponsors the event. Neither NARA nor the library may be a sponsor. • The library director must approve the candidate event, but cannot participate in the subject matter of the event nor can any of the library's employees. They may not suggest candidates to participate in the debates. Library directors should consult with Office of Presidential Libraries management and the NARA General Counsel before agreeing to allow candidate events.
Library director working in support of foundation activities	• Directors may fundraise for their library's gift fund or their foundation when the purpose is to support the library. The directors cannot fundraise for the foundations for nonlibrary purposes. • Library directors and employees cannot attend political fundraisers for the purpose of raising funds for the library or identify themselves as library employees at political fundraisers, even if they attend the fundraisers during off-duty hours.

Source: GAO analysis of NARA policy documents.

Library–Foundation Agreements Further Define Their Relationship

Each presidential library has a written agreement with its associated foundation and, if applicable, the associated university that governs aspects of the relationship between the entities.[14] These agreements differ in format; content; and the extent to which they address use of facilities, library and foundation staff relationships, and political activities. These agreements must be consistent with the applicable statutes and NARA regulations. At some libraries, the library–foundation relationship is addressed by more than one agreement due to the updating or supplementing of original documents, or to the changing format of the agreements over time. Some of the oldest agreements are primarily a series of Letters of Offer and Acceptance between the foundation and the General Services Administration (GSA), with later agreements taking the form of a mutually signed agreement between the foundation and NARA. For example, the Ford museum and the Hoover, Truman, Eisenhower, and Kennedy library agreements (from 1957 to 1980) include one or more Letters of Offer and Acceptance between the foundation and the GSA. Later agreements from more-recently established libraries, as well as earlier libraries that updated their agreements, include mutually signed agreements between the foundation and NARA. Of these later agreements, some focus on a specific project or aspect of the library–foundation relationship, while some focus broadly on the library–foundation relationship.

We reviewed the library–foundation agreements and found that, over time, the agreements have become increasingly more detailed, especially regarding staff, each entity's use and control of the different parts of the facilities, and political activities. Earlier agreements are largely focused on the transfer of property from the foundation to the United States, while later agreements address additional aspects of the library–foundation relationship. For example, later agreements address which entity controls specific parts of the facilities, including details related to one entity's use of the other's space (such as the permitted purposes for using the other's space, and reimbursing the other entity for costs associated with using its space). Later agreements are also more likely to clarify the different roles and responsibilities of library and foundation staff, and address activities or tasks that library staff are not allowed to perform. Some of the later agreements also address potential conflicts of interest between the library and the foundation. For example, two of the later agreements state that foundation staff are to act in the best interests of the foundation, and NARA staff are to act in the best interests of NARA and the United States. Regarding political activities, two of the later agreements state that library space is not allowed to be used for partisan political activities. Also, NARA regulations give library directors the authority to establish supplemental policies. According to NARA officials, these supplemental policies may provide further detail on the library–foundation relationship regarding facilities, staff, and political activities. Our review was limited to NARAwide policies and library–foundation agreements and we did not review any local library supplemental policies.

NARA officials explained that the written agreements between individual libraries and the foundations are important, but that they also do not fully prescribe the relationships between the entities. They said that the relationships are shaped over time and by factors such as the particular foundation's interest in collaborating with the library or doing charitable work elsewhere. For example, the Harry S. Truman Library and Museum and its associated foundation, the Truman Library Institute, are colocated and often collaborate on educational programs. The foundation describes itself as working with the library to "fulfill the Truman Library's commitment to research and education." In contrast, the mission of the foundation associated with the Jimmy Carter Library and Museum, The Carter Center, does not directly focus on the library, but rather "to advance peace and health worldwide." NARA officials said that interaction between individual libraries and their foundations vary, but they also stressed that no one foundation's emphasis is more correct than another. These are examples of differences among foundations and how those differences shape the level of involvement by a foundation with a library.

AGENCY COMMENTS

We provided a draft of this report to NARA. NARA had no substantive comments and provided technical comments by e-mail, which we incorporated as appropriate. NARA's letter is reprinted in appendix I.

We will send a copy of this report to the Archivist of the United States. This report will also be available at no charge on GAO's Web site at http://www.gao.gov. If you or your staff have any questions about this report, please contact me at (202) 512-9110 or brostekm@gao.gov. Contact points for our Offices of Congressional Relations and Public Affairs may be found on the last page of this report. Key contributors to this report are listed in appendix II.

Michael Brostek
Director, Tax Issues Strategic Issues Team

APPENDIX I. COMMENTS FROM THE NATIONAL ARCHIVES AND RECORDS ADMINISTRATION

NATIONAL ARCHIVES

ARCHIVIST of the
UNITED STATES

DAVID S. FERRIERO
T 202.357.5900
F 202.357.5901
david.ferriero@nara.gov

February 23, 2010

Michael Brostek,
Director, Strategic Issues
Government Accountability Office
Director of Information Technology Management Issues
441 G Street NW
Washington DC, 20548

Dear Mr. Brostek:

Thank you for the opportunity to comment on the draft report GAO-11-390, *National Archives: Framework Governing Use of Presidential Library Facilities and Staff*. We appreciate the thorough work by your staff to gain an understanding of the complex and individual relationships between NARA and the foundations that support each of our Presidential Libraries.

Under separate cover, we provided several technical comments. We have no substantive comments for this report. If you have any questions regarding this memo or our action plan process, please contact Mary Drak, NARA's Audit Liaison at 301-837-1668 or via email at mary.drak@nara.gov.

David S. Ferriero
Archivist of the United States

NATIONAL ARCHIVES and
RECORDS ADMINISTRATION
700 PENNSYLVANIA AVENUE, NW
WASHINGTON, DC 20408-0001
www.archives.gov

End Notes

[1] Some presidential libraries are located on university campuses and the libraries have ongoing relationships with those institutions. Because this report concerns the libraries and their associated private foundations, it does not go into detail on library–university relationships where they exist. Generally, the framework governing library–foundation relationships also applies to any library–university relationships.

[2] The George W. Bush Presidential Library and Museum is under construction in Texas. The library currently operates in a temporary facility leased by NARA.

[3] These foundations are 501(c)(3) tax-exempt charitable organizations. At some libraries, the foundation created to build a library went out of business after completing that task, with another foundation created to further the library's activities and programs, other charitable missions of interest to the president or his supporters, or both.

[4] While the 1986 act does not specify who must raise the endowment funds, for both libraries currently subject to the requirement—the Clinton and George H.W. Bush Libraries—NARA told us that the library foundations raised and donated the monies that form the principal portion of the endowments, and NARA expects the same to occur for the George W. Bush Library.

[5] As discussed later, the amount of the endowment required from foundations has increased over time.

[6] The Archivist consults with the library's associated foundation or other representative of the former president after the president's death.

[7] A fourth statute, the Consolidated Appropriations Resolution, 2003, Pub. L. No. 108-7, div. J, title V, § 513, 117 Stat. 11, 462 (Feb. 20, 2003), increased the endowment funding requirement from 20 percent to 40 percent of the assessed value of the library for Presidents who take the oath of office for the first time after July 1, 2002. This statute is not listed in table 2 because no libraries were constructed under the 40 percent requirement, and the requirement was subsequently increased (to 60 percent) by the Presidential Historical Records Preservation Act of 2008.

[8] 36 C.F.R. § 1280.94(d).

[9] 44 U.S.C. § 2112(e).

[10] 36 C.F.R. § 1280.94(c). The Application for Use of Space in Presidential Libraries has Office of Management and Budget control number 3095-0024, and its agency number is NA Form 16011.

[11] 5 U.S.C. §§ 1501-1508.

[12] The U.S. Office of Special Counsel (OSC) is an independent federal investigative and prosecutorial agency whose primary mission is to safeguard the merit system by protecting federal employees and applicants from prohibited personnel practices. OSC promotes compliance by government employees with legal restrictions on political activity by providing advisory opinions on, and enforcing, the Hatch Act.

[13] 5 C.F.R. pt. 2635.

[14] The George W. Bush Presidential Library is currently under construction and GAO did not review any agreements related to it.

In: Presidential Libraries: Elements and Considerations
Editor: Jamie D. Reynolds

ISBN: 978-1-61324-581-1
© 2011 Nova Science Publishers, Inc.

Chapter 6

REPORT ON ALTERNATIVE MODELS FOR PRESIDENTIAL LIBRARIES, ISSUED IN RESPONSE TO THE REQUIREMENTS OF PL 110-404

National Archives and Records Administration

OVERVIEW

The Presidential Historical Records Preservation Act of 2008 [PL 110-404] requires that the Archivist of the United States submit to Congress a report on alternative models for Presidential archival depositories that:

- Reduces the financial burden on the Federal Government,
- Improves the preservation of Presidential records, and
- Reduces the delay in public access to all Presidential records.

In preparing this report, NARA explored a range of issues relating to Presidential Libraries. This report will provide an overview of the history of the Library system and the statutory and other legal frameworks which govern Presidential Library operations. This context will inform the discussion of proposed alternative models for a Presidential Library that might reduce the financial burden to the Government and improve preservation and public access to Presidential records. In addressing the requirements of the Act, it should be noted that there is a tension among the three charges. Alternative models for a Presidential Library that reduce the Government's financial burden may not necessarily result in better preservation or quicker public access to Presidential records. Likewise, improvements in both of these areas could result in increased costs to the Federal Government. The models proposed in the report have tried to consider and balance this tension.

To fulfill the 2008 Act's mandate, NARA undertook an internal review of the current Presidential Library system, its programs, associated costs, and alternatives for the future of the system. NARA requested input on its web site for suggestions for the development of alternative models for a Presidential Library, and received over 100 comments.

The complexity of this assignment is illustrated by a brief look at the broad array of strong opinions NARA received on the Presidential Library system. Many comments were supportive of the current Presidential Library system and its programs. Some comments called for centralization of the Presidential Library system and/or digitization of all Presidential records.

Others favored centralization of key functions such as declassification, while still others were supportive of the importance of maintaining the regional diversity of the current system. Some comments were supportive of the Presidential museums while others called for their privatization or elimination. Further comments stressed the importance of maintaining the right to make Freedom of Information Act (FOIA) requests five years after the President leaves office as a right of requesting Presidential records.

A detailed summary of the external comments is located in Appendix A.

The 2008 Presidential Historical Records Preservation Act has tasked us with envisioning new ideas for funding, preserving, and making Presidential records available more quickly. Based on NARA's internal review, including reflecting on the evolution of the Presidential library system and the external comments received from individuals and organizations, this report will explore five specific alternatives.

Model 1: The current model (in which both the archival depository and museum are donated to NARA by the Library Foundation), with revisions to the endowment calculation that would require an endowment based on the total size of the building. This model also explores a new basis for the charter between NARA and the Library Foundations.

Model 2: The Presidential archival depository leased by the Government, with a separate Museum managed by the Foundation.

Model 3: The Presidential archival depository donated to NARA by the Foundation, a university, or other non-Federal entity, with a separate Museum managed by the Foundation.

Model 4: A centralized Presidential archival depository funded and managed by NARA, with no museum. Presidential Foundations may build and manage their own museums in a location of their choice.

Model 5: A centralized Presidential archival depository funded and managed by NARA and a Museum of the Presidency built and staffed by NARA. Private funds through a separate Foundation or through other fund-raising would be required to build and sustain the exhibits and the educational and public programs of the Museum.

We also considered an option that would place a Presidential collection in a currently existing NARA regional facility. However, because the geographic area from which future Presidents will come is unpredictable, it is impossible to determine which regional facilities would, in the future, house Presidential collections. While NARA believes that the size of the textual collections of future presidential administrations will decline, textual holdings will nonetheless remain substantial and therefore continue to require a significant amount of space at any future archival depository. A sizeable archival staff is required to process the textual and electronic records, which would require extensive changes to the infrastructure of the regional facility or even necessitate its relocation. Further infrastructure changes would be needed to house both the artifact holdings, which require customized stack configurations and special shelving and cabinets, and the secure compartmented information facilities, known as SCIFs, for classified records. The cost of making these infrastructure changes to an existing regional archives facility or moving to a larger facility proved too costly and too unpredictable for this to be a viable option for further study.

In proposing these five models, we are aware that the paradigm shift to preserving and making accessible electronic records is still in its infancy. In fact, President Obama's reliance on technology to conduct his everyday business, and his administration's focus on the use of Web 2.0 and social networking technologies to promote Americans' involvement in the governing process creates a challenge not yet met by NARA or the rest of government, both in implementation of his directives and in the management of the electronic records created through these initiatives. In addition, predicting what the storage requirements for Presidential records will be in the next 50 years is not yet possible. Finally, initial digitization projects undertaken by NARA have demonstrated the intensive cost in time and resources required to create, store, retrieve, and make accessible digital surrogates via the web. It is clear that management of electronic records is a process different from creation and management of digital surrogates, both of which are crucial to the success of any future model of a Presidential Library. Adequate infrastructure is critical to the future management of Presidential records.

Whether the current model or a variation remains or whether, in the future, Presidential records are retained in depositories that are very different from the Presidential Libraries we now have does not alter NARA's primary mission of preserving and providing access to Presidential records. Regardless of the ultimate outcome, an open and transparent discussion of Presidential Libraries and their futures serves everyone – the President and former Presidents, NARA, its stakeholders, and the American people.

A BRIEF HISTORY OF PRESIDENTIAL LIBRARIES

Seventy years ago, only five years after the establishment of the National Archives, Franklin D. Roosevelt proposed creating the first Presidential Library to house the Presidential papers and gifts accumulated during his administration. He wanted this Library to be a part of the National Archives, an institution he had nurtured from its establishment in 1934. He created a private foundation to raise funds for the construction of the Library building, which was then donated to the National Archives for operation as a Federal facility. On June 30, 1941, as the war in Europe threatened democracy, Roosevelt dedicated his Library at Hyde Park to the benefit of "future generations" who would use the records of his presidency. His words of dedication remain important today:

To bring together the records of the past and to house them in buildings where they will be preserved for the use of men and women in the future, a Nation must believe in three things.
It must believe in the past.
It must believe in the future.
It must, above all, believe in the capacity of its own people so to learn from the past that they can gain judgment in creating their own future.

With its extensive collection of Roosevelt historical materials available to researchers and its museum experience for the general public, the Roosevelt Library, including its public/private partnership, established the current model for the Presidential Library system.

By the early 1950s, with President Truman planning a Library and President Eisenhower clearly intending to do so, Congress codified the model in the Presidential Libraries Act of 1955. The Act outlined the legal authority of the Archivist of the United States to accept the gift of a Presidential archival depository. The legislation had full bipartisan support and was hailed by scholars and educators for formalizing an approach to caring for and making available the records of a President and his Administration. Fundamental to the Act was the public/private partnership. The Truman Institute, established for the purpose of constructing the Truman Library, became the model for future foundations in its support of research grants and conferences. To this day, the Truman Institute remains true to its original mission of supporting exhibits and Library programs, including the White House Decision Center, an immersive education experience that teaches critical thinking skills by having students confront the same decisions faced by President Truman.

The Presidential Libraries Act also authorized the Archivist of the United States to collect certain fees for the benefit of the Library and deposit the fees in a Trust Fund to help defray operating costs. Clearly Congress recognized even then the need for additional revenue sources. The Act provided flexibility for the Archivist to enter into agreements with state or political subdivisions, universities or institutions of higher learner, and institutes or foundations for the purposes of "utilizing land, buildings, and equipment for a Presidential Archival Depository." The model was not static but dynamic in its development. It enabled a President and the National Archives to develop a Library with new partners and to pursue a broader mission to educate and inform the public about the President and his life and times.

The Presidential Library System as we know it today (now consisting of thirteen Libraries) has certainly evolved from its simple beginnings. Early on, a President usually located his Library in his hometown. Today, Libraries are most often located in places more associated with his adult life or career. Affiliation with a university has become common. The public/private partnership has at times expanded to include third and fourth parties - universities and communities - involved in some measure with the advancement of the Library's mission and role. The number and complexity of programs and exhibits and the synergy of multiple Libraries documenting Presidents and American history has resulted in system-wide projects. Conferences on the Vietnam War, the Supreme Court, and the Nuclear Age along with the on-line Presidential

Timeline, which brings together on one website the documents, images, and recordings of the Presidency are examples of this new synergy. As historian David McCullough said addressing an audience at the 50th Anniversary of the Truman Library in June of 2007:

Don't ever think our Presidential Libraries aren't worth everything that has been put into them, and then some, and the fact that they are spreading out to so many different locales in the country is wonderful. It's bringing history out into every part of our nation and that is very important for the education of our children and our grandchildren.

As cultural and educational institutions, the Libraries make unique and vital contributions to communities across the nation. They have unparalleled research collections which, when combined with a public museum and public programs, provide researchers, students, and the general public a rich opportunity for understanding individual Presidents, the historical context of the times in which they lived and served, and the nature of the American Presidency. The Libraries also provide forums where scholars and citizens across the nation interact, ponder, and discuss the highest actions of our Federal Government, and consider issues both domestic and global in scope. Presidential Libraries represent less than 16% of NARA's budget yet account for 63% of visitors to the National Archives. Outreach opportunities provided through the Libraries could be lost if future Presidential Libraries are not built in local communities across the country.

Presidential Libraries can foster civic life in their communities. For example, the Clinton Library helped provide the catalyst for the re-birth of downtown Little Rock. For more than 50 years, the Eisenhower Library has been a center of community life in Abilene, Kansas. These two Libraries are illustrative of the benefits that they, and the eleven other Libraries, bring to the community, to their students, and to citizens. Furthermore, through the strength of the public-private partnership, both NARA and the Foundations provide resources for diverse exhibits and public programs that reach people across the country. Highlights of these programs are provided in the following table.

EXAMPLES OF THE DIVERSITY OF PRESIDENTIAL LIBRARY EXHIBITS AND PUBLIC PROGRAMS

- National Issue Forums hosted by all Presidential Libraries allow local citizens to discuss complex issues such as the cost of health care, energy, and the economy.
- The Abraham Lincoln exhibit at the Ford Museum shattered attendance records, and received wide media coverage. The exhibit was accompanied by numerous programs featuring Lincoln scholars and special events targeting school children.
- A civil rights symposium in 2007 sponsored by the Clinton and Eisenhower Presidential Libraries brought together scholars in history, law, and education to discuss the integration of Little Rock Central High School and its impact on national civil rights. Students from Abilene High School and Little Rock's Central High School engaged in a role-playing exercise and discussions reprising the events of that dramatic time.
- Experiential educational programs such as the Truman Library's White House Decision Center, the Eisenhower Library's Five Star Leader Program, and the Reagan Library Air Force One Discovery Center all challenge students in role-playing exercises related to Presidential decisions. These programs reach students grades 5-12, as well as college students, and adults, and fully immerse

> participants in key Presidential decisions such as desegregating the military, dropping the atomic bomb, and military invasions.
> - Speaker series and special conferences hosted by the Presidential Libraries explore historical topics as seen by key historical figures, such as Madeleine Albright, Kofi Annan, Tom Brokaw, Ken Burns, Doris Kearns Goodwin, Henry Kissinger, Barack Obama, Sandra Day O'Connor, Nancy Pelosi, Condoleezza Rice, John Roberts, Karl Rove, Maria Shriver, and Theodore Sorenson.
> - Special exhibits feature pivotal and rare documents often not seen outside of the Washington, DC, area, including the Magna Carta at the Reagan Library and the Emancipation Proclamation at the Clinton Library.
> - Library programs promote civic literacy. The Kennedy Library's National Student/Parent Mock Election program during election years has allowed 75,000 students all over Massachusetts to analyze party positions on diverse issues and pose their questions to party representatives during presidential, gubernatorial, and senatorial elections. Over the last thirteen years, the Hoover Library has had up to 30,000 students participate annually in interactive live virtual conferences featuring videos, artifacts, and original documents. Notably, schools located outside of driving distance or schools that cannot afford bus fare are able to experience Library offerings through this program.

CURRENT GOVERNING APPLICABLE STATUTES FOR PRESIDENTIAL HOLDINGS AND LIBRARIES

The two key statutes dealing with Presidential Libraries are the Presidential Libraries Act (PLA), 44 U.S.C. §§ 2111 and 2112, and its subsequent amendments, and the Presidential Records Act (PRA), 44 U.S.C. §§ 2201-2207. The PLA primarily deals with the facility and the endowment provisions for establishing new Presidential Libraries. The alternative models discussed below will suggest changes to the PLA that could reduce future costs for maintaining the Libraries. The Presidential Records Act specifies the access framework for Presidential Records. (We refer to Libraries that hold Presidential records as "PRA Libraries." Libraries established before Government ownership of Presidential records are referred to as "Deed of Gift" Libraries.) The alternative models will also include suggested changes to the PRA that could help to open Presidential records more quickly.

The Presidential Libraries Act

As noted above, Congress passed the Presidential Libraries Act in 1955 to codify the means by which the Archivist could accept a Presidential archival depository on behalf of the United States. By the early 1980s, Congress had become concerned about the size and costs of Presidential Libraries. The Senate Subcommittee on Treasury, Postal Service, and General Government, under the chairmanship of Senator Lawton Chiles, proposed new legislation to amend the Presidential Libraries Act of 1955. The resulting Presidential Libraries Act of 1986 includes the following key points:

1. A requirement for the Archivist to promulgate architectural and design standards applicable to Presidential archival depositories in order to ensure that such depositories preserve Presidential records and contain adequate research facilities;
2. The requirement that the donor of a Presidential archival depository must provide an endowment equal to 20% of the cost of the facility, land, or other improvements for the purpose of offsetting Library operations and maintenance costs (not program costs) for facilities up to 70,000 square feet. The endowment would increase dramatically if the Library exceeded 70,000 square feet, ultimately reaching 100% of the cost of the facility.

By effectively limiting Libraries to 70,000 square feet or less, the endowment provision failed to distinguish between the space requirements necessary for a two, versus a one, term President or to allow now for the needed growth of space for a larger staff, as electronic records have greatly increased the size and complexity of Presidential records holdings. Later legislation passed in 2003 increased the endowment provision first to 40% (not to go into effect until the President after George W. Bush) while also providing opportunities to reduce the endowment through credits for construction features or equipment that would result in long-term savings to the Government. The endowment requirement was changed again in 2008 to 60% of the cost of a facility up to 70,000 square feet and it too will not affect the George W. Bush Library.

The 20% endowment provision first applied to the George H. W. Bush Library in 1997. Prior to the acceptance of the Library by the National Archives, the Bush Foundation provided to the National Archives an endowment totaling $4,000,000. In 2004, the Clinton Foundation provided an endowment of $7,200,000 which represented 20% of the $32,000,000 cost of NARA's portion of the Library. These endowments have been based on the cost of the usable square footage transferred to NARA's control. The 60% endowment provision will first apply to a Barack Obama Library. As required by the statute, NARA uses the income to offset facility operations and maintenance costs.

The Archivist also promulgated the required architecture and design standards for Presidential Libraries. The first comprehensive draft was not completed until 1999. Previous versions had essentially been a program document with some technical data related to environmental conditions for holdings storage areas. The standards have now grown to include detailed technical specifications for HVAC systems, security infrastructure, and shelving. The Clinton Library was built to these new, more detailed standards. The latest version of the updated standards was promulgated in May 2008. When renovating existing Libraries, the standards are applied to the fullest extent technically possible in existing buildings.

The Presidential Records Act

The other main statutory authority dealing with Presidential Library holdings is the Presidential Records Act (PRA) of 1978. Throughout the 18th, 19th, and well into the 20th century, few questions were raised regarding the private ownership of Presidential papers by the President (just as the official papers of each Member of Congress and Supreme Court Justice remain privately owned to this day). Former Presidents could donate them to a library or archives, or not, as they saw fit. Fortunately, the Library of Congress undertook major collecting efforts, saving many Presidential papers (see Appendix B for the location of Presidential Papers from Washington to Bush 43). On the other hand, many were accidentally or purposely destroyed. As initiated by Franklin Roosevelt, the precedent of donating Presidential papers to the Government worked very well. Although the Presidential Libraries Act, which established the Libraries, did not mandate that Presidents systematically preserve their Presidential papers, the legislation assured a President who donated his materials to the National Archives that the integrity of a Presidential collection would be preserved in one place, and that the papers would be cared for by a professional archival staff and made available for research and study. A deed of gift for the President's papers was a pre-condition for the acceptance of a Presidential Library by the Government.

President Richard Nixon's resignation in 1974 prompted an examination of the tradition of private ownership of Presidential papers. That year Congress enacted the Presidential Recordings and Materials Preservation Act (PRMPA), which seized the Nixon Presidential materials and gave the National Archives legal custody and control over them. Title II of the PRMPA established the National Study Commission on Records and Documents of Federal Officials to explore topics of ownership, control, disposition, and preservation of historic materials created by Government officials. The report of the Commission, completed in March 1977, made two key recommendations:

1. All documentary materials received or made by Federal Officials in discharge of their official duties should be considered the property of the United States.
2. Presidents should be given additional rights to control access to their Presidential records up to 15 years after the end of their administration. (Congress changed this to 12 years in the subsequently enacted PRA legislation.)

In 1978, Congress acted on the report and passed the PRA, which clearly established public ownership of the official records of a President upon their creation. The PRA further established that immediately upon the conclusion of a President's tenure, the legal custody of Presidential records would be transferred to the National Archives. Government archivists would then be responsible for preserving, processing, and providing access to the records. Although NARA's process for providing access to donated historical materials and the process for providing access to Presidential records under the PRA varies somewhat in implementation because of the statutory and regulatory requirements, the mission of the Government staff in each Library is the same – to preserve and process the materials and provide access as fully and promptly as the law or deed and resources permit.

Basic Legal Authorities for Presidential Gifts

Besides large collections of papers and records of the President and others associated with him, each Presidential Library also houses tens of thousands of artifacts and gifts given to the President. There are several statutory authorities dealing with Presidential gifts.

Head of State and other foreign official gifts are regulated under the Foreign Gifts and Decorations Act, 22 U.S.C. 26, upon their receipt by the President. These foreign official gifts along with the gifts received by the President from private citizens for eventual deposit in his

Presidential Library are received under the provision of the Archivist's receivable authority (44 U.S.C. 2111 and 2112). Some of these gifts are also received as Presidential records (44 U.S.C. 2201). These gift collections have become a key part of the holdings of the Presidential Library and Museum and are used in museum exhibits to bring the Presidency to life.

THE CURRENT MODEL FOR THE PRESIDENTIAL LIBRARY SYSTEM

Though no President is required to establish a Presidential Library, each President from Herbert Hoover through George W. Bush has embraced the model first established by Franklin D. Roosevelt. In order to understand the proposed alternative models, it is essential to consider current Library funding sources, ongoing preservation efforts, and access to Presidential papers and records in the current Library system.

Current Funding Sources for the Presidential Libraries

Presidential Libraries rely upon multiple funding sources:

1. Base Appropriations: Funds appropriated by Congress for the operation of NARA that provide for staffing, administration, security, upkeep, maintenance, and renovation projects at the Presidential Libraries.
2. Trust Fund Revenue: Funds generated through museum admission fees, museum store sales, and duplication fees provide for admissions staff and help support exhibit-related and public programming expenses.
3. Gift Funds: Funds donated to a Library, usually for specific projects or programs.
4. Endowments: Funds required through the Presidential Libraries Act of 1986, as amended, offset a portion of the Library's operations and maintenance costs.
5. Foundation Funds: Funds provided by a Library support organization for programming, exhibits, staff, or special projects. These funds may be provided by the Foundation annually based on the Library's budget request, awarded on a project-by-project basis, or expended directly by the Foundation for the support of the Library. These funds may also be used to support staff performing governmental functions and library renovation projects.

Base Appropriations – FY2008 Cost for Operating Presidential Libraries

The cost of operating the Presidential Library system in FY2008 was $63,944,800 in NARA's base appropriation. This amount included funding for operating expenses, salaries and benefits, security, operations and maintenance, and facility-related repairs or other infrastructure needs. The overall number includes not only the monies budgeted for each Library, but also funding for the Office of Presidential Libraries and the Presidential Materials Staff, as well as the new George W. Bush Temporary Library Site. In FY2008,

Congress also provided special appropriations for the following Libraries: Roosevelt Library, $750,000; Kennedy Library, $8 million; Johnson Library, $3.76 million; and the Nixon Library $7.432 million. The following chart provides an overview of funding for each of the Presidential Libraries and the Central Office overseeing the Libraries.

Repair and renovation funds within NARA's base appropriation provide for ongoing upkeep and maintenance of Presidential Libraries; support projects aimed at bringing older Libraries as closely as possible into compliance with NARA standards; and offer opportunities to reduce operating costs through the addition of more efficient building systems. NARA has undertaken a series of building condition reports (BCR) for each Library to identify necessary repairs and improvements and to provide a basis for prioritizing Library projects.

Development of Capital Improvement Plans

In 2006, NARA recognized the need to identify immediate and long-term repair and renovation projects and developed a Capital Improvement Plan for projects over $1,500,000. A plan was also required through the Presidential Historical Preservations Act of 2008. Renovations, additions, or other capital projects can provide NARA with opportunities to create more secure, environmentally appropriate spaces for holdings and to address infrastructure needs that inevitably arise as facilities age. The Capital Improvement Plan is an incremental approach that enables NARA to address major projects in a systematic fashion within the context of overall agency needs. Major capital projects currently underway include the renovation of the Roosevelt Library (Phase 1, $17,500,000) and construction of an addition at the Kennedy Library (Phase 1 and 2, $30,000,000) to increase holdings storage capacity and provide education programming space. Currently, a new storage addition is under construction at the Nixon Library to house holdings now stored in College Park, MD. Major improvements to the Johnson Library plaza and education and public programming space are also underway with expected completion in 2010. NARA's Capital Improvement Plan prioritizes a series of potential major renovation and repair projects for Libraries through 2018 that are outlined in the list below:

NARA Capital Improvements Plan Projects: First Tier
Projects Roosevelt Library Renovation Construction, Phase 2

NARA Capital Improvements Plan Projects: Second Tier Projects
Eisenhower Center Renovations and Visitor Center Expansion (Design)
Johnson Library Space Alteration (Design)
Ford Library Roof Replacement

NARA Capital Improvements Plan: Third Tier Projects
Eisenhower Center Renovations and Visitor Center Expansion (Construction Phase 1)
Johnson Library Space Alterations (Construction)
Ford Museum Roof Replacement
Hoover Library Mechanical Repairs and Building Renovations (Construction)

NARA also incorporates new Federal mandates for the reduction of energy consumption when constructing and improving facilities. Better designed and renovated facilities and more efficient equipment do result in savings. The architectural and design standards for Presidential Libraries require new Libraries to meet LEED[9] silver standards. Systematic renovations, repairs, and maintenance of equipment and building systems will ultimately result in long-term savings in operating Presidential Libraries.

Foundation Support

Foundation support has been critical to the operation of the Libraries since their inception. When adjusted for inflation, the National Archives has received almost $400,000,000 in new facilities and equipment paid for by non-Federal funds.[10] NARA has also received additional non-Federal funds through Foundation contributions and gifts for the purposes of updating permanent exhibits, adding additional program space, and supporting staff to undertake public outreach efforts as well as core mission activities. This support varies from year to year but ranges from less than $100,000 to several million dollars in direct and indirect contributions to each Library by their foundation.

Table 1. FY 2008 Presidential Library Actual Costs

	O&M (Including Security)	Program Including Salary	Minor R&R	Major R&R[1]	Total
Hoover	899,000	1,269,800	21,200	20,900	**2,210,900**
Roosevelt	2,847,300	1,597,800	55,300	378,000	**4,878,400**
Truman	1,969,200	1,879,600	36,200	342,400	**4,227,400**
Eisenhower	1,159,600	2,004,800	23,900	180,900	**3,369,200**
Kennedy	3,846,600	2,206,100	14,200	1,600	**6,068,500**
Johnson	2,880,600	2,159,200	900	3,000	**5,043,700**
Nixon[2]	1,513,100	2,298,600	10,600	47,300	**3,869,600**
Ford	1,973,800	1,874,200	38,300	181,500	**4,067,800**
Carter	1,578,500	2,941,900	24,800	422,200	**4,967,400**
Reagan	3,082,000	2,013,600	57,800	273,700	**5,427,100**
Bush 41	2,595,500[3]	1,662,500	12,700	900	**4,271,600**
Clinton	2,261,700[4]	1,936,200	7,700	132,800	**4,438,400**
Bush 43[5]	460,600	3,086,200	0	0	**3,546,800**
Central Office[6]	0	4,606,200	0	0	**4,606,200**
Presidential Materials Staff[7]	0	1,404,500	0	0	**1,404,500**
Nixon Presidential Materials Staff[8]	0	1,547,300	0	0	**1,547,300**
Totals	**26,706,900**	**34,488,500**	**303,600**	**1,985,200**	**63,944,800**

The need for private funding to enhance government support for library programs was felt early on. The Truman Library Institute began raising money to support scholars visiting the Library as soon as it opened in 1957, and former President Truman frequently turned over his modest honoraria for lectures to the Institute. In 1958, the Institute secured its first major grant from the Rockefeller Foundation in the amount of $48,700. However, funding support for exhibits and public programs was limited or non-existent since the resources of the Truman Institute and the Foundations for the other three existing Libraries (Hoover, Roosevelt, and Eisenhower) had been exhausted by the building of the Libraries. President Johnson departed from the original public/private foundation model when he decided his Foundation would be endowed to provide on-going private financial support for exhibits, public programs, and other needs of the Library.[11] This financial support model became the paradigm.

Trust and Gift Funds

The Presidential Libraries Act specifically authorizes the Archivist to collect fees, solicit donations, and accept bequests for the benefit of Presidential Libraries. The monies generated at or for a Library are deposited into the National Archives Trust for use by that Library. Thus, since the beginning of the Presidential Library system in 1941, NARA has used revenue from ticket admissions, museum store sales, and duplications to pay for admissions staff and for other staff which support exhibit, education and public program activities. In FY2008, trust fund revenue offset $7.9 million in operating costs—costs not borne by the Federal Government.

Although these trust funds do not provide sufficient income to offset entirely the need for Federal appropriations, the Libraries derive considerable benefit from income generated through stores and ticket revenues. The income provides a measure of support for museum and public program activities and covers the salaries of those who work in admission and museum stores. In FY2008, even with the decline in revenue reflecting the broader economic downturn, Presidential

Libraries as a system generated a trust fund surplus of $810,000 and posted retained earnings of $13,665,295. Retained earnings are used to fund programs that are not covered by appropriated monies and to cover future deficits resulting from lower revenues. For the 2008 Trust Fund statement, please see Appendix D.

Endowment Funds

Endowments required by the Presidential Libraries Act of 1986 and first applied to the George H. W. Bush Library have offset some costs to the Federal Government. Conservatively invested to protect the principal, incomes range from two to four percent annually. In FY2008, the endowments yielded $248,122 and $383,477 for the Bush and Clinton Libraries, respectively. Current security and operation and maintenance contracts for these two Libraries are $2,530,220 for Bush and $2,981,606 for Clinton. The revenue from the endowments offset these contract costs for the Bush Library by a little more than 10% and for Clinton by a little less than 13%.

If the endowments had been 60 percent of the cost of the Library, as now required, the yield at 4% would produce $480,000 for Bush and $864,000 for Clinton, which would cover less than 20% of the Bush contracts and about one-third of the Clinton contracts. This strategy does not permit any reinvestment to grow the endowment fund. While the endowment would remain essentially flat (barring any losses), operating costs would increase over time while the annual offset from the endowment income would remain fairly static with conservative investments. Suggestions for increasing the base on which the endowment is calculated and expanding the use of the endowment to accumulate funds for major projects will be discussed in more detail in the section concerning Alternative Model 1.

PRESERVATION OF HOLDINGS

NARA's preservation program has evolved significantly over the past 25 years. From facility design and renovation to treatment of holdings, both through holdings maintenance and more directed individual object conservation, preservation is now a major priority of the agency. The agency's first strategic plan in the early nineties identified preservation as a key goal, stating that "all records will be preserved in appropriate space for use as long as needed." Preservation activities have evolved in Presidential Libraries as well, most notably as a result of the

Architecture and Design Standards for Presidential Libraries and through internal efforts to identify materials at risk and contract vehicles to treat these materials.

The *Architecture and Design Standards for Presidential Libraries* mandated by the Presidential Libraries Act of 1986 reflect NARA's commitment to oversee the design and construction,[12] as well as the renovation and repair of its facilities to provide space appropriate for the preservation of invaluable archival and artifact holdings.

Almost every aspect of the design standards relates to the preservation of holdings. The standards mandate site requirements; general structural criteria; heating, ventilation, and air conditioning standards; fire safety; security; floor loadings; finishes; lighting; and glazing criteria. Most importantly, the standards outline specific temperature and humidity criteria to ensure the longterm protection of Presidential records. These stringent requirements have resulted in preservation-quality spaces at the Clinton Library and are being incorporated into the design of the new Bush Library, as well as at older Libraries undergoing renovations or repairs. These requirements have significantly increased the cost of building Presidential Libraries. Conversely, these standards will greatly reduce NARA's future costs, since the new Libraries are less likely to need extensive renovations to meet preservation standards.

Yet the facility itself is only one part of preservation activities in the current Library model. NARA's Preservation Office and the Office of Presidential Libraries provide funds to treat textual, non-textual, and artifact holdings. In particular, non-textual funding enables the Libraries to create preservation copies of photographs, films, and audio tapes. At the Kennedy, Nixon, and Johnson Libraries, the ongoing review of Presidential tape collections has resulted not only in better access to holdings, but also improved preservation of the original tapes. The Office of Presidential Libraries, in conjunction with NARA's Preservation

Office, has also begun a major preservation assessment and treatment program at the Roosevelt Library. This effort, focused on textiles, prints, and paintings, will serve as a model for future projects at other Libraries. These projects underscore NARA's commitment to the preservation of Library holdings.

In 1998, the Office of Presidential Libraries added a professional curatorial staff as part of its Washington, DC based Presidential Materials Staff. The purpose of the curatorial staff is to work on a regular basis with the White House, particularly the White House Gift Office, on issues relating to artifacts. NARA now works with the White House in determining what gifts are appropriate for transfer to the Archives. The Presidential Materials Staff catalogues all incoming Presidential and Vice Presidential gifts and artifacts as they arrive, identifies condition issues, and applies preservation treatment to materials at risk. On the first day of an Administration, the gift unit of the Presidential Materials Staff begins tracking and packing artifacts according to curatorial standards. This staff has worked with two administrations in providing disposal guidance for Presidential gifts, and at the end of the George W. Bush Administration provided a complete inventory of all Bush artifacts. The result of these new protocols is full intellectual control over the Presidential gift holdings and completed risk assessments that will enable NARA to identify conservation treatment priorities and greatly enhanced control over their physical preservation.

NARA has also had to rely on its partners, the Library Foundations, to offset some preservation costs. For example, the Truman Institute provided $1,400,000 to construct a pavilion outside President Truman's office at the Library. The addition supports the preservation of the office and its contents and provides the public with an opportunity to view the office. The Institute also received a *Saving America's Treasures* grant to undertake conservation treatment of artifacts on exhibit in President Truman's office. The Kennedy Foundation has long supported preservation efforts at the Library. It has established an endowment specifically for preservation, which pays for approximately $36,000 worth of artifact conservation treatment annually. The Kennedy Foundation also received a $150,000 *Saving America's Treasures* grant for conservation treatment and another $50,000 for supplies and intern labor. An intern program supported by the Foundation funds approximately $75,000 in staff salaries for holdings maintenance, the most basic level of conservation treatment. A donor is funding the conversion of Johnson Library tapes and Kennedy Library news footage related to Robert Kennedy to digital formats. This project will ultimately amount to an estimated $200,000 gift. Without this private support through Library Foundations, it is unlikely that these items at risk would have received such timely conservation treatment. The Johnson Foundation has, over the past decade, provided much of the funding required for the preservation of the Johnson tapes (which were originally recorded on obsolete dictabelts) and supported preservation of other audiovisual materials in the collections.

CURRENT EFFORTS TO IMPROVE ACCESS TO PRESIDENTIAL RECORDS

This section of the report addresses Congress's request that NARA consider how to "reduce the delay in public access to all Presidential records." When the Presidential Records

Act (PRA) changed the ownership of Presidential papers from private to public, it incorporated several access provisions to ensure the Act's constitutionality and to balance the President's loss of private ownership of his papers.

One of the many changes established by the PRA was the application of the FOIA to Presidential records. The PRA also provided each President the discretion to impose, while in office, each of six Presidential restrictions to last up to 12 years after the President leaves office (which all Presidents have done). The Presidential restrictions, at 44 U.S.C. § 2204(a), known as P1 (classified national security information), P3 (required by a statute), P4 (trade secrets and other confidential business information), and P6 (clearly unwarranted invasion of personal privacy), are identical to FOIA exemptions (b)(1), (b)(3), (b)(4), and (b)(6). Two PRA restrictions are different. The P2 restriction applies to information "relating to appointments to Federal office." The P5 restriction applies to information containing "confidential communications requesting or submitting advice, between the President and his advisers, or between such advisers," and is similar to, but distinct from, the FOIA (b)(5) exemption (deliberative process and other privileges). Moreover, when the P5 restriction expires after twelve years, the FOIA (b)(5) exemption does not apply to Presidential records, thus allowing NARA to release most confidential advice records at that point in time unless a former or incumbent President raises a claim of executive privilege.

The PRA does not mandate these restrictions, but rather makes clear that they may be narrowed or waived even after the President leaves office. Moreover, in the legislative history, Congress advised the Archivist and former Presidents to do just that:

> It is also expected that the Archivist will follow past practice in applying the restrictive categories in former Presidents' deeds of gift, and negotiate with the ex-President or his representative on an on-going basis to lessen the number of years chosen for particular mandatory restriction categories, to eliminate entire categories, or to permit release of particular records otherwise restricted.[13]

Former Presidents Reagan, George H. W. Bush, and Clinton have all responded to this authority and narrowed the scope of PRA exemptions P2 and P5, allowing significantly more records to be opened. Such narrowing is voluntary by the former President, and may be withdrawn or revised at will during the 12-year period in which the restrictions can be applied.

The PRA restricts any public access for a five-year period, unless the Archivist decides to open an integral file segment. After five years, the PRA gives the public a right of access through FOIA requests. Significantly, the PRA also mandates that "[t]he Archivist shall have an affirmative duty to make such records available to the public as rapidly and completely as possible consistent with the provisions of this Act." *Id.* § 2203(f)(1). In mandating that Presidential records would not be available to the public for the first five years after a President leaves office, Congress expected that a significant portion of the Presidential records could be processed and ready for opening at the time they became available to FOIA requests. Unfortunately, this assumption on how quickly and effectively records would be processed and opened under the PRA has not been realized. The sheer size and complexity of the collections, coupled with the numerous special access requests by the incumbent and former Presidents, the Courts, and the Congress, have made this an unrealistic goal. As an illustration of this fact, at their respective five-year points, the Reagan and Bush Library staff had processed less than five percent of their Presidential records and Clinton less than one percent.

Therefore, at the point when Presidential records have become subject to request under FOIA, the vast majority of records have not yet been reviewed and publicly released. This fact, along with the significant number of FOIA requests filed at each of the libraries for access to these records, has resulted in dramatic FOIA backlogs. This problem was not unanticipated. Indeed, in the 1978 hearings on the PRA, then Archivist of the United States James B. Rhoads raised a serious archival concern about subjecting Presidential records to FOIA requests:

> [P]rofessional archivists have expressed concerns that efforts to systematically process the records and make them available would be severely hampered by numerous Freedom of Information Act requests and associated lawsuits. . . . We share these concerns. It is likely that Presidential records would attract a large number of Freedom of Information Act requests because of the President's extreme public visibility. . . . The threat of immediate, excessive litigation would divert considerable staff time from processing the records in order to search out isolated bits and pieces of information.[14]

Not only is the volume of FOIA requests problematic, but also the administrative and archival requirements of processing records in response to FOIA requests has led to significant delays in opening records. In the pre-PRA donor Libraries, NARA processes and opens records systematically, meaning that archivists start at the beginning of a collection or file series and review it through to its end. However, in processing FOIA requests, archivists must pull files and/or documents from multiple collections and series that relate to the request. This approach requires an extensive search to identify relevant files and records. Further, in order to maintain the provenance, or order, of the documents, archivists must carefully document the removal of records from their original file location and prepare withdrawal sheets for each closure, which further contributes to the time required to process FOIA requests.

The actual review of the records prior to release has become increasingly more complicated including the processing of electronic records. The line-by-line review by NARA archivists prior to release under the PRA requires applying two different sets of restrictions: the Presidential restrictive categories and eight of the nine FOIA exemptions. Additionally, because of the new regulations dealing with protecting personally identifiable information (PII) and the greater likelihood that Presidential records can or are being posted on the internet, NARA has intensified its efforts to redact this information from Presidential records, particularly the more recent records. Because a large amount of PII is in the records, doing so is labor intensive and significantly slows down processing.

Finally, since the enactment of the PRA, Presidential Libraries also experienced an explosive growth in the volume of electronic records, especially White House email. In 1994, the Clinton White House implemented a form of electronic recordkeeping for email known as the Automatic Records Management System or "ARMS" system. Utilizing that system, the Clinton Administration transferred approximately 20 million Presidential record emails to NARA in January 2001. This year, NARA received over 150 million Presidential emails from the George W. Bush Administration, as well as numerous other classified and unclassified electronic systems containing Presidential records. Presidential Library holdings in electronic form are now much larger than the paper holdings. Indeed, the email system for the George W. Bush Administration alone is many times larger than the entire textual holdings of any other Presidential Library. These electronic holdings bring new challenges to processing and making available Presidential records. The sheer volume exponentially increases what archivists have to search and isolate as relevant to a request, a lengthy process in and of itself before the review begins. Once review begins, the more informal communication style embodied in Presidential record emails often blends personal and record information in the same email necessitating more redactions.

NARA has now been processing Presidential records in response to FOIA requests for 15 years, and has explored through the years many ways to streamline and speed this process. In particular, since 2007, NARA's Office of Presidential Libraries has worked, and continues to work, with the PRA Libraries to change how Presidential records are processed, with the purpose of facilitating quicker access to Presidential records. Following a conference in March 2008 of PRA Libraries to examine our processing of Presidential records and determine the most effective use of newly allocated archival staff, the Libraries are implementing the following changes:

1. The Libraries added an additional processing queue based on frequently requested records. This type of review—reviewing an entire series or collection of documents from beginning to end—is known as systematic processing and is significantly faster than FOIA processing.
2. Libraries will move to a more standardized FOIA request queue structure across the Libraries, with page limitations, that will make useful volumes of records available for research while allowing the archivists to address more requests in a timely manner.
3. The Libraries will devote some portion of the archival staff to processing systematically entire series or sub-series of historically significant files, a process more efficient than FOIA processing.
4. The Libraries will make the folder titles for both processed and unprocessed textual Presidential records available on the web. Providing the public such a detailed view of the Presidential records in a Library will ensure that future FOIA requests are more targeted to the needs of the requesters.
5. Finally, Libraries will take some less sensitive series (routine requests for Presidential messages, bulk public mail, etc.) through the PRA-mandated notification processes and make them available for "review on request" access review. The Libraries estimate that more than 11 million pages can be provided to the public using this process.

NARA believes a statutory change to the PRA would be of some help in limiting the time delay and the NARA resources required for providing notice to the former and incumbent Presidents of our intent to open records. NARA recommends a statutory cut-off period for notice which we suggest should coincide with the death or disability of the former President or after 25 years, whichever is later. As the Supreme Court made clear in *Nixon v. Administrator of General Services*, 433 U.S. 425, 451 (1977), executive privilege is "subject to erosion over time after an administration leaves office." It is well established in archival practice, and codified into the Federal Records Act (FRA), that restrictions in archival records to protect deliberative processes and other privileges cease no later than 30 years after creation. The FRA states that "[s]tatutory and other restrictions referred to in this subsection shall remain in force until the records have been in existence for thirty years ..." 44 U.S.C. § 2108(a). Similarly, Executive Order 12958, as amended, established a 25-year automatic declassification requirement. Given that Presidential records will already be as much as eight years old when NARA receives them, 25 years is a reasonable cut-off time.[15] Eliminating the privilege review process after the passage of time will reduce some of the delay in making Presidential records available to the public.

Congress has funded a key resource change that should significantly help the PRA Libraries in addressing their FOIA backlogs. In FY2009, Congress appropriated funding for 15 additional archival positions for the existing Libraries with Presidential records – Reagan, Bush 41, and Clinton. Congress also appropriated funding for 18 archivists to process the George W. Bush and Cheney records. These positions, combined with improvements in the way NARA processes Presidential records, should result in the opening of significantly more records. As the chart that follows shows, by 2010 these innovations in processing should increase the Libraries' rate of processing by at least 1.3 million pages a year.

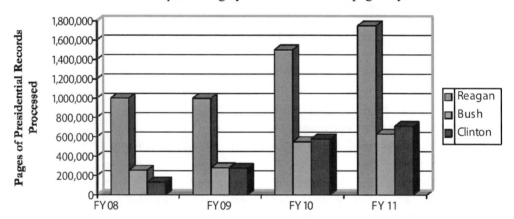

While this represents significant progress, it should be noted that the Presidential record collections of each of these three Presidents are significant in size and it will still take many decades to complete the processing of these important records.[16]

Ultimately, the ability to open Presidential records to the public is resource driven. It is the case throughout the National Archives that the more archivists available to review and redact records that are subject to statutory restrictions and constitutional review processes, the more NARA can open such records and satisfy FOIA requests. The review process generally speeds up as time passes, because many of the sensitivities in the records recede with the passage of time.

The explosion of email and other electronic records means that NARA will use FOIA requests and our own selective processing to open specific records on topics requested from the tens of terabytes of information we have now and the hundreds we expect to have in future. Accordingly, processing vast amounts or even the majority of these electronic records along with millions of textual records will remain a significant challenge for the foreseeable future. Also, given the complexities inherent in processing these records under the statutory and regulatory requirements, NARA faces another significant challenge in balancing its mandate to make Presidential records available as quickly as possible while at the same time safeguarding against the untimely release of sensitive information contained in these records.

FACILITATING THE DECLASSIFICATION OF PRESIDENTIAL PAPERS AND RECORDS

The Presidential Libraries hold nearly 40 million pages of classified records. The foreign policy materials in Presidential collections are among the highest-level, most historically-significant documents in the Federal Government. Presidential files include the records of the National Security Council and materials from all departments and agencies in the Federal Government that are sent into the White House.

Given the importance of these files and the automatic declassification provision of Executive Order 12958, as amended, a key priority for the Presidential Libraries was to establish a better approach for the declassification of approximately eight million classified pages from the administrations of President Hoover through President Carter. NARA's Presidential Libraries teamed with the Central Intelligence Agency to create the Remote Archives Capture Project (RAC), under which all 25-year-old classified documents would be scanned at the Libraries so they could be made available electronically to the equity holding agencies in the Washington, DC, area for a declassification review – i.e., a centralized declassification program. The RAC has, to date, scanned 4,205,005 pages of material from the Truman through the first part of the Reagan Administration. Nearly one million pages will have been reviewed for declassification and returned to the Libraries by the end of 2009. This includes decisions on documents through the Carter administration.

Further, the Presidential Libraries have begun the process of making new RAC declassification decisions quickly available to researchers on stand-alone unclassified computers in Library research rooms. This process started at the Carter Library, and the Office of Presidential Libraries plans to have similar unclassified computers at each of the Libraries from Truman through Reagan in order to make newly declassified documents available to researchers without delay.

FACILITATING ACCESS TO PRESIDENTIAL ELECTRONIC RECORDS AT THE PRA LIBRARIES

The Clinton Administration was the first to conduct much of its official business on computers. NARA, therefore, had to establish an electronic archival preservation and processing system to handle these new formats. For the main body of Clinton Presidential electronic records, NARA developed a system known as the Presidential Electronic Records Library (PERL), which allows search and retrieval of records for archival processing, access requests, and reference.

The much larger volume of electronic records from the George W. Bush Administration was well beyond the capabilities of the PERL infrastructure. NARA worked instead to speed the development of the Electronic Records Archive (ERA) program to accommodate these Presidential records.

The Executive Office of the President (EOP) instance of ERA focuses on immediate needs for search and access and the need to respond to special access requests while at the same time providing a basis for future development to handle PRA/FOIA review. EOP ERA allows NARA for the first time to store electronic records in a common format and eliminates the need to update and migrate proprietary software.

FACILITATING BROADER ACCESS TO PRESIDENTIAL RECORDS AND PAPERS

Over the last 20 years, the Internet has transformed information delivery and public expectations. It has also provided an opportunity for the Presidential Libraries to expand the knowledge of Presidential records to a much broader audience. Since the early 1990s, the Presidential Libraries have partnered with corporations, foundations, universities, and offices in the National Archives and their partners to use technology to make Presidential records and papers more accessible on the Internet with non-Federal funding. These partnerships have led to the creation of many useful sites. One such partnership has produced the Presidential Timeline (www.presidentialtimeline.org) with over 20 online exhibits, more than 1,000 digital objects, and a growing number of education modules for teachers. This partnership has allowed the Libraries to create a seamless presentation of issues and themes, such as Civil Rights and the Cold War, that cut across Presidential Administrations.

Corporations and universities have partnered with the Roosevelt, Truman, Kennedy, and Bush 41 Libraries to digitize full collections of Presidential materials, responses to FOIA requests, and declassified materials. Some of these collections are available on the web now. The Libraries will continue to use the digital world to reach broader audiences and to complement their successful public programming and outreach efforts, a cornerstone of the Presidential Library System.

PROPOSED ALTERNATIVE MODELS

As discussed in the overview of this report, NARA is presenting five models. NARA estimates all but one reduce Government costs, some more than others. The most significant cost savings are estimated to be achieved through the elimination of museum, public outreach, and educational programs, with NARA providing Governmental support only for the archival and collections management functions for both archives and artifacts. The difficult and most crucial question which NARA and others must resolve before adopting any changes is what the focus of NARA's mission for the Presidential Libraries and the study of the Presidency should be? Should NARA focus exclusively on the needs of the scholarly community or should NARA seek to reach a broader community to educate them about the American Presidency and our Government?

To achieve significant cost savings, NARA would need to shift the cost for renovating, staffing and maintaining Presidential museums to the Foundations. NARA would then necessarily cede the responsibility for exhibits, education, and public programming in museums to the Foundations that run them, thus eliminating these programs from NARA's mission. On balance, we believe that NARA's influence has brought a more nuanced perspective to the content and interpretation in exhibits and programming in our spaces, even as the Foundations have borne the major responsibility for funding them. The museums provide a stepping stone to many education activities and public programs of the Libraries. Without this important cultural resource and educational tool, NARA would not be able to present a richer, more contextual presentation of the Presidency.

ALTERNATIVE MODEZL 1: CURRENT MODEL WITH REVISIONS TO FURTHER REDUCE THE COST TO THE FEDERAL GOVERNMENT

This model builds on the current public-private partnership developed over the past 75 years. Potential revisions provide for greater revenue through the endowment and further clarify the relationship between the Library and the Foundation. This model would also suggests changes needed to the Presidential Libraries Act or NARA regulations to codify these new requirements.

The existing model for Presidential Libraries has served both Libraries and Foundations well, though sometimes in different ways. It provides the Government with a new, state-of-the-art facility to house Presidential records and offsets costs to the Government for certain types of activities primarily related to exhibits and public programs. For the Foundation, the model provides a former President and his supporters with an opportunity to showcase the Administration in a place chosen by the former President. The importance of the Presidential Library, museum, and education and outreach resources to local communities and to the universities that host them is easily evident in the great demand and competition to be the location selected for a new Presidential Library. Recently, more and more communities and universities are willing to expend considerable resources and provide significant financial incentives to convince the President to select their location for the Library.

As in a current Presidential Library, this model houses in the Library the official records that exist in paper form, along with complementary private collections and oral histories, the latter of which are largely funded with private money. This model preserves the tradition established with Franklin Delano Roosevelt of bringing together the official records with other historical pre- and post-presidential materials that illuminate the life of the President. This compilation of official and personal papers in one place could easily be lost in a centralized model as discussed below. A centralized model could result in the personal papers of the President being dispersed in the best case and lost or destroyed in the worst case.

Model 1 provides for a flexible institution that adapts to the changing world of records. As Presidential records become increasingly electronic, Model 1 would evolve toward a smaller building, but retain the archival expertise, the museum and civil literacy functions, and the private funding for the building and public program support. Even in an increasingly electronic world, records need to be contextualized. Since Presidential electronic records are already centralized and maintained in Washington, DC, area facilities, with the majority of the staff having access to these records at the Library site, this model would continue to build on the current structure. This model preserves and provides access to both the official records and personal papers of the Presidency in one location, while preserving private funding for museum and public program components. NARA maintains the flexibility to provide additional support for processing electronic records by utilizing staff located in the DC area or in another Presidential library when needed.

Since this model preserves the Government's relationship with the Foundations, the following discussion makes suggestion that would strengthen and define this public-private partnership.

Defining the Relationship between the Government and the Foundation

NARA's relationship with Library Foundations is one of the oldest public-private partnerships in Government. Each relationship is different, continually evolving, and not easily defined. The Government's role is to run the Library, which involves preserving the collections, processing the records for public access within the statutory and legal framework, and working to ensure that the historical content of exhibits reflects an objective perspective of the Presidency – even as the private Foundations have carried a large part of the financial responsibility for the latter. Beyond providing financial support, the Foundations' roles have often been to further the work and strengthen the legacy of the former Presidents and, increasingly, to engage in non-Library funding of various national or global initiatives of the former Presidents. While there have been many positive benefits from this unique relationship, the Foundations' activities and goals, given that they are a private partner, are not always aligned with NARA's view of our stewardship responsibilities. Therefore, we are suggesting a specific charter to guide future

Library/Foundation Relationships

Before NARA accepts a new Presidential Library, a clearer understanding between the Foundation and the Government should be memorialized in a written agreement. Given the inherent complexities in this relationship, the partnership would benefit from an established set of principles. Legislative changes to the PLA and new regulations to codify the relationship would serve both partners and the public interest. The following principles need to guide this partnership:

1. Greater clarity in the roles, goals, and priorities, as well as in the responsibility and authority of each partner, in order to minimize friction and maximize success in the relationship between the Presidential Library and its non-profit partner and to assure the sound and responsible stewardship of archival and historical materials held in the public trust.
2. Commitment from the Foundation for continued financial support of museum, outreach, and educational programs in order to make the Library a viable model in the present and into the future.
3. Library participation in the planning and decision-making of the Foundation as it relates to the Library, typically by having the Library director serve as an *ex officio* member of the board of the Foundation.[17]

To formalize the public/private partnership, NARA recommends the following changes to the Presidential Libraries Act, in Section 44 U.S.C 2112 and/or to NARA's regulations.

1. The Presidential archival depository should be built solely for the purpose of operating the Library and museum. Foundation spaces co-located in the Presidential archival depository should be in direct support of the Presidential Library museum program (*e.g.,* museum store, restaurant, auditorium, etc.). Sub-metering must be provided for all Foundation spaces located in the Presidential archival depository.
2. The Foundation must provide an endowment of 60% of the cost of the entire Library building (previously the endowment was only applied to the NARA program space or usable space and was not applied to support space, *e.g.* mechanical rooms, needed to operate the NARA program space or to Foundation-retained spaces within the Library) of which no more than 20% may be offset by credits. For example, a credit may be provided for energy saving features. To receive credits, the Foundation must document through an independent technical and cost analysis any savings to the Government.
3. NARA must determine its space needs based on program requirements for staffing and for the processing, accessibility, and storage of our collections. The endowment would cover the entire Library building. Since NARA needs to determine its space needs, the escalation clause for increasing the usable square footage of the building above 70,000 square feet should be eliminated from the PLA.
4. The Archivist should be provided with the authority to accumulate some or all of the interest earned by a Presidential Library endowment over several years for expenditure on higher cost repair or maintenance items. Currently, interest is used to offset only a relatively minor amount of operations and maintenance contracts. This authority to accumulate interest from the endowment should be capped at a predetermined dollar amount. In cases where the cap is exceeded, the Archivist must spend the excess amount on the affected Library's current facility operational costs or public and education programming. Currently, the entire endowment interest is used to offset operations and maintenance contracts, which is a relatively small amount of the costs.
5. The Foundation must provide a separate endowment, or agree to an annual commitment to support museum, public, and educational programming at the Library. The endowment should be $10 million or, alternatively, at least $400,000 to be provided annually to NARA

Model 1 Advantages

There are certain advantages for sustaining and improving the current model for Presidential Libraries.

- Foundations will continue to pay for the construction of the building with privately raised funds. NARA would determine space requirements to meet program needs and determine the size of the new Library. NARA would determine museum space requirements using A&D standards to meet program requirements. NARA standards would ensure that a high quality building is provided to or for the use of the Government.

- The decreasing physical size of textual collections as a result of the anticipated increase in electronic records will yield substantial facility operational cost savings to NARA, provided museum and other public spaces are not significantly expanded.
- The reinvestment of some endowment income for future use will make available funds to offset a portion of greater infrastructure expenses such as future modernization costs, new HVAC systems, roofs, and other large expenses.
- Presidential Libraries would continue to provide a NARA presence in communities as rich archival, cultural, historical, and educational centers providing a wide variety of diverse, non-partisan programming.
- The charter between the Government and the Foundation assures the long term viability of the Library. The roles and responsibilities of Presidential Foundations and the use of co-located foundation spaces in the NARA building would be more clearly defined.
- The Government role encourages diversity of views in a non-partisan environment while continuing private support of education programs and conferences that would not be possible with Government support alone.
- Housing Presidential records in Libraries around the country, provides "continuation of Government" advantages by dispersing holdings and ensuring that the highest policy level records documenting the Government survive any catastrophic event in the Washington, DC, area.
- NARA retains the relationship with the former President which is more likely to result in the donation of private papers of the President and others that will complement the official record and facilitate narrowing the application of PRA restrictions.

Model 1 Disadvantages

- This model is dependent on the viability of the Library Foundation's ability to raise money to build the Library and provide continued support for public programming and museum exhibits.
- Some future Presidents may not choose to raise the money required to build and sustain a Presidential Library, which would mean NARA would assume the responsibility for providing the space to house the Presidential records and the archival staff.
- The more structured relationship with the Foundation could lead to a loss of synergy with the Foundation and mere *pro forma* support from the Foundations.
- Researchers must travel to multiple cities to conduct research across Presidential Administrations, though the increasing availability of records on-line will diminish this disadvantage in the future.
- Model 1 assumes an agreement can be reached between NARA and the Foundation in time for NARA to plan for the move and storage of the Presidential holdings.
- This model requires some duplicative staff support (as opposed to a centralized model) for management and administrative functions.

For the detailed cost analysis of this model, along with all others, see the separate section on cost analysis. The analysis showed that over time (75 years) this model represents a substantial savings of $394 million over the baseline (the projected cost of future Presidential Libraries if no changes are made). In the current model, the 60% endowment only applies to 70,000 square feet; in Model 1, the 60% endowment applies to the entire building.

ALTERNATIVE MODEL 2: A PRESIDENTIAL ARCHIVAL DEPOSITORY LEASED AND MANAGED BY THE NATIONAL ARCHIVES, WITH A SEPARATE MUSEUM MANAGED BY THE FOUNDATION

This model allows for a continued regional presence for the National Archives, by placing the records and artifacts in a geographic area where a Foundation-operated museum may be located. The Library would become an archives-only facility, which maintains the archival program functions by continuing to store, preserve, and provide access to Presidential records and artifacts.

In this model, NARA would lease and operate an archival facility long-term, just as it does now for the short period when a President leaves office until the Library is completed. For example, the National Archives currently leases a facility in Lewisville, Texas, to store the George W. Bush Presidential records, which is approximately 20 miles from the new Library site on the campus of Southern Methodist University. The annual lease amounts to $2,100,000, which includes the cost of completely renovating the warehouse facility to meet NARA's archival storage standards.

In a long-term lease scenario, the leased facility would need to include some additional spaces not usually provided for in our temporary leases used while the Foundation builds the new Library -- i.e., research and conference rooms. The leased facility would include holdings storage for artifacts and artifact processing rooms, but it would not include any program spaces associated with the operation of a museum, such as exhibit galleries and exhibit production shops. The focus of a leased facility would be on collections management and research. Located in the same vicinity as any privately run museum, NARA could continue to build an ongoing relationship with the Presidential Foundation and encourage the donation of additional related collections to support the Library's core holdings. However NARA would no longer provide public and educational programming, because these components would be part of the Foundation's museum program.

In such a long-term lease scenario, NARA would renovate a facility according to the full architecture and design standards, to provide a preservation-quality environment for archival and artifact holdings. Although this would increase NARA's initial costs, it would reduce NARA's administrative overhead and some operational costs, because operations and maintenance, along with repairs and renovations, would be the responsibility of the property owner. This approach, however, could lead to a less-than-optimum preservation environment over time, because NARA would be reliant solely on the lessor to maintain and repair building systems. In the event of a disagreement, NARA holdings and program activities could be at risk until the dispute is settled. At the end of the initial lease period, NARA would negotiate new lease terms. If NARA and the lessor could not agree on price or other terms,

NARA might be forced to relocate its operation. To keep costs down, this option would require Congressional action to give NARA full lease authority.

Model 2 Advantages

- The records and artifacts are located in proximity to the private museum.
- NARA controls the initial renovation of the facility to meet our standards.
- NARA is not responsible for long-term upkeep and maintenance of the facility, thus reducing its capital costs.
- A lease provides NARA with long-term flexibility, including the flexibility to close a facility that is no longer viable.
- The continued regional presence and the proximity to the Foundation retain the opportunity to obtain additional historical collections that supplement the official records.
- Housing Presidential records in facilities around the country provides "continuation of Government" advantages by dispersing holdings and ensuring that the highest level policy records documenting governmental activities survive any catastrophic event in the Washington, DC area.
- Housing Presidential records in facilities around the country continues to assure the benefits to local communities and to the public as stated in Model 1.

Model 2 Disadvantages

- The leased facility would most likely not be directly adjacent to the Presidential museum, but rather located in a lower rent "warehouse" area.
- NARA would not offer museum, public and educational programs.
- This model also assumes a Presidential Foundation would be established to build a museum. A President may well choose not to assume the responsibility for raising funds to build and operate a museum.
- Future increases in rent could force NARA to relocate records, putting the collection at greater risk.
- NARA must rely on a private lessor for maintenance and upkeep.
- Because it takes a year to lease and renovate a facility to meet NARA standards, this model works best when a President serves two terms or announces an intent not to seek re-election.
- Privately managed museums could potentially be the subject of future congressional earmarks, thus still incurring a government expense.
- This model requires some duplicative staff support (as opposed to a centralized model) for management and administrative functions.

The cost analysis for this model shows it to be more expensive than all the other models. Given this also means the loss of the museum, public program, and education components, this model does not lessen the cost of managing Presidential Libraries over Model 1 because lease costs are only favorable in the short-term. Over the long-term, it is more expensive to lease space than it is to have a government-owned building.

ALTERNATIVE MODEL 3: FOUNDATION, UNIVERSITY, OR OTHER NON-FEDERAL ENTITY PROVIDED ARCHIVES WITH A MUSEUM MANAGED BY A FOUNDATION

Under this scenario, a Presidential Foundation, university, or other non-Federal entity would construct a Library-only building with no museum component. The building would be made available to the Government under a no-cost, perpetual use arrangement favorable to the Government.[18] Since the building is being donated for NARA to use in meeting statutory mandates for preserving Presidential records, and the Presidential Foundation would be building their own museum, no additional Foundation support in the form of an endowment is envisioned in this model. As in Model 2, the facility would contain no exhibit, exhibit support, or public and educational programming spaces, only archives and artifact holdings storage, processing rooms, and archival and administrative support offices. A Foundation or other partner may choose to co- locate the Library with the non-NARA museum or in the same general vicinity. NARA would be responsible for overall operations and maintenance, as well as major capital repairs or renovations. NARA would have the future option to vacate the facility if the agency so chose according to the perpetual use agreement. Though a Library-only operation, NARA would operate in a state-of-the-art facility, fostering the preservation and access to holdings, and maintain a presence in a local community.

Model 3 Advantages

- The records and artifacts are located in proximity to the private museum.
- This model most closely resembles the present model, but eliminates the museum program.
- This building is constructed according to NARA standards.
- NARA has the option of vacating the facility under the terms of the perpetual use agreement.
- Continued regional presence and the proximity to the Foundation continue the opportunity to obtain additional historical collections that supplement the official records.
- The continued relationship between NARA and the Foundation provides opportunities for exploring the use of technology and other innovative programs to increase the accessibility of the historical collections to a greater audience.
- Housing Presidential records in facilities around the country, provides "continuity of Government" advantages by dispersing records and ensuring that the highest level policy records documenting governmental activities survive any catastrophic event in the Washington, DC area.
- Housing Presidential records in facilities around the country continues to assure the benefits to local communities and to the public as stated in Model 1.

Model 3 Disadvantages

- This model works best provided a President chooses to have a privately operated museum. A President may well choose not to assume the responsibility for raising funds to build and operate a museum.
- The NARA facility might not be adjacent to the Presidential museum, which would causes challenges in coordinating programs.
- NARA would not offer museum, public, and educational programs. Because of NARA's ongoing partnership and potential proximity to the Foundation museum, there will be confusion as to whether the Foundation programs are NARA programs.
- Without the museum, public program, or educational components, NARA serves a much smaller group of users.
- NARA would have the ongoing responsibility for maintenance and upkeep of the facility.
- Privately managed museums could potentially be the subject of future congressional earmarks, thus still incurring a government expense.
- Unless the facility is built in advance of the President leaving office, NARA would need to store the records in a temporary facility before transfer to the permanent Library, just as is currently the case.
- This model requires some duplicative staff support (as opposed to a centralized model) for management and administrative functions.

Overall this model is less costly than the baseline and more costly than Model 1, but not significantly so considering the loss of the museum and public programs. Cost savings for this model over the baseline would begin in 2033.

ALTERNATIVE MODEL 4: CENTRALIZED PRESIDENTIAL ARCHIVAL DEPOSITORY FUNDED AND MANAGED BY NARA

The concept of a centralized depository for Presidential records would be a major departure from the current Presidential Libraries model. In this model, Presidential records and artifacts would be housed in a central archival depository in the Washington, DC area.

Unlike Models 1 and 3, the Government would bear the full cost of building the depository. A single, centralized depository for future Presidential records and donated materials would also require NARA to assume full responsibility for the cost of preserving, processing, and providing access to all Presidential materials in paper and digital formats. To date, much of the cost of digitizing Presidential records so as to provide web-based access has been provided by the Library Foundations, universities, and grants, and not by NARA's federal funds. While this private funding has been important for specific projects, it has not enabled wide-spread electronic access to the majority of Presidential materials. The cost of providing any enhanced access to Presidential records using web-based technologies has not been factored into the cost analysis.[19]

A centralized Presidential facility would also eliminate the costs for maintaining Sensitive Compartmentalized Information Facilities (SCIFs) at each individual Presidential

Library. The centralized depository would only need one SCIF for the storage of all classified Presidential records. With the potential development of a planned National Declassification Center (NDC) initiative, the systematic declassification review of these records at the 25-year point (when they are ready for automatic declassification review) could be facilitated by using the resources and expertise of a potential NDC initiative. However, this centralization of declassification review is also incorporated in the models that retain the Libraries in field locations through the current RAC program.[20]

To provide public access to these records as quickly as possible, the centralized facility would need additional archival staff with each new collection of Presidential records. In fact, this model would not result in a decrease in the size of the current archival or the curatorial staff.[21] Indeed, due to their large volume and complexity, it will continue to take decades to process the Presidential records of each administration even with improved processes. Though we did not assume that all cost savings from a centralized model would be used for archival processing, we did assume that any staff savings achieved in a centralized model would be used to hire more archivists for processing records Therefore, we have computed the staffing costs at the level of Model 1. This model also facilitates the temporary re-assignment of archivists from one collection to another to meet special access requests including those from the incumbent President, the Courts, and the Congress.

An important element to be considered in this model is the fact that it eliminates the museums and associated education and public programs along with the regional diversity that is a hallmark of the present system. NARA would be able to stage occasional exhibits on the Presidency or individual Presidents in the Lawrence O'Brien temporary gallery at the National Archives Building, but these would need to be small, given the size of the O'Brien gallery.

A centralized model for Presidential Libraries would not preclude a former President from building an independently operated museum dedicated to his or her Presidency. The President's museum could be operated by his or her Foundation or by a city, state, or academic institution. There is no limit to the type of partnership a Presidential Foundation could employ for the operation of its museum. As we do today with non-NARA museums, NARA would work cooperatively with the former President on the loan of documents and artifacts for display in a museum environment that meets our standards. The privately operated museum facility might also include a research component, which could provide access to the digital copies of materials maintained at the NARA Presidential Libraries or the centralized depository.

Scholars interested in the study of the Presidency would benefit from a centralized model. Conversely, those interested in studying individual Presidents would be disadvantaged by the loss of individual Presidential Libraries that house the personal, political and donated collections that complement the content of the presidential record. While the National Archives would not be precluded from soliciting personal collections, these collections could just as likely end up being geographically distant and located with the President's Foundation or another archival depository in a location near the President's chosen community. Potential donors who were prominent during a former President's administration are more likely to donate their papers to the Foundation or an institution that engenders their loyalty than to donate them to the National Archives.

Model 4 Advantages

- As records become more predominately digital in format, a centralized depository for Presidential records would be consistent with the evolution of the records life cycle, especially given that electronic-based records are already centralized in digital storage solutions.
- A centralized model reduces the need for facility management and administrative staff.
- The centralized facility provides researchers the opportunity to conduct complementary research in Federal agency records and the opportunity to consult with NARA experts in numerous areas. This model also facilitates comprehensive research, such as in issues that continue across administrations, or study in decision-making styles of different Presidents.
- Proximity to declassification activities could facilitate the coordination for declassification of Presidential records.

Model 4 Disadvantages

- The Government would have to fund the total cost of building a new facility and the continued operational expenses with no private endowment. Archives I and Archives II are presently near capacity, which already means that NARA may have to build an Archives III facility. A third NARA facility built to house Presidential records could, for the near future, also hold Federal agency records until such time as the space is needed for future administrations. NARA would then need to build a fourth facility in the Washington, DC area to house the Federal agency records temporarily stored in the central Presidential facility.
- This model will also lose the unique museum and education programs that the Libraries offer, allowing the Presidency to reach millions of visitors each year.
- This model probably cedes the personal, political and donated collections, which complement the Presidential collection, to the Foundations or other institutions.
- This model would mean a loss of Foundation funding to help support the cost of digitization, web-based programs, preservation, and other programs.
- In this model the present system of Presidential Libraries becomes static and looses the synergy from new Presidential Libraries entering the system.

Our cost analysis shows a cost savings over the baseline costs would not begin to be realized until 23 years after the establishment of the centralized depository, since this model assumes an initial outlay of nearly $100 million for design and construction of a new facility. However, over 75 years, assuming there is a new President every eight years, the cost savings would be $850 million over the baseline and $458 million over Model 1.

MODEL 5. A MUSEUM OF THE PRESIDENCY IN ASSOCIATION WITH THE CENTRALIZED DEPOSITORY

This model would add a Museum of the Presidency to the centralized archival depository. Unlike the suburban located depository, the Museum would be located in an area of Washington, DC easily accessible to tourists, ideally on or near the National Mall. The Museum of the Presidency would be built by the Government and have a strong NARA identity, NARA could seek partners interested in promoting our historical resources without aligning with any one President. NARA would have opportunities to partner with the Congressional Visitors Center and the White House Visitors Center on exhibits and programs that document much of our national experience from the perspective of the Congress and the President, thereby providing visitors with a balanced perspective on Government involvement in selected issues.

As with the exhibits in the National Archives Building, exhibits in the Museum of the Presidency would be dependent on Foundation funding. Since this is unlikely to be sustained by any individual Presidential Foundation, the National Archives Foundation or a dedicated Presidential Museum Foundation would need to take on the funding responsibility. NARA would provide a staff of 25 curators, educators, and other professionals to support the Museum. Artifacts and documents stored in the centralized depository would be brought to the Museum for display. The Museum would also borrow items from other Presidential Libraries and from any privately established and operated Presidential Museums of future Presidents.

A Museum of the Presidency would attract a large number of tourists from all over the world, but the immersive education experience and the vast range of public programs would be available only to those who live in or were able to visit the Washington, DC, area. However, the DC metropolitan area is saturated with museums, many of which explore similar themes – the American History Museum, the Capitol Visitors Center, the Newseum, the White House Visitors Center, the Portrait Gallery, to name a few.

Model 5 Advantages

- A centralized Museum of the Presidency offers visitors an exhibit that focuses on several Presidents and the institution of the Presidency.
- The initial and later exhibits in the Museum would not be created by a President and his supporters or be subject to their concerns about content.
- The centralized staff of the Museum would have a greater ability to focus on building web-based exhibits and educational programming and have access to multiple collections.

Model 5 Disadvantages

- This model becomes a Washington, DC-centric model and the economic and cultural benefits of a Presidential Library would remain focused in one city already saturated with museums and other civic and cultural offerings.

- Financially, NARA would lose the Library Foundations' support not only for programs and exhibits, but also to help forward the Government's mission to preserve, protect, and make accessible the records.
- Government funding would be required to design, build, and maintain the Museum at an initial outlay of $55 million for the museum (plus another $100 million for the depository).
- Any privately funded and operated Presidential museums would be in direct competition for content and private money with the Museum of the Presidency, as would the already existing NARA-operated Presidential Libraries.
- This model requires consistent fund-raising to support exhibits and programs not funded by the Government.
- This model makes it more difficult o provide an in-depth focus on individual Presidents and their administrations.
- As in Model 4 the present system of Presidential Libraries loses the synergy and dynamic growth resulting from the establishment of new Presidential Libraries.

It would require more than 50 years to realize any cost savings over the baseline. At the 75-year point, Model 5 saves $418 million over the baseline cost. The savings over the cost of Model 1 would be only $24 million, or an average savings of $320,000 per year for 75 years.

SUMMARY OF THE COST ANALYSIS

This section addresses one of the three mandates in the Presidential Historical Records Preservation Act – the mandate for reducing the financial burden on the Federal Government for the Presidential Library system. The spread sheets for the full cost analysis of each model are located in Appendix E.

The need to preserve, maintain, and make accessible the records of a President for posterity requires a long-term commitment of resources. While a cost analysis can help us estimate the monetary cost to the Government of different approaches to Presidential Libraries, unlike an economic model it does not capture the intangible benefits of the Presidential Library system, the economic benefits to communities and other sectors, or reflect the shifting of significant costs to the Library Foundations. If the Government requires considerably more from the Foundations, in the form of an endowment when the Libraries are built, or if the cost for building, maintaining, and operating Presidential Museums is shifted completely to the Foundations, the Presidential Library system may cease to exist. It is not hard to imagine future Presidents deciding not to participate in the public/private partnership.

The Libraries are more than places of historical research. The museum, education, and public programs in the Libraries reflect a commitment of resources dedicated to increasing the public's knowledge and understanding of the Presidency as a whole and the life and times of each President. All models benefit from the predicted shift from textual to electronic format and subsequent savings in storage costs. None of the models, however, takes into account the high cost of maintaining records in electronic format. Those costs, now currently centralized in the Electronic Records Archives (ERA) and its predecessor, the Presidential Electronic Record Library (PERL), have not been factored into any of the models, since these costs are necessary to each model. NARA is addressing the funding for maintaining and accessing electronic records more globally through its ERA initiative, which addresses Presidential and Federal records.

NARA conducted a preliminary cost analysis at both the 40-year cycle and the 75-year life cycle. We selected the 75-year cycle because it showed costs until the end of the century and therefore more accurately addressed the long term preservation needs for Presidential records. Additionally, while the 40-year cycle showed some cost benefits, the appreciable cost benefits did not really occur until closer to the end of the 75-year period. The 75-year life cycle cost analysis is an attempt to quantify the financial commitment that each model would require for new Presidential Libraries between FY2025 and FY2099. The costs were all calculated in constant FY2009 dollars.

A conservative approach was taken in developing the analysis, and therefore the amounts needed should be viewed as comparisons between the five models and not as a prediction of the actual costs. In an actual scenario, NARA would expect that the costs would be higher, though we would also expect that the increases would maintain the basic ratio of one model to another. For example, construction costs vary widely across the country as do operation and maintenance costs and lease costs. A future Presidential Library constructed in Alaska would be expected to have considerably higher construction, operational, and maintenance costs than the base line costs which were based on the Clinton and Bush 41 libraries. A lease in downtown New York City would be considerably higher than the Bush 43 lease costs in suburban Dallas, which formed the basis for the leased cost model. Additionally, costs for the centralized archival model in the Washington, DC area and an additional museum in downtown Washington, DC may be significantly higher than the costs used at the time these facilities are actually built.

Any cost savings to be achieved over the current Presidential Library model will happen over the long term. Cost savings can be identified between the models, but the impact on the budget will be small for many years to come or in some cases, more costly in the short term. A new model would likely not be in place before FY2017, even assuming passage of legislation in the next two years. All previous changes to the Presidential Libraries Act have not applied to the incumbent president, but take effect with the next administration. Assuming, therefore for the purpose of this report, that a new approach would not apply to President Obama, and that he serves two terms, we projected the changes to take effect with the Presidential term that starts in January 2017 and ends in January 2025. Our cost model also assumes that all the Presidents serve two- terms for the rest of this century (meaning 12 presidencies every 96 years); the historical average, however, has been 18 presidencies per 100 years, which would increase the cost model by about 50%.

Properly maintaining Presidential records is, like maintaining any of NARA's permanent holdings, a costly endeavor no matter what the model. NARA recognizes that costs for the system will continue to increase, and that cost control efforts are essential. Over time, both NARA and Congress have put in measures to control these costs. The five models attempt to explore how costs could be further contained with different approaches. Additional analysis will be required before making a decision on proceeding in any new direction for Presidential Libraries.

Model 1 maintains the current Presidential Library system with suggested changes to control future costs. Over a 75-year period starting in FY2025 and ending in FY2099, Model

1 would cost an estimated $2.36 billion for new Libraries starting with the successor to President Obama. This represents a savings of $394 million over the baseline.

Model 2, the Leased Option, essentially eliminates the Government presence at the Presidential Foundation museum, but maintains full programs in the archival and collections management area. Model 2, even though it is in leased space, would cost an estimated $2.86 billion in the same 75-year period. This is actually $111 million more than the baseline.

Model 3, in which the archival space is donated to NARA, with a separate Foundation built and managed museum, would cost an estimated $2.5 billion over 75 years. This represents a savings of $254 million over the baseline, but would be $140 million more than Model 1.

Model 4, a Centralized Presidential Library, replicates Models 2 and 3 in that it does not provide for public, educational, and museum programs managed by NARA. This model would cost an estimated $1.9 billion over the same 75-year period, including an initial outlay of nearly $100 million to construct the depository. This represents a savings of $850 million over the baseline and $458 million over Model 1 (or an annual savings of $11.33 million over the baseline or $6.1 million per year over Model 1).

Model 5, which combines Model 4's centralized depository with a Museum of the Presidency, would cost $2.33 billion over the 75-year period, including an initial outlay of $155 million to build the depository and museum. This represents a savings of $419 million over the baseline, and $25 million over Model 1. Over the baseline, Model 5 saves $418 million for an average savings of $5.57 million per year.

As the above cost analysis shows, the only way to reduce costs is to eliminate programs. Centralizing the facility does not achieve appreciable cost savings without a program reduction. Model 1, which is most similar to the current library system, maintains all existing programs, while Models 2 and 3 eliminate the Governmental role in providing public, educational, and museum programs in the various locations where the Presidential Libraries would be constructed. This does not necessarily mean that those programs would be eliminated – we assume that most presidents will continue to want to have a Presidential Museum constructed, operated, and maintained by their Presidential Foundation – but it does mean that the Federal Government would not have any say in the message developed by the Foundations. While Government funding and staffing is provided for a centralized Museum of the Presidency in Model 5, NARA cannot predict how robust the private funding would be for sustaining the museum exhibits and the educational and public program components.

Table 2. The 75-Year Cost for Each Model (All Costs in 2009 Dollars)

Model	Total 75-year cost	Average savings per year for 75 years over baseline	Average savings per year for 75 years over Model 1	Annual operating cost in FY 2099	First year of cost savings over baseline
Baseline	$2,752,000,000	n/a	+$5,250,000	$66,438,000	n/a
Model 1	$2,358,000,000	-$ 5,253,000	n/a	$55,795,000	FY 2031
Model 2	$2,863,000,000	+$ 1,480,000	+$6,730,000	$74,376,000	n/a
Model 3	$2,499,000,000	-$ 3,370,000	+$1,880,000	$60,238,000	FY 2033
Model 4	$1,900,000,000	-$11,360,000	-$6,106,000	$42,153,000	FY 2045
Model 5	$2,334,000,000	-$ 5,570,000	-$320,000	$46,966,000	FY 2076

The cost analysis shows that there is no savings for pursuing a leased permanent location as laid out in Model 2. In fact, the leased option is estimated to be the most expensive. In general, leased locations are cost effective for providing temporary Government space. However, in the case of permanent space needs, leased locations cost more in the long term. Leased locations trade higher yearly costs for lower upfront costs by avoiding the large one year budget impact of funding the initial construction (including land acquisition and design and construction oversight). Also, Budget procedures may require that the cost of a long-term lease be realized up front. Accordingly, Model 2 is not recommended. It has the highest costs but with the lowest benefits. Model 3, in which just the archival facility is donated, is also more costly, particularly because it does not include an endowment. Some cost savings would be realized if an endowment were part of the transfer. However, because the building is being donated solely for NARA to meet its statutory mandates for preserving Presidential records, and the Presidential Foundation would still be expected to build its own museum, we did not think additional Foundation support, even in the form of an endowment, could be expected.

Model 4 – the Centralized Presidential Library – clearly offers the potential for significant cost savings over the long term. It represents the most significant cost savings to the Government, approximately 30% less than the baseline over the 75-year period. However, it would require an initial outlay of nearly $100 million, in 2022 (so the new depository could be completed by 2025) and would not realize any cost savings over the baseline until 2045. If a Museum of the Presidency is included (Model 5), the cost savings will be much less since Model 5 would require an additional $55 million to construct the Museum of the Presidency. It would take over 50 years to realize any cost savings.

Model 4 also offers the best opportunity to benefit from some staff reductions because of economies of scale: *e.g.,* fewer personnel devoted to facility operations and administrative support because all functions are in the same location and reductions in research room staffs because there would only be one large research room rather than many. However, in constructing this model, NARA shifted these positions and others from the museum, education, and public program staff to processing and other collection management functions to help meet the mandate for processing records more quickly. Finally, Model 4 is based on the construction standards reached in the Archives II construction, where the building efficiency is 80%, versus the 50% to 70% efficiencies attained in the newer Presidential Libraries. (Note: the lower efficiencies attained in the Presidential Libraries are not attributed to poorer construction standards, but to the need to provide spaces to meet all building needs, including large entrance lobbies, auditoriums, cafeterias, etc. Archives II is a larger building but has much less space devoted to these functions, primarily due to economies of scale.)

Model 1 contains several recommendations that can help to reduce the cost of the system as a whole. The recommendations to tighten the commitments of the Foundations for each Library will help reduce the burden on the Government. The change in how the endowment is calculated from the current method, which bases it on the program requirements of the NARA space – essentially 70,000 square feet per building – to the total size of the building that will be transferred to the Government, will have a substantial impact on the costs to operate the Libraries. If implemented, during the 75-year period it will generate over $330 million in income, which in turn would reduce the operating expenses by 12% over that time period. (Income is estimated at 4% of the amount invested.) By modifying the Architectural and Design Standards to require that the Foundation space in the Library be restricted to those areas that only directly support the Library (versus the Foundation), NARA will reduce the size of the buildings and their operating costs.

CONCLUSION

There is no more important question to consider in evaluating alternative models for Presidential Libraries than to know or decide who the system is designed to serve. The models laid out in this report provide very different experiences for very different groups of users. In evaluating this report, the reader needs to consider how broad NARA's mission should be, what audiences should be served, and what their experience with a Presidential Library should be. The Presidential collections are among the most vital and valuable of our Nation's historical assets. We have no more important mission than to preserve and make them accessible to those who need them. There is a higher cost associated with making these collections accessible not only to a diverse constituency of scholars who discuss and analyze these records and their impact on future policy decisions, but also to an extended audience of museum visitors, middle and secondary school students, not to mention a vast number of curious citizens who visit our websites. Public conferences, museum exhibits, immersive educational experiences and content-rich websites require more staff, larger buildings, and greater funding at an increased cost to the Government and the Foundations.

Finally, we understand that Presidential Libraries are considered by some to be costly monuments to past Presidents. Others consider them to be vital links to the narrative of American history. Presidential Libraries are peculiarly and inalterably American institutions. In our open democracy we are free to judge our Presidents. That freedom to judge extends to the Presidential Libraries as they are now or in whatever form they may take in the future. Our mission, through our archival collections, education, and museum programs, is to ensure that these invaluable collections facilitate historical understanding of our national experience to the widest possible audience. Presidential Libraries help to shape our memories or knowledge of a certain period of time, individual Presidents and the institution of the Presidency. The core question in evaluating the future model of Presidential Libraries is to determine if this mission should be redefined.

APPENDIX A. SUMMARY OF PUBLIC COMMENTS REGARDING ALTERNATIVE MODELS FOR PRESIDENTIAL LIBRARIES

Through Friday, May 22nd, 2009, 104 comments were received.

General Categories of Comments

Professional Societies and Public-Interest Groups

This category of respondents provided NARA with nearly 9% of all comments received. These groups offered a variety of suggestions, but the majority urged that NARA find more effective and transparent ways to provide quicker access and availability to Presidential records, particularly through digital means. Respondents in this category provided detailed feedback concerning access issues handled by the Presidential Library system, with the primary areas of concern including the following issues:

- Providing for faster releases of Presidential records pursuant to FOIA requests.
- Further analysis of whether the centralization of Presidential records could speed processing.
- Further analysis of the 2007 report of the Public Interest Declassification Board (PIDB) when considering any alternative models for Presidential Libraries.
- The development of long-term technological plans that will enable NARA to use new technologies in the management of Presidential electronic records. Specifically, many of these organizations expressed concerns about the Electronic Records Archives' ability to handle processing electronic records.
- Several professional organizations and public interest groups questioned whether operating museums is part of NARA's core mission and advocated separating the museum function from the archival function as a cost-saving measure, which would not negatively impact access to records.
- Many of these respondents urged that when considering any alternative models for Presidential Libraries, NARA should carefully weigh the needs of future researchers and how archival description, preservation, and declassification would be affected by any changes.

Community Partners, Civic Leaders, and Presidential Foundations

Another 9% of all respondents comprised this category. These respondents discussed the importance of the educational benefits that their local Presidential Library provides to their community schools and the overall economic benefits their Library brings through jobs, publicity, etc. A survey of the comments includes the following:

- Community leaders cited the economic, cultural, and educational impact on the entire community. These respondents argued that the presence of the Library offers a unique cultural and educational asset that provides an important historical experience for locals and visitors alike. Many respondents cited economic data that details how the Libraries have impacted the surrounding communities.
- Respondents in this category noted that, in addition to providing vital economic benefits and increasing tourism revenue, the Library offers a sense of pride, connection, and identity for area residents.
- Presidential Foundations expressed a strong desire to keep the Presidential Libraries operating as they currently do, with the belief that the current model serves the Government and taxpayer well. This group noted the success of the public/private partnership and that Foundations provide critical financial support, creative resources, and staffing for their respective Presidential Libraries. The Foundations argued that in the current model they fund a variety of archival functions, including internships, research grants, digitization initiatives, marketing and public information projects, and nationally-recognized public programs. The Foundations argued that

the increase in the endowment should significantly off-set operating expenses of Libraries in the future.

Educational Community

This category of respondents comprised 41.5% of the total comments received and included principals, teachers, school librarians, and members of the homeschool community. Educators of all grade levels denoted the value of bringing Presidential history into local communities throughout our country. Specific comments included the following:

- Teachers lauded the archival resources and student programs in their local communities and cited the multiple field trips their schools participate in every year.
- Educators noted the research expertise of Library staff members and how educational programs offered by the Libraries support their curricula.
- Many respondents – including concerned parents of schoolchildren and members of homeschool associations – cited the value of their own individual experiences with the Libraries and expressed a desire for continued support of the current system. These parents and educators often discussed specific visits to the Libraries and the benefit of particular Presidential exhibits to their children's development.
- Respondents in this group noted that without regional Presidential Libraries, many students located outside Washington, DC, and without the means to visit our nation's Capital, would not have access to the valuable resources offered in the Libraries that help shape our understanding of our country, our democracy, and our political and cultural heritage.

Users of Presidential Libraries and Other Members of the General Public

These comments comprised 40.5% of all responses. Respondents in this category included regular users of Presidential Libraries, former NARA employees, historians, and other members of the archival and library community. These suggestions reflect a wide range of feedback, including calls for centralization, increased digitization efforts, and appreciation for the educational and cultural opportunities afforded by Presidential Libraries. Comments in this category include the following:

- Many respondents encouraged NARA to make documents available electronically and to centralize the system as a cost-saving measure.
- Other members of the general public response group expressed their support for the public programming at the individual Libraries, including speakers and film series that would otherwise be unavailable in their communities.
- Some respondents expressed their view of the Libraries as monoliths to former Presidents and recommended that NARA not support the museum component of the program.
- Few respondents advocated a specific model; but instead, most offered commentary on digitization efforts and current educational opportunities.
- Individual members of the archival and library community offered a variety of opinions, almost all of which advocated digital initiatives as a priority. Many respondents agreed that centralization was the best option, both for cost-saving

measures and for more efficient processing. Others noted the value of the research expertise offered by archivists at the individual Libraries and the importance of contact with original documents in traditional research settings.
- Several respondents from the archival community urged NARA to take more time in preparing the report, so that all stakeholders could have adequate time to respond.

APPENDIX B. LOCATION OF PRESIDENTIAL PAPERS AND LIBRARIES FROM WASHINGTON TO BUSH

George Washington –Library of Congress has 95% of extant Washington papers; also Huntington Library; Historical Societies of Virginia and Pennsylvania; Virginia State Library; Yale University; and the Detroit Public Library.

John Adams –Massachusetts Historical Society

Thomas Jefferson – Library of Congress; also University of Virginia; Massachusetts Historical Society; National Archives; Missouri Historical Society; Historical Society of Pennsylvania; College of William and Mary; Henry E. Huntington Library; American Philosophical Society; New York Historical Society; Virginia State Library; William Clements Library; Yale University; and other smaller repositories and private hands

James Madison – Library of Congress; also University of Virginia; Huntington Library; the Historical Societies of Virginia and Pennsylvania; New York Public Library; William L. Clements Library (U. of Michigan); and Princeton University

James Monroe – Library of Congress; also James Monroe Memorial Library; College of William and Mary; University of Virginia; and Virginia State libraries

John Quincy Adams – Massachusetts Historical Society

Andrew Jackson – Library of Congress; also Tennessee State Library; Tennessee Historical Society; Chicago Historical Society; New York Public Library; and New York Historical Society

Martin Van Buren – Library of Congress; also New York State Library; Columbia County Historical Society; Pierpont Morgan Library; and Massachusetts Historical Society

William Henry Harrison – almost all were lost in a fire that destroyed the Harrison home 1858, but friends sent material to the grandson, President Benjamin Harrison, which was then later donated to the Library of Congress. Other repositories include historical societies of Indiana, New York, Pennsylvania, Virginia, and Wisconsin; and the William Clements and University of North Carolina libraries.

John Tyler – Library of Congress; also College of William and Mary Library; Gardiner Family Papers at Yale University, Duke University, and Pierpont Morgan Library

James Polk – Library of Congress; also Chicago Historical Society; Yale University; and Tennessee State Libraries

Zachary Taylor – personal papers destroyed or dispersed in 1862, but Library of Congress accumulated items over the next 90 years; other surviving material wildly scattered among collectors, libraries, and historical societies

Millard Fillmore – Buffalo Historical Society and College of Oswego

Franklin Pierce – New Hampshire Historical Society; Henry E. Huntington Library; Library of Congress; Bowdoin College; William L. Clements Library; Concord Public Library; New York Public Library; and historical societies of New Jersey and Pennsylvania

James Buchanan – Historical Society of Pennsylvania; Lancaster County Historical Society; Franklin and Marshall College Library; Princeton University; Pierpont Morgan and Rutherford B. Hayes Libraries; New York Historical Society; and the Pennsylvania Historical and Museum Commission

Abraham Lincoln – Library of Congress; substantial collections at the Illinois Historical Society and Brown University

Andrew Johnson – Library of Congress; also Henry E. Huntington Library; and Tennessee State Library

Ulysses S. Grant – Library of Congress, Huntington Library; and New York Historical Society Library

Rutherford B. Hayes – Rutherford B. Hayes Memorial Library administered by the Ohio Historical Society and the Hayes Foundation

James Garfield – Library of Congress; also Ohio Historical Society; and Rutherford B. Hayes Library

Chester A. Arthur – bulk of papers are missing; Library of Congress (only 1,413 documents); also New York State Library; New York Historical Society; Boston Public and Rutherford B. Hayes Libraries

Grover Cleveland – Library of Congress; also Detroit Public Library; Buffalo Historical Society; New York Historical Society; Princeton University; and Pierpont Morgan Library

Benjamin Harrison – Library of Congress; also Indiana State Library; and the Rutherford B. Hayes Library

William McKinley – Library of Congress; also Western Reserve Historical Society in Cleveland; and Rutherford B. Hayes Library

Theodore Roosevelt – Library of Congress (over 275,000 items) making it one of the largest presidential collections with other important papers at Harvard University

William Howard Taft – Library of Congress (over 500,000 items) making it one of the most complete presidential collections in existence; also Yale University; Princeton University; Western Reserve University; and the Ohio Historical Society

Woodrow Wilson – Library of Congress; substantial collections at Princeton University; Columbia University; and the University of Virginia

Warren G. Harding – Ohio Historical Society

Calvin Coolidge – Library of Congress; substantial pre-presidential documents in the Calvin Coolidge Memorial Room of the Forbes Library, Massachusetts

Herbert C. Hoover – Hoover Institution Archives at Stanford University; when Mr. Hoover decided to establish a Presidential Library in accordance with the provisions of the Presidential Libraries Act of 1955, he offered all his public service and related papers to the Government. Theses papers were withdrawn from Stanford in 1962 and transferred to Herbert Hoover Presidential Library in West Branch, Iowa.

Franklin D. Roosevelt – Franklin D. Roosevelt Library and Museum in Hyde Park, New York, the first Presidential Library administered by the National Archives

Harry S. Truman – Harry S. Truman Library in Independence, Missouri

Dwight D. Eisenhower – Dwight D. Eisenhower Library in Abilene, Kansas

John F. Kennedy – John F. Kennedy Library in Boston, Massachusetts

Lyndon B. Johnson – Lyndon B. Johnson Library in Austin, Texas

Richard M. Nixon – Richard Nixon Library in Yorba Linda, California and the National Archives at College Park, Maryland (2007)

Gerald R. Ford – Gerald R. Ford Library in Ann Arbor, Michigan and the Gerald R. Ford Museum in Grand Rapids, Michigan

Jimmy Carter – the Jimmy Carter Library and Museum within the Jimmy Carter Center in Atlanta, Georgia

Ronald W. Reagan – Ronald Reagan Library in Simi Valley, California

George Bush – George Bush Library and Museum in College Station, Texas

William J. Clinton – William J. Clinton Library and Museum in Little Rock, Arkansas

George W. Bush – George W. Bush Library to be built on the campus of Southern Methodist University, Dallas, Texas

Sources: *Records of the Presidency: Presidential Papers and Libraries from Washington to Reagan* by Frank L. Schick with Renee Schick and Mark Carroll, (Oryx Press, Phoenix, AZ, 1989); and National Archives Presidential Libraries web sites

APPENDIX C. PRESIDENTIAL LIBRARY COSTS AND IMPROVEMENTS[22]

This appendix includes cost information relating to the construction of each Presidential Library operated by NARA as well as the source of funds for the design and construction of major renovations of or additions to Presidential Libraries. Information about major exhibit renovations paid for with private funds is also included. This appendix does not include future projects that are captured through the NARA Capital Improvements Plan.

I. Hoover Library

Dedication
August 10, 1962

Construction
$1,000,000, inflation factor, $7,043,000

Expansions/Renovations
A. 1965, design and addition of storage space
   Cost: $900,000, private funding,
B. 1969 and 1974/1975, design and addition of auditorium and other renovations
   Cost: $1,074,000, Federal funding
C. 1992, design, expansion, and remodeling of facility
   Cost: $4.9 million, Federal funding $1.6 million, private funding

II. Roosevelt Library

Dedication
July, 4, 1940

Construction
$369,000, inflation factor, $5,647,000

Expansions/Renovations
  A. 1971-1972, addition of Eleanor Roosevelt wings
      Cost: $882,000, Federal funding
          $769,000, private funding
  B. 1997-1998, construction of Visitor Center and renovation of Library north wing
      Cost: $8,000,000, Federal (NARA) funding
          $7,800,000, Federal (NPS) funding
          $3,050,000, private funding
  C. 2005, design of FDR renovation
      Cost: $750,000, Federal funding
  D. 2008, complete design of FDR renovation
      Cost: $750,000, Federal funding
  E. 2009, Phase 1 construction of FDR renovation
      Cost: $17,500,000, Federal funding

III. Truman Library

Dedication
July 6, 1957

Construction
$1,670,000, inflation factor, $12,641,424

Expansions/Renovations
  A. 1968, design and construction of east gallery
      Cost: $1,000,000, Federal funding
  B. 1979, enclosure of courtyard, space for educational programs, office space, museum workshop, and space for holdings storage
      Cost: $2,750,000, Federal funding
  C. 1997-1998, renovation of almost entire facility, including new permanent exhibit
      Cost: $8,000,000, Federal funding
          $2,400,000, private funding for infrastructure, design, fabrication, and installation of new exhibit
  D. 2008-2009, design and construction of Truman Working Office addition
      Cost: $1,300,000, private funding

IV. Eisenhower Library

Dedication
May 1, 1962

Construction
$2,956,000, inflation factor, $20,280,125

Expansions/Renovations
- A. 1966, construction of the Place of Meditation
  Cost: $176,000, private funds
- B. 1971, museum expansion
  Cost: $500,000, Federal funding
- C. 1975, construction of Visitor Center
  Cost: $980,000, Federal funding
- D. 2002, renovation of library and museum stacks and new Presidential gallery
  Cost: $1,288,000, Federal funding for infrastructure changes
  $2,750,000, private funding for design, fabrication, and installation of new Presidential gallery exhibit

V. Kennedy Library

Dedication
October 20, 1979

Construction
$18,000,000, inflation factor, $52,737,768

Expansions/Renovations
- A. 1985, 1989, and 1991, construction of Smith Center, renovation of museum, and facility improvements
  Cost: $17,300,000, Federal funding
  $2,000,000, private funding
- B. 2001, repair of plaza, seawall
  Cost: $6,610,000, Federal funding
- C. 2005, design of renovation and addition for holdings storage
  Cost: $1,000,000, Federal funding
- D. 2006, design of renovation and addition for holdings storage
  Cost: $990,000, Federal funding
- E. 2008, purchase of land and site work for addition for holdings storage
  Cost: $8,000,000, Federal funding
- F. 2009, Phase 1 construction of addition for holdings storage
  Cost: $22,000,000, Federal funding

VI. Johnson Library

Dedication
May 22, 1971

Construction
$10,000,000, inflation factor, $52,520,740

Expansions/Renovations
  A. 1980s, enclosure of courtyard by UT
     Cost: unknown, all borne by UT
  B. 2003, design, repair, and improvements of LBJ plaza
     Cost: $3,250,000, Federal funding
  C. 2004, design, repair, and improvements of LBJ plaza
     Cost: $5,000,000, Federal funding
  D. 2005, design, repair, and improvements of LBJ plaza
     Cost: $2,000,000, Federal funding
  E. 2006, design, repair, and improvements of LBJ plaza
     Cost: $990,000, Federal funding
  F. 2008, renovations and improvements to the LBJ plaza
     Cost: $3,760,000, Federal funding
  G. 2009, further renovations and improvements to the LBJ plaza Cost: $2,000,000, Federal funding

VII. Nixon Library

Dedication
July 19, 1990
Transferred to the Federal Government, July 11, 2007

Construction
$29,000,000, inflation factor, $47,190,795

Expansion/Renovations
  A. 2004, Loker Center addition
     Cost: $14,000,000, private funding
  B. 2005-2006, design of addition for archival holdings
     Cost: $647,580 Federal funding
  C. 2006, Federal community development grant to the Nixon Library Foundation for improvements to the Nixon Library
     Cost: $2,000,000, Federal funding
  D. 2008-2009, construction of addition for archival holdings
     Cost: $7,432,000, Federal funding

VIII. Ford Library and Museum (Two Separate Facilities)

Dedication
Library, April 27, 1981
Museum, September 18, 1981

Construction
$1 1,400,000*, inflation factor, $26,676,376 *Cost of both Library and Museum

Expansions/Renovations
A. 2001-2002, addition to museum and renovation of existing space
   Cost: $5,105,000, Federal funding
   $250,000 private funding for Cabinet Room infrastructure
   $500,000, private funding for Cabinet Room exhibit design, fabrication, and installation

IX. Carter Library

Dedication
October 1, 1986

Construction
$26,000,000, inflation factor, $50,460,164

Expansions/Renovations
A. 2009, renovation and replacement of permanent exhibit
   Cost: $10,000,000, private funding

X. Reagan Library

Dedication
November 4, 1991

Construction
$42,000,000, inflation factor, $65,593,083

Expansions/Renovations
A. 2000, addition to facility and some modifications to existing structure
   Cost: $8,000,000, Federal funding

XI. George H. W. Bush Library

Dedication
November 6, 1997

Construction
$22,386,166, inflation factor, $29,668,155

Expansions/Renovations
A. 2007, renovation of permanent exhibit
   Cost: $8,200,000, private funding

XII. Clinton Library

Dedication
November 18, 2004

Construction
$36,000,000, inflation factor, $40,537,448

XIII. George W. Bush Library
The Library currently operates in a temporary facility leased by NARA.

APPENDIX D. 2008 TRUST FUND STATEMENT

Library	Revenues	Operating Expense	Net Operating. Income - (loss)	Interest Income	Other Income	Realized Gain on Investments	Unrealized Loss on Investments	Net Income - Loss
Hoover	$180,000	($184,000)	($4,000)	$10,000		$2,000	($21,000)	($13,000)
Roosevelt	$1,029,000	($895,000)	$134,000	$29,000		$1,000	($83,000)	$81,000
Truman	$773,000	($577,000)	$196,000	$2,000		$1,000	($1,000)	$198,000
Eisenhower	$440,000	($449,000)	($9,000)	$7,000				($2,000)
Kennedy	$3,353,000	($3,032,000)	$321,000	$179,000	$165,000	$7,000	($638,000)	$34,000
Johnson	$28,000	($144,000)	($116,000)	$12,000	$131,000		($17,000)	$10,000
Nixon	$278,000	($86,000)	$192,000	$4,000				$196,000
Ford	$507,000	($426,000)	$81,000	$18,000			($2,000)	$97,000
Carter	$378,000	($391,000)	($13,000)	$2,000				($11,000)
Reagan	$952,000	($937,000)	$15,000	$83,000		$3,000	($143,000)	($42,000)
Bush	$459,000	($348,000)	$111,000	$8,000	$40,000		($18,000)	$141,000
Clinton	$596,000	($445,000)	$151,000	$92,000		$3,000	($125,000)	$121,000
Totals	$8,973,000	($7,914,000)	$1,059,000	$446,000	$336,000	$17,000	($1,048,000)	$810,000

APPENDIX E. COST ANALYSIS SPREADSHEETS

The Cost Analysis of the five models was performed in an effort to quantify how much funding each model might require under tightly controlled circumstances. The comparisons of the costs for the different models made an attempt to account for the changes recommended in the report for each model when compared to the current system. The process used was as follows:

1. After the model parameters were decided upon, standardized costs for the major cost components were developed using currently available NARA cost data to provide the services in similar systems.
2. Life Cycle Costs: This sheet develops the costs for each model plus the baseline (i.e., the existing system, with a 60% endowment as stipulated in the current law governing Presidential Libraries) for a 42 year period. The period is the two years prior to a president leaving office when the staff for the library starts to be hired and ends 40 years after the president leaves office. The yearly costs starting 40 years after leaving office were assumed to be constant. By that point the facility operation and costs had stabilized, with the only changes being major renovations. Renovations for the Government owned as well as the leased facilities had taken place in the time frame of 35 to 40 years. The facilities should not require major renovations until after the 75 year period of time, and no other changes that would impact the costs were envisioned. Consequently, the yearly cost to complete the full 75 year cycle used the 40th year costs for years 41 through 75. Notes showing where the specific numbers came from are on the Life Cycle Cost. The spreadsheet consisted of all of the major cost components identified in NARA's budget for the library system, and include: Program Costs, Move and Lease Build Out Costs, Operation and Maintenance (O&M) Costs, Overtime Utility Costs (24/7 utilities above the standard leased costs), Repair and Restoration Costs, and future Renovation costs. The Life Cycle Costs were developed in this format for the 40 year post presidency period (42 year total costs, to include the transition).
3. Model Costs: The Life Cycle cost table reflects the total for one library for each of the six conditions: baseline and Models One through Five. In order to accurately reflect the total 75 year cost for each of the six scenarios, the Model Cost spreadsheets were developed and reflect the funding for 10 presidencies, each starting at an 8 year interval.
4. Model Cost Totals by FY: These tables take the projected yearly costs for each model and show the costs by year and cumulative, permitting comparisons of the projected costs for each model when compared to the baseline.

This appendix contains the following tables which show baseline and model costs:
1. Model Cost Totals by Fiscal Year and Cumulative
2. NL Model Life Cycle Cost Estimate
3. Baseline
4. Model One
5. Model Two

6. Model Three
7. Model Four
8. Model Five

Model Cost Totals by Fiscal Year and Cumulative All Cost Figures ($) in Thousands (000)

		Baseline		Model One		Model Two		Model Three		Model Four		Model Five	
		Total by FY	Cumulative	Total by FY	Cumulative	Total by FY	Cumulative	Total by FY	Cumulative	Total by FY	Cumulative	Total by FY	Cumulative
FY	2022	$0	$0	$0	$0	$0	$0	$0	$0	$99,510	$99,510	$154,510	$154,510
FY	2023	$524	$524	$524	$524	$524	$524	$524	$524	$524	$99,510	$524	$155,034
FY	2024	$1,112	$1,636	$1,112	$1,636	$1,112	$1,636	$1,112	$1,636	$1,112	$100,622	$1,112	$156,146
FY	2025 election	$8,995	$10,631	$8,995	$10,631	$8,995	$10,631	$8,995	$10,631	$3,225	$103,847	$6,682	$162,828
FY	2026	$6,316	$16,947	$6,316	$16,947	$6,316	$16,947	$6,316	$16,947	$4,159	$108,006	$8,863	$171,691
FY	2027	$6,316	$23,263	$6,316	$23,263	$6,316	$23,263	$6,316	$23,263	$4,159	$112,166	$8,863	$180,554
FY	2028	$6,316	$29,579	$6,316	$29,579	$6,316	$29,579	$6,316	$29,579	$4,159	$116,325	$8,863	$189,416
FY	2029	$6,316	$35,895	$6,316	$35,895	$6,316	$35,895	$6,316	$35,895	$4,159	$120,485	$8,863	$198,279
FY	2030	$6,634	$42,529	$6,634	$42,529	$8,265	$44,160	$8,265	$44,160	$4,159	$124,644	$8,863	$207,142
FY	2031	$7,035	$49,564	$5,853	$48,382	$7,228	$51,388	$6,404	$50,564	$4,745	$129,390	$9,559	$216,701
FY	2032	$7,623	$57,187	$6,441	$54,822	$7,816	$59,205	$6,992	$57,556	$5,333	$134,723	$10,147	$226,847
FY	2033 election	$15,506	$72,693	$14,324	$69,146	$15,699	$74,904	$14,875	$72,432	$7,446	$142,170	$12,260	$239,107
FY	2034	$12,827	$85,521	$11,645	$80,790	$13,020	$87,924	$12,196	$84,628	$8,381	$150,551	$13,194	$252,301
FY	2035	$12,827	$98,348	$11,645	$92,435	$13,020	$100,945	$12,196	$96,824	$8,381	$158,932	$13,194	$265,496
FY	2036	$13,017	$111,365	$11,835	$104,270	$13,123	$114,068	$12,321	$109,145	$8,381	$167,312	$13,194	$278,690
FY	2037	$13,017	$124,382	$11,835	$116,104	$13,123	$127,191	$12,321	$121,466	$8,381	$175,693	$13,194	$291,884
FY	2038	$13,335	$137,718	$12,153	$128,257	$15,072	$142,264	$14,270	$135,737	$8,381	$184,074	$13,194	$305,078
FY	2039	$13,736	$151,454	$11,371	$139,629	$14,036	$156,299	$12,409	$148,146	$8,967	$193,041	$13,780	$318,858
FY	2040	$14,324	$165,779	$11,959	$151,588	$14,624	$170,923	$12,997	$161,143	$9,555	$202,596	$14,368	$333,227
FY	2041 election	$22,207	$187,986	$19,842	$171,430	$22,615	$193,538	$20,880	$182,024	$11,668	$214,264	$16,481	$349,708
FY	2042	$19,528	$207,515	$17,163	$188,594	$19,936	$213,474	$18,201	$200,225	$12,602	$226,866	$17,416	$367,124
FY	2043	$19,528	$227,043	$17,163	$205,757	$19,936	$233,410	$18,201	$218,427	$12,602	$239,469	$17,416	$384,539
FY	2044	$19,719	$246,762	$17,353	$223,110	$20,039	$253,448	$18,326	$236,753	$12,602	$252,071	$17,416	$401,955
FY	2045	$19,719	$266,480	$17,353	$240,464	$20,039	$273,487	$18,326	$255,079	$12,602	$264,674	$17,416	$419,371
FY	2046	$20,037	$286,517	$17,671	$258,135	$22,101	$295,589	$20,275	$275,355	$12,602	$277,276	$17,416	$436,786
FY	2047	$20,438	$306,955	$16,890	$275,026	$21,065	$316,653	$18,415	$293,769	$13,188	$290,464	$18,002	$454,788

(Continued)

		Baseline		Model One		Model Two		Model Three		Model Four		Model Five	
		Total by FY	Cumulative	Total by FY	Cumulative	Total by FY	Cumulative	Total by FY	Cumulative	Total by FY	Cumulative	Total by FY	Cumulative
FY	2048	$21,026	$327,980	$17,478	$292,504	$21,653	$338,306	$19,003	$312,772	$13,776	$304,241	$18,590	$473,378
FY	2049 election	$28,909	$356,889	$25,361	$317,865	$29,644	$367,950	$26,886	$339,658	$15,889	$320,130	$20,703	$494,080
FY	2050	$26,230	$383,119	$22,682	$340,547	$26,965	$394,915	$24,207	$363,864	$16,824	$336,954	$21,637	$515,717
FY	2051	$26,230	$409,349	$22,682	$363,229	$27,466	$422,380	$24,207	$388,071	$16,824	$353,778	$21,637	$537,355
FY	2052	$26,420	$435,769	$22,872	$386,101	$27,569	$449,949	$24,332	$412,402	$16,824	$370,602	$21,637	$558,992
FY	2053	$26,420	$462,188	$22,872	$408,973	$27,569	$477,518	$24,332	$436,734	$16,824	$387,425	$21,637	$580,629
FY	2054	$26,738	$488,926	$23,190	$432,164	$29,631	$507,149	$26,281	$463,015	$16,824	$404,249	$21,637	$602,266
FY	2055	$27,139	$516,065	$22,409	$454,572	$28,595	$535,744	$24,420	$487,434	$17,410	$421,659	$22,223	$624,489
FY	2056	$27,727	$543,792	$22,997	$477,569	$29,471	$565,215	$25,008	$512,442	$17,998	$439,657	$22,811	$647,300
FY	2057 election	$35,610	$579,403	$30,880	$508,449	$37,462	$602,677	$32,891	$545,333	$20,111	$459,768	$24,924	$672,224
FY	2058	$32,931	$612,334	$28,201	$536,650	$34,783	$637,461	$30,212	$575,545	$21,045	$480,813	$25,859	$698,083
FY	2059	$32,931	$645,265	$28,201	$564,851	$35,284	$672,745	$30,212	$605,757	$21,045	$501,858	$25,859	$723,942
FY	2060	$33,121	$678,386	$28,391	$593,242	$35,387	$708,132	$30,337	$636,093	$21,045	$522,904	$25,859	$749,800
FY	2061	$33,121	$711,507	$28,391	$621,633	$35,387	$743,519	$30,337	$666,430	$120,555	$643,459	$125,369	$875,169
FY	2062	$33,439	$744,946	$28,709	$650,342	$37,450	$780,969	$32,286	$698,716	$21,045	$664,504	$25,859	$901,027
FY	2063	$33,840	$778,787	$27,928	$678,269	$36,413	$817,382	$30,425	$729,141	$21,631	$686,136	$26,445	$927,472
FY	2064	$34,428	$813,215	$28,516	$706,785	$37,290	$854,671	$31,013	$760,154	$22,219	$708,355	$27,033	$954,505
FY	2065 election	$66,955	$880,170	$61,042	$767,827	$45,281	$899,952	$55,696	$815,850	$34,748	$743,103	$58,042	$1,012,546
FY	2066	$39,632	$919,803	$33,720	$801,547	$42,602	$942,554	$36,217	$852,067	$25,267	$768,370	$30,080	$1,042,626
FY	2067	$39,632	$959,435	$33,720	$835,267	$43,103	$985,656	$36,217	$888,284	$25,267	$793,637	$30,080	$1,072,706
FY	2068	$39,823	$999,258	$33,910	$869,176	$43,206	$1,028,862	$36,342	$924,626	$25,267	$818,903	$30,080	$1,102,786
FY	2069	$39,823	$1,039,080	$33,910	$903,086	$43,206	$1,072,067	$36,342	$960,968	$25,267	$844,170	$30,080	$1,132,866
FY	2070	$40,141	$1,079,221	$34,228	$937,314	$45,268	$1,117,336	$38,291	$999,259	$25,267	$869,437	$30,080	$1,162,947
FY	2071	$40,542	$1,119,762	$33,446	$970,760	$44,231	$1,161,567	$36,430	$1,035,689	$25,853	$895,290	$30,666	$1,193,613

		Baseline		Model One		Model Two		Model Three		Model Four		Model Five	
		Total by FY	Cumulative	Total by FY	Cumulative	Total by FY	Cumulative	Total by FY	Cumulative	Total by FY	Cumulative	Total by FY	Cumulative
FY	2072	$41,130	$1,160,892	$34,034	$1,004,794	$45,108	$1,206,675	$37,018	$1,072,707	$26,441	$921,731	$31,254	$1,224,867
FY	2073 election	$73,656	$1,234,548	$66,561	$1,071,356	$53,099	$1,259,774	$61,701	$1,134,409	$38,970	$960,700	$43,783	$1,268,650
FY	2074	$46,334	$1,280,882	$39,238	$1,110,594	$50,420	$1,310,194	$42,222	$1,176,631	$29,488	$990,189	$34,302	$1,302,951
FY	2075	$46,334	$1,327,216	$39,238	$1,149,832	$50,921	$1,361,115	$42,222	$1,218,853	$29,488	$1,019,677	$34,302	$1,337,253
FY	2076	$46,524	$1,373,740	$39,428	$1,189,261	$51,024	$1,412,139	$42,347	$1,261,200	$29,488	$1,049,165	$34,302	$1,371,554
FY	2077	$46,524	$1,420,263	$39,428	$1,228,689	$51,024	$1,463,163	$42,347	$1,303,548	$29,488	$1,078,653	$34,302	$1,405,856
FY	2078	$46,842	$1,467,105	$39,746	$1,268,436	$53,087	$1,516,250	$44,296	$1,347,844	$29,488	$1,108,141	$34,302	$1,440,157
FY	2079	$47,243	$1,514,348	$38,965	$1,307,401	$52,050	$1,568,300	$42,435	$1,390,279	$30,074	$1,138,216	$34,888	$1,475,045
FY	2080	$47,831	$1,562,179	$39,553	$1,346,954	$52,926	$1,621,226	$43,023	$1,433,303	$30,662	$1,168,878	$35,476	$1,510,520
FY	2081 election	$80,358	$1,642,537	$72,080	$1,419,034	$60,918	$1,682,144	$67,706	$1,501,009	$43,191	$1,212,069	$48,005	$1,558,525
FY	2082	$53,035	$1,695,572	$44,757	$1,463,791	$58,239	$1,740,383	$48,227	$1,549,236	$33,710	$1,245,779	$38,523	$1,597,048
FY	2083	$53,035	$1,748,607	$44,757	$1,508,548	$58,739	$1,799,122	$48,227	$1,597,464	$33,710	$1,279,488	$38,523	$1,635,571
FY	2084	$53,225	$1,801,832	$44,947	$1,553,495	$58,842	$1,857,964	$48,352	$1,645,816	$33,710	$1,313,198	$38,523	$1,674,094
FY	2085	$53,225	$1,855,057	$44,947	$1,598,442	$58,842	$1,916,807	$48,352	$1,694,169	$33,710	$1,346,908	$38,523	$1,712,617
FY	2086	$53,543	$1,908,600	$45,265	$1,643,708	$60,905	$1,977,712	$50,301	$1,744,470	$33,710	$1,380,617	$38,523	$1,751,140
FY	2087	$53,944	$1,962,545	$44,484	$1,688,191	$59,868	$2,037,580	$48,441	$1,792,911	$34,296	$1,414,913	$39,109	$1,790,249
FY	2088	$54,532	$2,017,077	$45,072	$1,733,263	$60,745	$2,098,325	$49,029	$1,841,939	$34,884	$1,449,797	$39,697	$1,829,946
FY	2089 election	$87,059	$2,104,136	$77,599	$1,810,862	$68,736	$2,167,061	$73,712	$1,915,651	$47,413	$1,497,209	$52,226	$1,882,172
FY	2090	$59,736	$2,163,872	$50,276	$1,861,138	$66,057	$2,233,118	$54,233	$1,969,883	$37,931	$1,535,141	$42,744	$1,924,916
FY	2091	$59,736	$2,223,608	$50,276	$1,911,413	$66,558	$2,299,676	$54,233	$2,024,116	$37,931	$1,573,072	$42,744	$1,967,661
FY	2092	$59,926	$2,283,535	$50,466	$1,961,879	$66,661	$2,366,337	$54,358	$2,078,474	$37,931	$1,611,003	$42,744	$2,010,405
FY	2093	$59,926	$2,343,461	$50,466	$2,012,345	$66,661	$2,432,998	$54,358	$2,132,831	$37,931	$1,648,934	$42,744	$2,053,149
FY	2094	$60,244	$2,403,706	$50,784	$2,063,129	$68,723	$2,501,721	$56,307	$2,189,138	$37,931	$1,686,865	$42,744	$2,095,894
FY	2095	$60,646	$2,464,351	$50,003	$2,113,132	$67,687	$2,569,408	$54,446	$2,243,584	$38,517	$1,725,382	$43,330	$2,139,224
FY	2096	$61,234	$2,525,585	$50,591	$2,163,723	$68,563	$2,637,971	$55,034	$2,298,617	$39,105	$1,764,487	$43,918	$2,183,143
FY	2097 election	$93,760	$2,619,345	$83,117	$2,246,840	$76,554	$2,714,526	$79,717	$2,378,334	$51,634	$1,816,122	$56,447	$2,239,590
FY	2098	$66,438	$2,685,783	$55,795	$2,302,635	$73,875	$2,788,401	$60,238	$2,438,572	$42,153	$1,858,274	$46,966	$2,286,556
FY	2099	$66,438	$2,752,221	$55,795	$2,358,429	$74,376	$2,862,778	$60,238	$2,498,810	$42,153	$1,900,427	$46,966	$2,333,522

NL Model Life Cycle Cost Estimate Model Cost Totals By FY All Cost Figures ($) in Thousands (000)

	Baseline Status Quo	Model One Status Quo ++	Model Two Leased	Model Three Provided	Model Four Centralized	Model Five Centralized with Museum
Building Size in sf	152,122	152,122 [1]	70,000 [2]	70,000 [2]	62,000 [3]	110,000
Efficiency Factor				0.7		
new building size				100,000		
Initial Construction Investment for 5 presidencies.					$99,510 [6]	$55,000 [6]
Year 40 Facility Expansion for an additional 5 presidencies.					$99,510 [6]	
A. Transition Period						
-staff at -2 years	$524 [4]	$524 [4]	$524 [4]	$524 [4]	$524 [4]	
-staff at -1 year	$1,112 [4]	$1,112 [4]	$1,112 [4]	$1,112 [4]	$1,112 [4]	
-staff in last year in office	$3,225 [4]	$3,225 [4]	$3,225 [4]	$3,225 [4]	$3,225 [4]	$3,457 [10]
-staff savings for centralized facility	$0	$0	$0	$0	-$90 [5]	
-Move/lease/build out	$5,770 [4]	$5,770 [4]	$5,770 [4]	$5,770 [4]	$0	
	$0	$0	$0	$0		
-Centralized O&M @ $10.33/sf	$0	$0	$0	$0	$640 [7]	$1,136 [7]
Total Transition	$10,631	$10,631	$10,631	$10,631	$5,411	$4,593
B Years 2 - 6 Costs in Temporary Space; years 2 - 6 after leaving office						
-base lease	$1,766 [8]	$1,766 [8]	$1,766 [8]	$1,766 [8]	$0	
-O&M costs	$0	$0	$0	$0	$640 [7]	$1,136 [7]
-program	$3,547 [9]	$3,547 [9]	$3,547 [9]	$3,547 [9]	$3,457 [10]	$3,457 [10]
-guards	$439 [11]	$439 [11]	$439 [11]	$439 [11] in O&M		
-leased O&M and taxes	$364 [12]	$364 [12]	$364 [12]	$364 [12]		
-add in 24/7 utilities	$200 [13]	$200 [13]	$200 [13]	$200 [13]		
-non renovation R&R @ 50%					$62 [14]	$110
subtotal per year	$6,316	$6,316	$6,316	$6,316	$4,159	$4,703
Total years two through six	$31,580	$31,580	$31,580	$31,580	$20,797	$23,517
C. Move to Permanent Location						
-move/build out	$318 [15]	$318 [15]	$749 [16]	$749 [16]		
-security & shelving replacement	by foundation	by foundation	$1,200 [17]	$1,200 [17]		
Total Move to Permanent Space	$318	$318	$1,949	$1,949	$0	
D. Costs per year: years 0 - 5 Permanent Space; years 6 - 10 after leaving office						
-program costs	$3,547 [9]	$3,547 [9]	$3,547 [9]	$3,547 [9]	$3,457 [10]	$3,457 [10]
-add in education specialists	$400 [18]	$400 [18]	$0	$0	$0	
-O&M costs	$2,982 [19]	$2,982 [19]	$0	$2,208 [20]	$640 [7]	$1,136 [7]
-base lease	$0	$0	$2,060 [21]	$0	$0	
-leased operational costs	$0	$0	$425 [22]	$0	$0	
-add in 24/7 utilities	$0	$0	$233 [23]	$0	$0	
-guards	in O&M	in O&M	$439 [11]	in O&M	in O&M	
-non renovation R&R @ 50%	$190 [14]	$190 [14]	$0	$125 [14]	$0	
-non renovation R&R @ 100%					$124 [24]	$220 [24]
-endowment deduction @ 60%	-$608 [25]	-$1,791 [25]	$0	$0	$0	
subtotal costs per year	$6,511	$5,329	$6,704	$5,880	$4,221	$4,813
Total years 0 through 5	$32,556	$26,643	$33,522	$29,401	$21,107	$24,067
E. Costs per year: years 6 - 10 Permanent Space; years 11 - 15 after leaving office						
-program costs	$3,547 [9]	$3,547 [9]	$3,547 [9]	$3,547 [9]	$3,457 [10]	$3,457 [10]
-add in education specialists	$400 [18]	$400 [18]	$0	$0	$0	
-O&M costs	$2,982 [19]	$2,982 [19]	$0	$2,208 [20]	$640 [7]	$1,136 [7]
-base lease costs	$0	$0	$2,060 [21]	$0		
-5% lease increase			$103 [26]			
-leased operational costs			$425 [22]			
-add in 24/7 utilities			$233 [23]			
-guards	in O&M	in O&M	$439 [11]	in O&M		
-non renovation R&R @ 100%	$380 [24]	$380 [24]	$0	$250 [24]	$124 [24]	$220 [24]
-endowment deduction @ 60%	-$608 [25]	-$1,791 [25]				
subtotal costs per year	$6,701	$5,519	$6,807	$6,005	$4,221	$4,813
Total years 6 - 10	$33,507	$27,594	$34,037	$30,026	$21,107	$24,067

	Baseline Status Quo	Model One Status Quo ++	Model Two Leased	Model Three Provided	Model Four Centralized	Model Five Centralized with Museum
Building Size in sf	152,122	152,122 [1]	70,000 [2]	70,000 [2]	62,000 [3]	110,000
Efficiency Factor				0.7		
new building size				100,000		
Initial Construction Investment for 5 presidencies.					$99,510 [6]	$55,000 [6]
Year 40 Facility Expansion for an additional 5 presidencies.					$99,510 [6]	
A. Transition Period						
-staff at -2 years	$524 [4]	$524 [4]	$524 [4]	$524 [4]	$524 [4]	
-staff at -1 year	$1,112 [4]	$1,112 [4]	$1,112 [4]	$1,112 [4]	$1,112 [4]	
-staff in last year in office	$3,225 [4]	$3,225 [4]	$3,225 [4]	$3,225 [4]	$3,225 [4]	$3,457 [10]
-staff savings for centralized facility	$0	$0	$0	$0	-$90 [5]	
-Move/lease/build out	$5,770 [4]	$5,770 [4]	$5,770 [4]	$5,770 [4]	$0	
	$0	$0	$0	$0		
-Centralized O&M @ $10.33/sf	$0	$0	$0	$0	$640 [7]	$1,136 [7]
Total Transition	$10,631	$10,631	$10,631	$10,631	$5,411	$4,593
B Years 2 - 6 Costs in Temporary Space; years 2 - 6 after leaving office						
-base lease	$1,766 [8]	$1,766 [8]	$1,766 [8]	$1,766 [8]	$0	
-O&M costs	$0	$0	$0	$0	$640 [7]	$1,136 [7]
-program	$3,547 [9]	$3,547 [9]	$3,547 [9]	$3,547 [9]	$3,457 [10]	$3,457 [10]
-guards	$439 [11]	$439 [11]	$439 [11]	$439 [11] in O&M		
-leased O&M and taxes	$364 [12]	$364 [12]	$364 [12]	$364 [12]		
-add in 24/7 utilities	$200 [13]	$200 [13]	$200 [13]	$200 [13]		
-non renovation R&R @ 50%					$62 [14]	$110
subtotal per year	$6,316	$6,316	$6,316	$6,316	$4,159	$4,703
Total years two through six	$31,580	$31,580	$31,580	$31,580	$20,797	$23,517
C. Move to Permanent Location						
-move/build out	$318 [15]	$318 [15]	$749 [16]	$749 [16]		
-security & shelving replacement	by foundation	by foundation	$1,200 [17]	$1,200 [17]		
Total Move to Permanent Space	$318	$318	$1,949	$1,949	$0	
D. Costs per year: years 0 - 5 Permanent Space; years 6 - 10 after leaving office						
-program costs	$3,547 [9]	$3,547 [9]	$3,547 [9]	$3,547 [9]	$3,457 [10]	$3,457 [10]
-add in education specialists	$400 [18]	$400 [18]	$0	$0	$0	
-O&M costs	$2,982 [19]	$2,982 [19]	$0	$2,208 [20]	$640 [7]	$1,136 [7]
-base lease	$0	$0	$2,060 [21]	$0	$0	$0
-leased operational costs	$0	$0	$425 [22]	$0	$0	$0
-add in 24/7 utilities	$0	$0	$233 [23]	$0	$0	$0
-guards	in O&M	in O&M	$439 [11]	in O&M	in O&M	
-non renovation R&R @ 50%	$190 [14]	$190 [14]	$0	$125 [14]	$0	
-non renovation R&R @ 100%					$124 [24]	$220 [24]
-endowment deduction @ 60%	-$608 [25]	-$1,791 [25]	$0	$0	$0	
subtotal costs per year	$6,511	$5,329	$6,704	$5,880	$4,221	$4,813
Total years 0 through 5	$32,556	$26,643	$33,522	$29,401	$21,107	$24,067
E. Costs per year: years 6 - 10 Permanent Space; years 11 - 15 after leaving office						
-program costs	$3,547 [9]	$3,547 [9]	$3,547 [9]	$3,547 [9]	$3,457 [10]	$3,457 [10]
-add in education specialists	$400 [18]	$400 [18]	$0	$0	$0	
-O&M costs	$2,982 [19]	$2,982 [19]	$0	$2,208 [20]	$640 [7]	$1,136 [7]
-base lease costs	$0	$0	$2,060 [21]	$0		
-5% lease increase			$103 [26]			
-leased operational costs			$425 [22]			
-add in 24/7 utilities			$233 [23]			
-guards	in O&M	in O&M	$439 [11]	in O&M		
-non renovation R&R @ 100%	$380 [24]	$380 [24]	$0	$250 [24]	$124 [24]	$220 [24]
-endowment deduction @ 60%	-$608 [25]	-$1,791 [25]				
subtotal costs per year	$6,701	$5,519	$6,807	$6,005	$4,221	$4,813
Total years 6 - 10	$33,507	$27,594	$34,037	$30,026	$21,107	$24,067

	Baseline Status Quo	Model One Status Quo ++	Model Two Leased	Model Three Provided	Model Four Centralized	Model Five Centralized with Museum
Total Life Cycle From end of 2nd term to 40 years post term	$300,768	$259,378	$294,520	$270,517	$184,376	$215,055

Annual costs after 40 years are assumed to be steady at the year 40 annual costs for the lifetime of the facility.

The **Baseline** differs from **Model One** only in the calculation of the endowment. The Baseline uses the current interpretation: 60% applied to the 70,000 sf of NARA program space.

The Model One endowment uses the proposed change of 60% applied to the entire building - in this case 152,122 sf.

Source of the Numbers. Unless otherwise stated, all numbers were provided by both Budget and Presidential Libraries.
1. Clinton Library is basis for size and costs
2. Bush43 leased space plus 10,000 sf for research room.
3. Calculated need if located in AII type space
4. Bush 43 FY2009 budget
5. Bush 43 cost for one facility manager not needed in a centralized facility.
6. Centralized Archives @ $321/sf for 5 modules; Centralized Museum @ $500/sf
7. From Budget (NAB): FY2009 All O&M costs/sf (calculated at $10.33/sf) for AII applied to sf needed for library
8. From Property Mgmt Branch (NASR): Bush 43 temp space lease cost per year (60,000 sf in temp space)
9. Bush 43 program costs
10. Bush 43 program costs less one facility manager
11. Bush 43 guard service for one year.
12. Bush 43 operating and tax costs for one year.
13. From NASR Contracting Officer: Bush 43 24/7 utility costs to be added to lease.
14. From Security Division (NAS): normal rate for repairs is $2/sf; 50% applied for 1st five years in a facility.
15. Clinton 2004 move cost to permanent space escalated to FY2009
16. Clinton 2004 move costs plus Bush 43 temporary space build out costs
17. Bush 43 shelving and security system costs for temp space.
18. Estimated future personnel costs for education program.
19. Clinton FY2009 O&M budget
20. Blended rate using Bush 41 and Johnson Libraries. Ford costs do not appear to be replicable at other locations.
21. Bush 43 base lease rate applied to 70,000 sf facility vice 60,000.
22. Bush 43 tax and operating costs escalated for 70,000 sf facility
23. Bush 43 24/7 utilities escalated to 70,000 sf facility
24. NAS: full rate for major repairs applied after 5 years
25. Clinton construction costs escalated to FY2009; 60% endowment earning 4% per year
26. NAS CO: lease provides for opportunity to raise rates at 5 year periods. Predicted that lessor will raise rates 5%.
27. NAS CO: Predicts lessor will raise rates 10% to accomplish repairs normally covered by renovation.
28. Predicted renovation costs using AI renovation $162/sf

Note: The Museum option is for multiple presidencies.
The museum option assumes that The Foundation of the National Archives - or one created just for the centralized museum of the presidency - would fully fund all exhibits and the construction of the exhibits. Staffing was assumed to be ten facilities personnel and 24 exhibit/education/support personnel. The museum would be operated by CFM plus guard contracts, all included in the O&M figure.

BASELINE: DONATED PRESIDENTIAL LIBRARY WITH MUSEUM AND PUBLIC PROGRAMS—CURRENT LAW AND ENDOWMENT INTERPRETATION
MODEL COST TOTALS BY FY —BASELINE
ALL COST FIGURES ($) IN THOUSANDS (000)

FY																									Baseline Total by Year	Baseline Cumulative Total
FY 2022																										
FY 2023	$524																								$524	$524
FY 2024	$1,112																								$1,112	$1,636
FY 2025 election	$8,995																								$8,995	$10,631
FY 2026	$6,316																								$6,316	$16,947
FY 2027	$6,316																								$6,316	$23,263
FY 2028	$6,316																								$6,316	$29,579
FY 2029	$6,316																								$6,316	$35,895
FY 2030	$6,634																								$6,634	$42,529
FY 2031	$6,511	$524																							$7,035	$49,564
FY 2032	$6,511	$1,112																							$7,623	$57,187
FY 2033 election	$6,511	$8,995																							$15,506	$72,693
FY 2034	$6,511	$6,316																							$12,827	$85,521
FY 2035	$6,511	$6,316																							$12,827	$98,348
FY 2036	$6,701	$6,316																							$13,017	$111,365
FY 2037	$6,701	$6,316																							$13,017	$124,382
FY 2038	$6,701	$6,634																							$13,335	$137,718
FY 2039	$6,701	$6,511	$524																						$13,736	$151,454
FY 2040	$6,701	$6,511	$1,112																						$14,324	$165,779
FY 2041 election	$6,701	$6,511	$8,995																						$22,207	$187,986
FY 2042	$6,701	$6,511	$6,316																						$19,528	$207,515
FY 2043	$6,701	$6,511	$6,316																						$19,528	$227,043
FY 2044	$6,701	$6,701	$6,316																						$19,719	$246,762
FY 2045	$6,701	$6,701	$6,316																						$19,719	$266,480

										Baseline Total by Year	Baseline Cumulative Total
FY 2046	$6,701	$6,634								$20,037	$286,517
FY 2047	$6,701	$6,511	$524							$20,438	$306,955
FY 2048	$6,701	$6,511	$1,112							$21,026	$327,980
FY 2049 election	$6,701	$6,511	$8,995							$28,909	$356,889
FY 2050	$6,701	$6,511	$6,316							$26,230	$383,119
FY 2051	$6,701	$6,511	$6,316							$26,230	$409,349
FY 2052	$6,701	$6,701	$6,316							$26,420	$435,769
FY 2053	$6,701	$6,701	$6,316							$26,420	$462,188
FY 2054	$6,701	$6,701	$6,634							$26,738	$488,926
FY 2055	$6,701	$6,701	$6,511	$524						$27,139	$516,065
FY 2056	$6,701	$6,701	$6,511	$1,112						$27,727	$543,792
FY 2057 election	$6,701	$6,701	$6,511	$8,995						$35,610	$579,403
FY 2058	$6,701	$6,701	$6,511	$6,316						$32,931	$612,334
FY 2059	$6,701	$6,701	$6,511	$6,316						$32,931	$645,265
FY 2060	$6,701	$6,701	$6,701	$6,316						$33,121	$678,386
FY 2061	$6,701	$6,701	$6,701	$6,316						$33,121	$711,507
FY 2062	$6,701	$6,701	$6,701	$6,634						$33,439	$744,946
FY 2063	$6,701	$6,701	$6,701	$6,511	$524					$33,840	$778,787
FY 2064	$6,701	$6,701	$6,701	$6,511	$1,112					$34,428	$813,215
FY 2065 election	$31,345	$6,701	$6,701	$6,511	$8,995					$66,955	$880,170
FY 2066	$6,701	$6,701	$6,701	$6,511	$6,316					$39,632	$919,803
FY 2067	$6,701	$6,701	$6,701	$6,511	$6,316					$39,632	$959,435
FY 2068	$6,701	$6,701	$6,701	$6,701	$6,316					$39,823	$999,258
FY 2069	$6,701	$6,701	$6,701	$6,701	$6,316					$39,823	$1,039,080
FY 2070	$6,701	$6,701	$6,701	$6,701	$6,634					$40,141	$1,079,221
FY 2071	$6,701	$6,701	$6,701	$6,701	$6,511	$524				$40,542	$1,119,762
FY 2072	$6,701	$6,701	$6,701	$6,701	$6,511	$1,112				$41,130	$1,160,892
FY 2073 election	$6,701	$6,701	$6,701	$6,701	$6,511	$8,995				$73,656	$1,234,548

(Continued)

											Baseline Total by Year	Baseline Cumulative Total
FY 2074	$6,701	$6,701	$6,701	$6,701	$6,701	$6,511	$6,316				$46,334	$1,280,882
FY 2075	$6,701	$6,701	$6,701	$6,701	$6,701	$6,511	$6,316				$46,334	$1,327,216
FY 2076	$6,701	$6,701	$6,701	$6,701	$6,701	$6,701	$6,316				$46,524	$1,373,740
FY 2077	$6,701	$6,701	$6,701	$6,701	$6,701	$6,701	$6,316				$46,524	$1,420,263
FY 2078	$6,701	$6,701	$6,701	$6,701	$6,701	$6,701	$6,634				$46,842	$1,467,105
FY 2079	$6,701	$6,701	$6,701	$6,701	$6,701	$6,701	$6,511	$524			$47,243	$1,514,348
FY 2080	$6,701	$6,701	$6,701	$6,701	$6,701	$6,701	$6,511	$1,112			$47,831	$1,562,179
FY 2081 election	$6,701	$6,701	$31,345	$6,701	$6,701	$6,701	$6,511	$8,995			$80,358	$1,642,537
FY 2082	$6,701	$6,701	$6,701	$6,701	$6,701	$6,701	$6,511	$6,316			$53,035	$1,695,572
FY 2083	$6,701	$6,701	$6,701	$6,701	$6,701	$6,701	$6,511	$6,316			$53,035	$1,748,607
FY 2084	$6,701	$6,701	$6,701	$6,701	$6,701	$6,701	$6,701	$6,316			$53,225	$1,801,832
FY 2085	$6,701	$6,701	$6,701	$6,701	$6,701	$6,701	$6,701	$6,316			$53,225	$1,855,057
FY 2086	$6,701	$6,701	$6,701	$6,701	$6,701	$6,701	$6,701	$6,634			$53,543	$1,908,600
FY 2087	$6,701	$6,701	$6,701	$6,701	$6,701	$6,701	$6,701	$6,511	$524		$53,944	$1,962,545
FY 2088	$6,701	$6,701	$6,701	$6,701	$6,701	$6,701	$6,701	$6,511	$1,112		$54,532	$2,017,077
FY 2089 election	$6,701	$6,701	$6,701	$31,345	$6,701	$6,701	$6,701	$6,511	$8,995		$87,059	$2,104,136
FY 2090	$6,701	$6,701	$6,701	$6,701	$6,701	$6,701	$6,701	$6,511	$6,316		$59,736	$2,163,872
FY 2091	$6,701	$6,701	$6,701	$6,701	$6,701	$6,701	$6,701	$6,511	$6,316		$59,736	$2,223,608
FY 2092	$6,701	$6,701	$6,701	$6,701	$6,701	$6,701	$6,701	$6,701	$6,316		$59,926	$2,283,535
FY 2093	$6,701	$6,701	$6,701	$6,701	$6,701	$6,701	$6,701	$6,701	$6,316		$59,926	$2,343,461
FY 2094	$6,701	$6,701	$6,701	$6,701	$6,701	$6,701	$6,701	$6,701	$6,634		$60,244	$2,403,706
FY 2095	$6,701	$6,701	$6,701	$6,701	$6,701	$6,701	$6,701	$6,701	$6,511	$524	$60,646	$2,464,351
FY 2096	$6,701	$6,701	$6,701	$6,701	$6,701	$6,701	$6,701	$6,701	$6,511	$1,112	$61,234	$2,525,585
FY 2097 election	$6,701	$6,701	$6,701	$6,701	$31,345	$6,701	$6,701	$6,701	$6,511	$8,995	$93,760	$2,619,345
FY 2098	$6,701	$6,701	$6,701	$6,701	$6,701	$6,701	$6,701	$6,701	$6,511	$6,316	$66,438	$2,685,783
FY 2099	$6,701	$6,701	$6,701	$6,701	$6,701	$6,701	$6,701	$6,701	$6,511	$6,316	$66,438	$2,752,221

MODEL ONE: STATUS QUO - DONATED PRESIDENTIAL LIBRARY WITH MUSEUM AND PUBLIC PROGRAMS
MODEL COST TOTALS BY FY - MODEL ONE ALL COST FIGURES ($) IN THOUSANDS (000)

	FY											Model One Total by Year	Model One Cumulative Total
FY	2022												
FY	2023	$524										$524	$524
FY	2024	$1,112										$1,112	$1,636
FY	2025 election	$8,995										$8,995	$10,631
FY	2026	$6,316										$6,316	$16,947
FY	2027	$6,316										$6,316	$23,263
FY	2028	$6,316										$6,316	$29,579
FY	2029	$6,316										$6,316	$35,895
FY	2030	$6,634										$6,634	$42,529
FY	2031	$5,329	$524									$5,853	$48,382
FY	2032	$5,329	$1,112									$6,441	$54,822
FY	2033 election	$5,329	$8,995									$14,324	$69,146
FY	2034	$5,329	$6,316									$11,645	$80,790
FY	2035	$5,329	$6,316									$11,645	$92,435
FY	2036	$5,519	$6,316									$11,835	$104,270
FY	2037	$5,519	$6,316									$11,835	$116,104
FY	2038	$5,519	$6,634									$12,153	$128,257
FY	2039	$5,519	$5,329	$524								$11,371	$139,629
FY	2040	$5,519	$5,329	$1,112								$11,959	$151,588
FY	2041 election	$5,519	$5,329	$8,995								$19,842	$171,430
FY	2042	$5,519	$5,329	$6,316								$17,163	$188,594
FY	2043	$5,519	$5,329	$6,316								$17,163	$205,757

(Continued)

							Model One Total by Year	Model One Cumulative Total
FY	2044	$5,519	$5,519	$6,316			$17,353	$223,110
FY	2045	$5,519	$5,519	$6,316			$17,353	$240,464
FY	2046	$5,519	$5,519	$6,634			$17,671	$258,135
FY	2047	$5,519	$5,519	$5,329	$524		$16,890	$275,026
FY	2048	$5,519	$5,519	$5,329	$1,112		$17,478	$292,504
FY	2049 election	$5,519	$5,519	$5,329	$8,995		$25,361	$317,865
FY	2050	$5,519	$5,519	$5,329	$6,316		$22,682	$340,547
FY	2051	$5,519	$5,519	$5,329	$6,316		$22,682	$363,229
FY	2052	$5,519	$5,519	$5,519	$6,316		$22,872	$386,101
FY	2053	$5,519	$5,519	$5,519	$6,316		$22,872	$408,973
FY	2054	$5,519	$5,519	$5,519	$6,634		$23,190	$432,164
FY	2055	$5,519	$5,519	$5,519	$5,329	$524	$22,409	$454,572
FY	2056	$5,519	$5,519	$5,519	$5,329	$1,112	$22,997	$477,569
FY	2057 election	$5,519	$5,519	$5,519	$5,329	$8,995	$30,880	$508,449
FY	2058	$5,519	$5,519	$5,519	$5,329	$6,316	$28,201	$536,650
FY	2059	$5,519	$5,519	$5,519	$5,329	$6,316	$28,201	$564,851
FY	2060	$5,519	$5,519	$5,519	$5,519	$6,316	$28,391	$593,242
FY	2061	$5,519	$5,519	$5,519	$5,519	$6,316	$28,391	$621,633
FY	2062	$5,519	$5,519	$5,519	$5,519	$6,634	$28,709	$650,342
FY	2063	$5,519	$5,519	$5,519	$5,329	$5,329	$524	$27,928	$678,269
FY	2064	$5,519	$5,519	$5,519	$5,329	$5,329	$1,112	$28,516	$706,785
FY	2065 election	$30,163	$5,519	$5,519	$5,329	$5,329	$8,995	$61,042	$767,827
FY	2066	$5,519	$5,519	$5,519	$5,329	$5,329	$6,316	$33,720	$801,547

								Model One Total by Year	Model One Cumulative Total
FY	2067	$5,519	$5,519	$5,519	$5,519	$5,329	$6,316	$33,720	$835,267
FY	2068	$5,519	$5,519	$5,519	$5,519	$5,519	$6,316	$33,910	$869,176
FY	2069	$5,519	$5,519	$5,519	$5,519	$5,519	$6,316	$33,910	$903,086
FY	2070	$5,519	$5,519	$5,519	$5,519	$5,519	$6,634	$34,228	$937,314
FY	2071	$5,519	$5,519	$5,519	$5,519	$5,329	$5,329	$524	$33,446	$970,760
FY	2072	$5,519	$5,519	$5,519	$5,519	$5,329	$5,329	$1,112	$34,034	$1,004,794
FY	2073 election	$5,519	$30,163	$5,519	$5,519	$5,329	$5,329	$8,995	$66,561	$1,071,356
FY	2074	$5,519	$5,519	$5,519	$5,519	$5,329	$6,316	$39,238	$1,110,594
FY	2075	$5,519	$5,519	$5,519	$5,519	$5,329	$6,316	$39,238	$1,149,832
FY	2076	$5,519	$5,519	$5,519	$5,519	$5,519	$6,316	$39,428	$1,189,261
FY	2077	$5,519	$5,519	$5,519	$5,519	$5,519	$6,316	$39,428	$1,228,689
FY	2078	$5,519	$5,519	$5,519	$5,519	$5,519	$6,634	$39,746	$1,268,436
FY	2079	$5,519	$5,519	$5,519	$5,519	$5,519	$5,329	$524	$38,965	$1,307,401
FY	2080	$5,519	$5,519	$5,519	$5,519	$5,519	$5,329	$1,112	$39,553	$1,346,954
FY	2081 election	$5,519	$5,519	$30,163	$5,519	$5,519	$5,329	$8,995	$72,080	$1,419,034
FY	2082	$5,519	$5,519	$5,519	$5,519	$5,519	$5,329	$6,316	$44,757	$1,463,791
FY	2083	$5,519	$5,519	$5,519	$5,519	$5,519	$5,329	$6,316	$44,757	$1,508,548
FY	2084	$5,519	$5,519	$5,519	$5,519	$5,519	$5,519	$6,316	$44,947	$1,553,495
FY	2085	$5,519	$5,519	$5,519	$5,519	$5,519	$5,519	$6,316	$44,947	$1,598,442
FY	2086	$5,519	$5,519	$5,519	$5,519	$5,519	$5,519	$6,634	$45,265	$1,643,708
FY	2087	$5,519	$5,519	$5,519	$5,519	$5,519	$5,519	$5,329	$524	$44,484	$1,688,191
FY	2088	$5,519	$5,519	$5,519	$5,519	$5,519	$5,519	$5,329	$1,112	$45,072	$1,733,263
FY	2089 election	$5,519	$5,519	$5,519	$30,163	$5,519	$5,519	$5,329	$8,995	$77,599	$1,810,862

									Model One Total by Year	Model One Cumulative Total
FY	2090	$5,519	$5,519	$5,519	$5,519	$5,519	$5,329	$6,316		$50,276	$1,861,138
FY	2091	$5,519	$5,519	$5,519	$5,519	$5,519	$5,329	$6,316		$50,276	$1,911,413
FY	2092	$5,519	$5,519	$5,519	$5,519	$5,519	$5,519	$6,316		$50,466	$1,961,879
FY	2093	$5,519	$5,519	$5,519	$5,519	$5,519	$5,519	$6,316		$50,466	$2,012,345
FY	2094	$5,519	$5,519	$5,519	$5,519	$5,519	$5,519	$6,634		$50,784	$2,063,129
FY	2095	$5,519	$5,519	$5,519	$5,519	$5,519	$5,519	$5,329	$524	$50,003	$2,113,132
FY	2096	$5,519	$5,519	$5,519	$5,519	$5,519	$5,519	$5,329	$1,112	$50,591	$2,163,723
FY	2097 election	$5,519	$5,519	$5,519	$30,163	$5,519	$5,519	$5,329	$8,995	$83,117	$2,246,840
FY	2098	$5,519	$5,519	$5,519	$5,519	$5,519	$5,519	$5,329	$6,316	$55,795	$2,302,635
FY	2099	$5,519	$5,519	$5,519	$5,519	$5,519	$5,519	$5,329	$6,316	$55,795	$2,358,429

Model Two: Leased Space - No Museum or Public Programs Model Cost Totals by FY - Model Two All Cost Figures ($) in Thousands (000)

												Model Two Total by Year	Model Two Cumulative Total
FY	2023	$524										$524	$524
FY	2024	$1,112										$1,112	$1,636
FY	2025 election	$8,995										$8,995	$10,631
FY	2026	$6,316										$6,316	$16,947
FY	2027	$6,316										$6,316	$23,263
FY	2028	$6,316										$6,316	$29,579
FY	2029	$6,316										$6,316	$35,895
FY	2030	$8,265										$8,265	$44,160
FY	2031	$6,704	$524									$7,228	$51,388
FY	2032	$6,704	$1,112									$7,816	$59,205
FY	2033 election	$6,704	$8,995									$15,699	$74,904
FY	2034	$6,704	$6,316									$13,020	$87,924
FY	2035	$6,704	$6,316									$13,020	$100,945
FY	2036	$6,807	$6,316									$13,123	$114,068
FY	2037	$6,807	$6,316									$13,123	$127,191
FY	2038	$6,807	$8,265									$15,072	$142,264
FY	2039	$6,807	$6,704	$524								$14,036	$156,299
FY	2040	$6,807	$6,704	$1,112								$14,624	$170,923
FY	2041 election	$6,915	$6,704	$8,995								$22,615	$193,538
FY	2042	$6,915	$6,704	$6,316								$19,936	$213,474
FY	2043	$6,915	$6,704	$6,316								$19,936	$233,410
FY	2044	$6,915	$6,807	$6,316								$20,039	$253,448
FY	2045	$6,915	$6,807	$6,316								$20,039	$273,487
FY	2046	$7,029	$6,807	$8,265								$22,101	$295,589
FY	2047	$7,029	$6,807	$6,704	$524							$21,065	$316,653

(Continued)

								Model Two Total by Year	Model Two Cumulative Total
FY	2048	$7,029	$6,807	$6,704				$21,653	$338,306
FY	2049 election	$7,029	$6,915	$6,704	$8,995	$1,112		$29,644	$367,950
FY	2050	$7,029	$6,915	$6,704	$6,316			$26,965	$394,915
FY	2051	$7,530	$6,915	$6,704	$6,316			$27,466	$422,380
FY	2052	$7,530	$6,915	$6,807	$6,316			$27,569	$449,949
FY	2053	$7,530	$6,915	$6,807	$6,316			$27,569	$477,518
FY	2054	$7,530	$7,029	$6,807	$8,265			$29,631	$507,149
FY	2055	$7,530	$7,029	$6,807	$6,704	$524		$28,595	$535,744
FY	2056	$7,818	$7,029	$6,807	$6,704	$1,112		$29,471	$565,215
FY	2057 election	$7,818	$7,029	$6,915	$6,704	$8,995		$37,462	$602,677
FY	2058	$7,818	$7,029	$6,915	$6,704	$6,316		$34,783	$637,461
FY	2059	$7,818	$7,530	$6,915	$6,704	$6,316		$35,284	$672,745
FY	2060	$7,818	$7,530	$6,915	$6,807	$6,316		$35,387	$708,132
FY	2061	$7,818	$7,530	$6,915	$6,807	$6,316		$35,387	$743,519
FY	2062	$7,818	$7,530	$7,029	$6,807	$8,265		$37,450	$780,969
FY	2063	$7,818	$7,530	$7,029	$6,807	$6,704	$524	$36,413	$817,382
FY	2064	$7,818	$7,818	$7,029	$6,807	$6,704	$1,112	$37,290	$854,671
FY	2065 election	$7,818	$7,818	$7,029	$6,915	$6,704	$8,995	$45,281	$899,952
FY	2066	$7,818	$7,818	$7,029	$6,915	$6,704	$6,316	$42,602	$942,554
FY	2067	$7,818	$7,818	$7,530	$6,915	$6,704	$6,316	$43,103	$985,656
FY	2068	$7,818	$7,818	$7,530	$6,915	$6,807	$6,316	$43,206	$1,028,862
FY	2069	$7,818	$7,818	$7,530	$6,915	$6,807	$6,316	$43,206	$1,072,067
FY	2070	$7,818	$7,818	$7,530	$7,029	$6,807	$8,265	$45,268	$1,117,336
FY	2071	$7,818	$7,818	$7,530	$7,029	$6,807	$6,704	$524	$44,231	$1,161,567
FY	2072	$7,818	$7,818	$7,818	$7,029	$6,807	$6,704	$1,112	$45,108	$1,206,675
FY	2073 election	$7,818	$7,818	$7,818	$7,029	$6,915	$6,704	$8,995	$53,099	$1,259,774
FY	2074	$7,818	$7,818	$7,818	$7,029	$6,915	$6,704	$6,316	$50,420	$1,310,194

										Model Two Total by Year	Model Two Cumulative Total
FY	2075	$7,818	$7,818	$7,530	$6,915	$6,704	$6,316			$50,921	$1,361,115
FY	2076	$7,818	$7,818	$7,530	$6,915	$6,807	$6,316			$51,024	$1,412,139
FY	2077	$7,818	$7,818	$7,530	$6,915	$6,807	$6,316			$51,024	$1,463,163
FY	2078	$7,818	$7,818	$7,530	$7,029	$6,807	$8,265			$53,087	$1,516,250
FY	2079	$7,818	$7,818	$7,530	$7,029	$6,807	$6,704	$524		$52,050	$1,568,300
FY	2080	$7,818	$7,818	$7,530	$7,029	$6,807	$6,704	$1,112		$52,926	$1,621,226
FY	2081 election	$7,818	$7,818	$7,818	$7,029	$6,915	$6,704	$8,995		$60,918	$1,682,144
FY	2082	$7,818	$7,818	$7,818	$7,029	$6,915	$6,704	$6,316		$58,239	$1,740,383
FY	2083	$7,818	$7,818	$7,818	$7,530	$6,915	$6,704	$6,316		$58,739	$1,799,122
FY	2084	$7,818	$7,818	$7,818	$7,530	$6,915	$6,807	$6,316		$58,842	$1,857,964
FY	2085	$7,818	$7,818	$7,818	$7,530	$6,915	$6,807	$6,316		$58,842	$1,916,807
FY	2086	$7,818	$7,818	$7,818	$7,530	$7,029	$6,807	$8,265		$60,905	$1,977,712
FY	2087	$7,818	$7,818	$7,818	$7,530	$7,029	$6,807	$6,704	$524	$59,868	$2,037,580
FY	2088	$7,818	$7,818	$7,818	$7,818	$7,029	$6,807	$6,704	$1,112	$60,745	$2,098,325
FY	2089 election	$7,818	$7,818	$7,818	$7,818	$7,029	$6,915	$6,704	$8,995	$68,736	$2,167,061
FY	2090	$7,818	$7,818	$7,818	$7,818	$7,029	$6,915	$6,704	$6,316	$66,057	$2,233,118
FY	2091	$7,818	$7,818	$7,818	$7,818	$7,530	$6,915	$6,704	$6,316	$66,558	$2,299,676
FY	2092	$7,818	$7,818	$7,818	$7,818	$7,530	$6,915	$6,807	$6,316	$66,661	$2,366,337
FY	2093	$7,818	$7,818	$7,818	$7,818	$7,530	$6,915	$6,807	$6,316	$66,661	$2,432,998
FY	2094	$7,818	$7,818	$7,818	$7,818	$7,530	$7,029	$6,807	$8,265	$68,723	$2,501,721
FY	2095	$7,818	$7,818	$7,818	$7,818	$7,530	$7,029	$6,807	$6,704	$524	$67,687	$2,569,408
FY	2096	$7,818	$7,818	$7,818	$7,818	$7,818	$7,029	$6,807	$6,704	$1,112	$68,563	$2,637,971
FY	2097 election	$7,818	$7,818	$7,818	$7,818	$7,818	$7,029	$6,915	$6,704	$8,995	$76,554	$2,714,526
FY	2098	$7,818	$7,818	$7,818	$7,818	$7,818	$7,029	$6,915	$6,704	$6,316	$73,875	$2,788,401
FY	2099	$7,818	$7,818	$7,818	$7,818	$7,818	$7,530	$6,915	$6,704	$6,316	$74,376	$2,862,778
										$0	$2,862,778

Model Three: Provided Space - No Museum or Public Programs
Model Cost Totals by FY - Model Three
All Cost Figures ($) in Thousands (000)

	FY													Model Three Total by Year	Model Three Cumulative Total
FY	2023	$524												$524	$524
FY	2024	$1,112												$1,112	$1,636
FY	2025 election	$8,995												$8,995	$10,631
FY	2026	$6,316												$6,316	$16,947
FY	2027	$6,316												$6,316	$23,263
FY	2028	$6,316												$6,316	$29,579
FY	2029	$6,316												$6,316	$35,895
FY	2030	$8,265												$8,265	$44,160
FY	2031	$5,880	$524											$6,404	$50,564
FY	2032	$5,880	$1,112											$6,992	$57,556
FY	2033 election	$5,880	$8,995											$14,875	$72,432
FY	2034	$5,880	$6,316											$12,196	$84,628
FY	2035	$5,880	$6,316											$12,196	$96,824
FY	2036	$6,005	$6,316											$12,321	$109,145
FY	2037	$6,005	$6,316											$12,321	$121,466
FY	2038	$6,005	$8,265											$14,270	$135,737
FY	2039	$6,005	$5,880	$524										$12,409	$148,146
FY	2040	$6,005	$5,880	$1,112										$12,997	$161,143
FY	2041 election	$6,005	$5,880	$8,995										$20,880	$182,024
FY	2042	$6,005	$5,880	$6,316										$18,201	$200,225
FY	2043	$6,005	$5,880	$6,316										$18,201	$218,427
FY	2044	$6,005	$6,005	$6,316										$18,326	$236,753
FY	2045	$6,005	$6,005	$6,316										$18,326	$255,079
FY	2046	$6,005	$6,005	$8,265										$20,275	$275,355
FY	2047	$6,005	$6,005	$5,880	$524									$18,415	$293,769
FY	2048	$6,005	$6,005	$5,880	$1,112									$19,003	$312,772

	FY								Model Three Total by Year	Model Three Cumulative Total
FY	2049 election	$6,005	$6,005	$5,880	$8,995				$26,886	$339,658
FY	2050	$6,005	$6,005	$5,880	$6,316				$24,207	$363,864
FY	2051	$6,005	$6,005	$5,880	$6,316				$24,207	$388,071
FY	2052	$6,005	$6,005	$6,005	$6,316				$24,332	$412,402
FY	2053	$6,005	$6,005	$6,005	$6,316				$24,332	$436,734
FY	2054	$6,005	$6,005	$6,005	$8,265				$26,281	$463,015
FY	2055	$6,005	$6,005	$6,005	$5,880	$524			$24,420	$487,434
FY	2056	$6,005	$6,005	$6,005	$5,880	$1,112			$25,008	$512,442
FY	2057 election	$6,005	$6,005	$6,005	$5,880	$8,995			$32,891	$545,333
FY	2058	$6,005	$6,005	$6,005	$5,880	$6,316			$30,212	$575,545
FY	2059	$6,005	$6,005	$6,005	$5,880	$6,316			$30,212	$605,757
FY	2060	$6,005	$6,005	$6,005	$6,005	$6,316			$30,337	$636,093
FY	2061	$6,005	$6,005	$6,005	$6,005	$6,316			$30,337	$666,430
FY	2062	$6,005	$6,005	$6,005	$6,005	$8,265			$32,286	$698,716
FY	2063	$6,005	$6,005	$6,005	$6,005	$5,880	$524		$30,425	$729,141
FY	2064	$6,005	$6,005	$6,005	$6,005	$5,880	$1,112		$31,013	$760,154
FY	2065 election	$22,805	$6,005	$6,005	$6,005	$5,880	$8,995		$55,696	$815,850
FY	2066	$6,005	$6,005	$6,005	$6,005	$5,880	$6,316		$36,217	$852,067
FY	2067	$6,005	$6,005	$6,005	$6,005	$5,880	$6,316		$36,217	$888,284
FY	2068	$6,005	$6,005	$6,005	$6,005	$6,005	$6,316		$36,342	$924,626
FY	2069	$6,005	$6,005	$6,005	$6,005	$6,005	$6,316		$36,342	$960,968
FY	2070	$6,005	$6,005	$6,005	$6,005	$6,005	$8,265		$38,291	$999,259
FY	2071	$6,005	$6,005	$6,005	$6,005	$6,005	$5,880	$524	$36,430	$1,035,689
FY	2072	$6,005	$6,005	$6,005	$6,005	$6,005	$5,880	$1,112	$37,018	$1,072,707
FY	2073 election	$6,005	$22,805	$6,005	$6,005	$6,005	$5,880	$8,995	$61,701	$1,134,409
FY	2074	$6,005	$6,005	$6,005	$6,005	$6,005	$5,880	$6,316	$42,222	$1,176,631
FY	2075	$6,005	$6,005	$6,005	$6,005	$6,005	$5,880	$6,316	$42,222	$1,218,853
FY	2076	$6,005	$6,005	$6,005	$6,005	$6,005	$6,005	$6,316	$42,347	$1,261,200

(Continued)

	FY Year										Model Three Total by Year	Model Three Cumulative Total
FY	2077	$6,005	$6,005	$6,005	$6,005	$6,005	$6,316				$42,347	$1,303,548
FY	2078	$6,005	$6,005	$6,005	$6,005	$6,005	$8,265				$44,296	$1,347,844
FY	2079	$6,005	$6,005	$6,005	$6,005	$6,005	$5,880	$524			$42,435	$1,390,279
FY	2080	$6,005	$6,005	$6,005	$6,005	$6,005	$5,880	$1,112			$43,023	$1,433,303
FY	2081 election	$6,005	$6,005	$22,805	$6,005	$6,005	$5,880	$8,995			$67,706	$1,501,009
FY	2082	$6,005	$6,005	$6,005	$6,005	$6,005	$5,880	$6,316			$48,227	$1,549,236
FY	2083	$6,005	$6,005	$6,005	$6,005	$6,005	$5,880	$6,316			$48,227	$1,597,464
FY	2084	$6,005	$6,005	$6,005	$6,005	$6,005	$6,005	$6,316			$48,352	$1,645,816
FY	2085	$6,005	$6,005	$6,005	$6,005	$6,005	$6,005	$6,316			$48,352	$1,694,169
FY	2086	$6,005	$6,005	$6,005	$6,005	$6,005	$6,005	$8,265			$50,301	$1,744,470
FY	2087	$6,005	$6,005	$6,005	$6,005	$6,005	$6,005	$5,880	$524		$48,441	$1,792,911
FY	2088	$6,005	$6,005	$6,005	$6,005	$6,005	$6,005	$5,880	$1,112		$49,029	$1,841,939
FY	2089 election	$6,005	$6,005	$6,005	$22,805	$6,005	$6,005	$5,880	$8,995		$73,712	$1,915,651
FY	2090	$6,005	$6,005	$6,005	$6,005	$6,005	$6,005	$5,880	$6,316		$54,233	$1,969,883
FY	2091	$6,005	$6,005	$6,005	$6,005	$6,005	$6,005	$5,880	$6,316		$54,233	$2,024,116
FY	2092	$6,005	$6,005	$6,005	$6,005	$6,005	$6,005	$6,005	$6,316		$54,358	$2,078,474
FY	2093	$6,005	$6,005	$6,005	$6,005	$6,005	$6,005	$6,005	$6,316		$54,358	$2,132,831
FY	2094	$6,005	$6,005	$6,005	$6,005	$6,005	$6,005	$6,005	$8,265		$56,307	$2,189,138
FY	2095	$6,005	$6,005	$6,005	$6,005	$6,005	$6,005	$6,005	$5,880	$524	$54,446	$2,243,584
FY	2096	$6,005	$6,005	$6,005	$6,005	$6,005	$6,005	$6,005	$5,880	$1,112	$55,034	$2,298,617
FY	2097 election	$6,005	$6,005	$6,005	$6,005	$22,805	$6,005	$6,005	$5,880	$8,995	$79,717	$2,378,334
FY	2098	$6,005	$6,005	$6,005	$6,005	$6,005	$6,005	$6,005	$5,880	$6,316	$60,238	$2,438,572
FY	2099	$6,005	$6,005	$6,005	$6,005	$6,005	$6,005	$6,005	$5,880	$6,316	$60,238	$2,498,810
											$0	$2,498,810

Model Four Centralized Archives - No Museum or Public Programs Model Cost Totals By FY - Model Three All Cost Figures ($) In Thousands (000)

				Model Four Total by Year	Model Four Cumulative Total
FY	2022	$99,510	construction cost for centralized archives.	$99,510	$99,510
FY	2023	$524	2nd module costs are in FY2061	$524	$99,510
FY	2024	$1,112		$1,112	$100,622
FY	2025 election	$3,225		$3,225	$103,847
FY	2026	$4,159		$4,159	$108,006
FY	2027	$4,159		$4,159	$112,166
FY	2028	$4,159		$4,159	$116,325
FY	2029	$4,159		$4,159	$120,485
FY	2030	$4,159		$4,159	$124,644
FY	2031	$4,221	$524	$4,745	$129,390
FY	2032	$4,221	$1,112	$5,333	$134,723
FY	2033 election	$4,221	$3,225	$7,446	$142,170
FY	2034	$4,221	$4,159	$8,381	$150,551
FY	2035	$4,221	$4,159	$8,381	$158,932
FY	2036	$4,221	$4,159	$8,381	$167,312
FY	2037	$4,221	$4,159	$8,381	$175,693
FY	2038	$4,221	$4,159	$8,381	$184,074
FY	2039	$4,221	$524	$8,967	$193,041
FY	2040	$4,221	$1,112	$9,555	$202,596
FY	2041 election	$4,221	$3,225	$11,668	$214,264
FY	2042	$4,221	$4,159	$12,602	$226,866
FY	2043	$4,221	$4,159	$12,602	$239,469
FY	2044	$4,221	$4,159	$12,602	$252,071
FY	2045	$4,221	$4,159	$12,602	$264,674

(Continued)

								Model Four Total by Year	Model Four Cumulative Total
FY	2046	$4,221	$4,221	$4,159				$12,602	$277,276
FY	2047	$4,221	$4,221	$4,221	$524			$13,188	$290,464
FY	2048	$4,221	$4,221	$4,221	$1,112			$13,776	$304,241
FY	2049 election	$4,221	$4,221	$4,221	$3,225			$15,889	$320,130
FY	2050	$4,221	$4,221	$4,221	$4,159			$16,824	$336,954
FY	2051	$4,221	$4,221	$4,221	$4,159			$16,824	$353,778
FY	2052	$4,221	$4,221	$4,221	$4,159			$16,824	$370,602
FY	2053	$4,221	$4,221	$4,221	$4,159			$16,824	$387,425
FY	2054	$4,221	$4,221	$4,221	$4,159			$16,824	$404,249
FY	2055	$4,221	$4,221	$4,221	$4,221	$524		$17,410	$421,659
FY	2056	$4,221	$4,221	$4,221	$4,221	$1,112		$17,998	$439,657
FY	2057 election	$4,221	$4,221	$4,221	$4,221	$3,225		$20,111	$459,768
FY	2058	$4,221	$4,221	$4,221	$4,221	$4,159		$21,045	$480,813
FY	2059	$4,221	$4,221	$4,221	$4,221	$4,159		$21,045	$501,858
FY	2060	$4,221	$4,221	$4,221	$4,221	$4,159		$21,045	$522,904
FY	2061	$4,221	$4,221	$4,221	$4,221	$4,159	$99,510	$120,555	$643,459
FY	2062	$4,221	$4,221	$4,221	$4,221	$4,159		$21,045	$664,504
FY	2063	$4,221	$4,221	$4,221	$4,221	$4,221	$524	$21,631	$686,136
FY	2064	$4,221	$4,221	$4,221	$4,221	$4,221	$1,112	$22,219	$708,355
FY	2065 election	$14,637	$4,221	$4,221	$4,221	$4,221	$3,225	$34,748	$743,103
FY	2066	$4,221	$4,221	$4,221	$4,221	$4,221	$4,159	$25,267	$768,370
FY	2067	$4,221	$4,221	$4,221	$4,221	$4,221	$4,159	$25,267	$793,637
FY	2068	$4,221	$4,221	$4,221	$4,221	$4,221	$4,159	$25,267	$818,903
FY	2069	$4,221	$4,221	$4,221	$4,221	$4,221	$4,159	$25,267	$844,170
FY	2070	$4,221	$4,221	$4,221	$4,221	$4,221	$4,159	$25,267	$869,437
FY	2071	$4,221	$4,221	$4,221	$4,221	$4,221	$4,221	$524	$25,853	$895,290
FY	2072	$4,221	$4,221	$4,221	$4,221	$4,221	$4,221	$1,112	$26,441	$921,731
FY	2073 election	$4,221	$14,637	$4,221	$4,221	$4,221	$4,221	$3,225	$38,970	$960,700
FY	2074	$4,221	$4,221	$4,221	$4,221	$4,221	$4,221	$4,159	$29,488	$990,189

										Model Four Total by Year	Model Four Cumulative Total
FY	2075	$4,221	$4,221	$4,221	$4,221	$4,159				$29,488	$1,019,677
FY	2076	$4,221	$4,221	$4,221	$4,221	$4,159				$29,488	$1,049,165
FY	2077	$4,221	$4,221	$4,221	$4,221	$4,159				$29,488	$1,078,653
FY	2078	$4,221	$4,221	$4,221	$4,221	$4,159				$29,488	$1,108,141
FY	2079	$4,221	$4,221	$4,221	$4,221	$4,221	$524			$30,074	$1,138,216
FY	2080	$4,221	$4,221	$4,221	$4,221	$4,221	$1,112			$30,662	$1,168,878
FY	2081 election	$4,221	$14,637	$4,221	$4,221	$4,221	$3,225			$43,191	$1,212,069
FY	2082	$4,221	$4,221	$4,221	$4,221	$4,221	$4,159			$33,710	$1,245,779
FY	2083	$4,221	$4,221	$4,221	$4,221	$4,221	$4,159			$33,710	$1,279,488
FY	2084	$4,221	$4,221	$4,221	$4,221	$4,221	$4,159			$33,710	$1,313,198
FY	2085	$4,221	$4,221	$4,221	$4,221	$4,221	$4,159			$33,710	$1,346,908
FY	2086	$4,221	$4,221	$4,221	$4,221	$4,221	$4,159			$33,710	$1,380,617
FY	2087	$4,221	$4,221	$4,221	$4,221	$4,221	$4,221	$524		$34,296	$1,414,913
FY	2088	$4,221	$4,221	$4,221	$4,221	$4,221	$4,221	$1,112		$34,884	$1,449,797
FY	2089 election	$4,221	$4,221	$14,637	$4,221	$4,221	$4,221	$3,225		$47,413	$1,497,209
FY	2090	$4,221	$4,221	$4,221	$4,221	$4,221	$4,221	$4,159		$37,931	$1,535,141
FY	2091	$4,221	$4,221	$4,221	$4,221	$4,221	$4,221	$4,159		$37,931	$1,573,072
FY	2092	$4,221	$4,221	$4,221	$4,221	$4,221	$4,221	$4,159		$37,931	$1,611,003
FY	2093	$4,221	$4,221	$4,221	$4,221	$4,221	$4,221	$4,159		$37,931	$1,648,934
FY	2094	$4,221	$4,221	$4,221	$4,221	$4,221	$4,221	$4,159		$37,931	$1,686,865
FY	2095	$4,221	$4,221	$4,221	$4,221	$4,221	$4,221	$4,221	$524	$38,517	$1,725,382
FY	2096	$4,221	$4,221	$4,221	$4,221	$4,221	$4,221	$4,221	$1,112	$39,105	$1,764,487
FY	2097 election	$4,221	$4,221	$4,221	$4,221	$4,221	$4,221	$4,221	$3,225	$51,634	$1,816,122
FY	2098	$4,221	$4,221	$4,221	$4,221	$4,221	$4,221	$4,221	$4,159	$42,153	$1,858,274
FY	2099	$4,221	$4,221	$4,221	$4,221	$4,221	$4,221	$4,221	$4,159	$42,153	$1,900,427

Model Five: Centralized Archives Plus Museum of the Presidency Model
Cost Totals by FY - Model Five
All Cost Figures ($) in Thousands (000)

	Presidential Terms				Museum	Model Five Total by Year	Model Five Cumulative Total
FY 2022	$99,510	Construction costs for initial archival module plus museum			55000	$154,510	$154,510
FY 2023	$524	2nd archival module construction in FY2061			0	$524	$155,034
FY 2024	$1,112				$0	$1,112	$156,146
FY 2025 election	$3,225				$3,457	$6,682	$162,828
FY 2026	$4,159				$4,703	$8,863	$171,691
FY 2027	$4,159				$4,703	$8,863	$180,554
FY 2028	$4,159				$4,703	$8,863	$189,416
FY 2029	$4,159				$4,703	$8,863	$198,279
FY 2030	$4,159				$4,703	$8,863	$207,142
FY 2031	$4,221	$524			$4,813	$9,559	$216,701
FY 2032	$4,221	$1,112			$4,813	$10,147	$226,847
FY 2033 election	$4,221	$3,225			$4,813	$12,260	$239,107
FY 2034	$4,221	$4,159			$4,813	$13,194	$252,301
FY 2035	$4,221	$4,159			$4,813	$13,194	$265,496
FY 2036	$4,221	$4,159			$4,813	$13,194	$278,690
FY 2037	$4,221	$4,159			$4,813	$13,194	$291,884
FY 2038	$4,221	$4,159			$4,813	$13,194	$305,078
FY 2039	$4,221	$4,221	$524		$4,813	$13,780	$318,858
FY 2040	$4,221	$4,221	$1,112		$4,813	$14,368	$333,227
FY 2041 election	$4,221	$4,221	$3,225		$4,813	$16,481	$349,708

	Presidential Terms						Museum	Model Five Total by Year	Model Five Cumulative Total
FY 2042	$4,221	$4,221	$4,159				$4,813	$17,416	$367,124
FY 2043	$4,221	$4,221	$4,159				$4,813	$17,416	$384,539
FY 2044	$4,221	$4,221	$4,159				$4,813	$17,416	$401,955
FY 2045	$4,221	$4,221	$4,159				$4,813	$17,416	$419,371
FY 2046	$4,221	$4,221	$4,159				$4,813	$17,416	$436,786
FY 2047	$4,221	$4,221	$4,221	$524			$4,813	$18,002	$454,788
FY 2048	$4,221	$4,221	$4,221	$1,112			$4,813	$18,590	$473,378
FY 2049 election	$4,221	$4,221	$4,221	$3,225			$4,813	$20,703	$494,080
FY 2050	$4,221	$4,221	$4,221	$4,159			$4,813	$21,637	$515,717
FY 2051	$4,221	$4,221	$4,221	$4,159			$4,813	$21,637	$537,355
FY 2052	$4,221	$4,221	$4,221	$4,159			$4,813	$21,637	$558,992
FY 2053	$4,221	$4,221	$4,221	$4,159			$4,813	$21,637	$580,629
FY 2054	$4,221	$4,221	$4,221	$4,159			$4,813	$21,637	$602,266
FY 2055	$4,221	$4,221	$4,221	$4,221	$524		$4,813	$22,223	$624,489
FY 2056	$4,221	$4,221	$4,221	$4,221	$1,112		$4,813	$22,811	$647,300
FY 2057 election	$4,221	$4,221	$4,221	$4,221	$3,225		$4,813	$24,924	$672,224
FY 2058	$4,221	$4,221	$4,221	$4,221	$4,159		$4,813	$25,859	$698,083
FY 2059	$4,221	$4,221	$4,221	$4,221	$4,159		$4,813	$25,859	$723,942
FY 2060	$4,221	$4,221	$4,221	$4,221	$4,159		$4,813	$25,859	$749,800
FY 2061	$4,221	$4,221	$4,221	$4,221	$4,159	$99,510	$4,813	$125,369	$875,169
FY 2062	$4,221	$4,221	$4,221	$4,221	$4,159		$4,813	$25,859	$901,027
FY 2063	$4,221	$4,221	$4,221	$4,221	$4,221	$524	$4,813	$26,445	$927,472
FY 2064	$4,221	$4,221	$4,221	$4,221	$4,221	$1,112	$4,813	$27,033	$954,505

(Continued)

	Presidential Terms							Museum	Model Five Total by Year	Model Five Cumulative Total
FY 2065 election	$14,637	$4,221	$4,221	$4,221	$3,225			$23,293	$58,042	$1,012,546
FY 2066	$4,221	$4,221	$4,221	$4,221	$4,159			$4,813	$30,080	$1,042,626
FY 2067	$4,221	$4,221	$4,221	$4,221	$4,159			$4,813	$30,080	$1,072,706
FY 2068	$4,221	$4,221	$4,221	$4,221	$4,159			$4,813	$30,080	$1,102,786
FY 2069	$4,221	$4,221	$4,221	$4,221	$4,159			$4,813	$30,080	$1,132,866
FY 2070	$4,221	$4,221	$4,221	$4,221	$4,159			$4,813	$30,080	$1,162,947
FY 2071	$4,221	$4,221	$4,221	$4,221	$4,221	$524		$4,813	$30,666	$1,193,613
FY 2072	$4,221	$4,221	$4,221	$4,221	$4,221	$1,112		$4,813	$31,254	$1,224,867
FY 2073 election	$14,637	$4,221	$4,221	$4,221	$4,221	$3,225		$4,813	$43,783	$1,268,650
FY 2074	$4,221	$4,221	$4,221	$4,221	$4,221	$4,159		$4,813	$34,302	$1,302,951
FY 2075	$4,221	$4,221	$4,221	$4,221	$4,221	$4,159		$4,813	$34,302	$1,337,253
FY 2076	$4,221	$4,221	$4,221	$4,221	$4,221	$4,159		$4,813	$34,302	$1,371,554
FY 2077	$4,221	$4,221	$4,221	$4,221	$4,221	$4,159		$4,813	$34,302	$1,405,856
FY 2078	$4,221	$4,221	$4,221	$4,221	$4,221	$4,159		$4,813	$34,302	$1,440,157
FY 2079	$4,221	$4,221	$4,221	$4,221	$4,221	$4,221	$524	$4,813	$34,888	$1,475,045
FY 2080	$4,221	$4,221	$4,221	$4,221	$4,221	$4,221	$1,112	$4,813	$35,476	$1,510,520
FY 2081 election	$4,221	$14,637	$4,221	$4,221	$4,221	$4,221	$3,225	$4,813	$48,005	$1,558,525
FY 2082	$4,221	$4,221	$4,221	$4,221	$4,221	$4,221	$4,159	$4,813	$38,523	$1,597,048
FY 2083	$4,221	$4,221	$4,221	$4,221	$4,221	$4,221	$4,159	$4,813	$38,523	$1,635,571
FY 2084	$4,221	$4,221	$4,221	$4,221	$4,221	$4,221	$4,159	$4,813	$38,523	$1,674,094
FY 2085	$4,221	$4,221	$4,221	$4,221	$4,221	$4,221	$4,159	$4,813	$38,523	$1,712,617
FY 2086	$4,221	$4,221	$4,221	$4,221	$4,221	$4,221	$4,159	$4,813	$38,523	$1,751,140
FY 2087	$4,221	$4,221	$4,221	$4,221	$4,221	$4,221	$4,221	$524	$4,813	$39,109	$1,790,249
FY 2088	$4,221	$4,221	$4,221	$4,221	$4,221	$4,221	$4,221	$1,112	$4,813	$39,697	$1,829,946

	Presidential Terms							Museum	Model Five Total by Year	Model Five Cumulative Total
FY 2089 election	$4,221	$4,221	$4,221	$14,637	$4,221	$4,221	$4,221	$3,225		$4,813	$52,226	$1,882,172
FY 2090	$4,221	$4,221	$4,221	$4,221	$4,221	$4,221	$4,221	$4,159		$4,813	$42,744	$1,924,916
FY 2091	$4,221	$4,221	$4,221	$4,221	$4,221	$4,221	$4,221	$4,159		$4,813	$42,744	$1,967,661
FY 2092	$4,221	$4,221	$4,221	$4,221	$4,221	$4,221	$4,221	$4,159		$4,813	$42,744	$2,010,405
FY 2093	$4,221	$4,221	$4,221	$4,221	$4,221	$4,221	$4,221	$4,159		$4,813	$42,744	$2,053,149
FY 2094	$4,221	$4,221	$4,221	$4,221	$4,221	$4,221	$4,221	$4,159		$4,813	$42,744	$2,095,894
FY 2095	$4,221	$4,221	$4,221	$4,221	$4,221	$4,221	$4,221	$4,221	$524	$4,813	$43,330	$2,139,224
FY 2096	$4,221	$4,221	$4,221	$4,221	$4,221	$4,221	$4,221	$4,221	$1,112	$4,813	$43,918	$2,183,143
FY 2097 election	$4,221	$4,221	$4,221	$4,221	$14,637	$4,221	$4,221	$4,221	$3,225	$4,813	$56,447	$2,239,590
FY 2098	$4,221	$4,221	$4,221	$4,221	$4,221	$4,221	$4,221	$4,221	$4,159	$4,813	$46,966	$2,286,556
FY 2099	$4,221	$4,221	$4,221	$4,221	$4,221	$4,221	$4,221	$4,221	$4,159	$4,813	$46,966	$2,333,522

End Notes

[1] Represents Major R&R from NARA base appropriations, not restricted appropriations for major projects.

[2] The addition of the Nixon textual holdings storage addition will result in an increase to O&M costs.

[3] Reflects $248,122 generated by the endowment required by the PLA for operating costs.

[4] Reflects $383,477 generated by the endowment required by the PLA for operating costs.

[5] Represents George W. Bush Library guard services, not included in total. In FY 2008, NARA only paid for one month of security guard services. That is why this security contract amount is not reflected in the total.

[6] O&M and R&R costs for the Office of Presidential Libraries (central office) in College Park, MD are not calculated separately from the cost of operations for NARA's facilities in Washington, DC, and College Park.

[7] O&M and R&R costs for the Presidential Materials Staff in Washington, DC, are not calculated separately from the cost of operations for NARA's facilities in Washington, DC, and College Park, MD.

[8] Until the completion of the archival storage addition at the Nixon Library in Yorba Linda, CA, NARA continues to maintain space in College Park, MD for Nixon records and staff. O&M and R&R costs for the Nixon staff are not calculated separately from the cost of operations for NARA's facilities in Washington, DC, and College Park, MD.

[9] Leadership in Energy and Environmental Design (LEED) Green Building Rating SystemTM encourages sustainable green building and development practices through the creation and implementation of universally understood and accepted tools and performance criteria.

[10] An inflation factor based on the Consumer Price Index inflation calculator was applied to original Library costs from dedication date through 2008.

[11] This year the Johnson Foundation will be contributing $1.8 million to the Library.

[12] The Architecture and Design Standards require that design and construction of any new Library be subjected to regular reviews by NARA to ensure that the standards are being met.

[13] H. Rep. 95-1487, at 15 (95th Cong., 2d Sess., Aug. 14, 1978).

[14] Hearings before a Subcommittee of the Committee on Government Operations, on H.R. 10998 and Related Bills on the Presidential Records Act of 1978, 95th Cong., 2d Sess., Feb. 23, 25, Mar. 2, 7, 1978, at 136.

[15] NARA recognizes that an incumbent President retains the constitutional authority to request that NARA provide him an opportunity to review Presidential records for constitutionally based privileges even after a statutorily established cut-off period for providing notice.

[16] The Reagan Library holds 57,552,000 pages of paper records; Bush 41 46,584,000 pages; and Clinton 73,834,000 pages. These numbers do not include the electronic holdings.

[17] Based in part on the article by Larry J. Hackman, The *Public Historian,* Vol. 28, No.3, pgs. 182 – 183.

[18] Currently, many of the Libraries are provided to the Government under perpetual use agreements at no cost to the Government. NARA does, however, assume all costs for upkeep of the NARA occupied portions of these facilities.

[19] We considered it premature, given the current state of technology, to cost out digitizing a majority of the collection in a preservation format that would allow for disposal of the paper records. Limiting the paper collection to items of great intrinsic value, e.g., records viewed or annotated by the President, correspondence with world leaders, and decision memoranda would save considerable space; however, given the cost of digitizing, storing digital media, and the staffing required to provide the metadata for each image, this is a more costly option at this time than storing the records in their original formats.

[20] Under the RAC program, through an interagency agreement between NARA and the CIA, classified records are scanned at each library, so that these materials can undergo declassification review in a centralized location in the Washington, DC area. NARA will incorporate the RAC into the NDC with the expectation that shared resources for declassification of Federal and Presidential records will lead to greater efficiencies and increased productivity.

[21] This model assumes that each new Presidential collection would require a staff equivalent to the size of the archival staff for the Bush 43 Library.

[22] The inflation factor is calculated using the Bureau of Labor Statistics, Consumer Price Index calculator.

In: Presidential Libraries: Elements and Considerations
Editor: Jamie D. Reynolds

ISBN: 978-1-61324-581-1
© 2011 Nova Science Publishers, Inc.

Chapter 7

STATEMENT OF SENATOR LIEBERMAN ON THE PRESIDENTIAL RECORDS ACT

Senate Homeland Security and Governmental Affairs Chairman Joe Lieberman, ID-Conn., entered the following statement into the record Tuesday on the Presidential Records Act:

Mr. President, recently the Obama Administration asked the National Archives to speed up its already planned release of Supreme Court nominee Elena Kagan's records from her time in the Clinton Administration.

I applaud the Administration's openness. But this speedy release of documents is not required by the current Presidential Records Act and might have been impossible under an executive order issued by former President George W. Bush. That order allowed former presidents, vice presidents, and their heirs to withhold the release of documents indefinitely by claiming executive privilege.

On his first day in office, President Obama repealed the Bush executive order, but a future President could just as easily change it back or add new impediments to the timely release of an Administration's records.

Mr. President, I have long championed legislation to make it clear that these documents are the property of the American people and therefore should be subject to timely release.

But we cannot move forward with this legislation because my friend, colleague and Ranking Member on the Judiciary Committee, Sen. Jeff Sessions, has placed a hold on it.

Regarding the release of the Kagan documents, Sen. Sessions recently told *The Washington Post*: "I think all the documents that are producible should be produced. The American people are entitled to know what kind of positions she took, and what kind of issues she was involved with during her past public service."

I agree with Senator Sessions and hope he will now release his hold on my legislation so this kind of speedy release of documents and the right of the American people to view them will be the legal standard for all future Presidents.

A little history will help explain how we got to where we are today.

Securing Presidential documents is a problem as old as the Republic. George Washington had planned to build a library on his estate at Mount Vernon to house his Presidential papers. But Washington died before he could get his plan underway and his heirs were not always careful stewards of our Founding President's legacy.

Some of the documents were so badly stored they were eaten by mice. Others were sold off or given away haphazardly. One of Washington's heirs even took to cutting the signature from Washington's correspondence and sending it to collectors.

In a letter, this heir wrote: "I am now cutting up fragments from old letters and accounts, some of 1760 ... to supply the call for anything that bears the impress of his venerated hand. One of my correspondents says, 'Send me only the dot of an *i* or the cross of a *t*, made by his hand, and I will be content.'"

Despite this inauspicious beginning in preserving our nation's history, for nearly two centuries it was presumed that the papers of former Presidents were their personal property to be disposed of however they or their heirs saw fit.

Think of all our national history that's been lost, destroyed or kept locked away far too long.

The bulk of Andrew Jackson's papers were scattered among at least 100 collections. Jackson's successor, Martin Van Buren, destroyed correspondence *he* decided was – I quote – "of little value."

The papers of Presidents Harrison, Tyler, Taylor, Arthur and Harding were destroyed in fires – sometimes by accident, sometimes intentional.

President Lincoln's son Todd burned his father's Civil War correspondence and threatened to burn all of his father's Presidential papers until a compromise was reached with the Library of Congress that kept most of the papers sealed until 1947. This delay helped fuel conspiracy theories that the papers were kept hidden because they would show that members of Lincoln's cabinet were part of the assassination plot – in effect, that Lincoln died in a coup.

Of course, when the papers were finally released, they showed that wasn't true, but it took 82 unnecessary years to put the rumor to rest.

These historical records are too valuable to be left to the judgment of former Presidents, the whims of their heirs, the caprice of nature or – as in George Washington's case – the appetite of rodents.

This situation finally began to change under President Franklin Roosevelt who, on Dec. 10, 1938, announced he would build a library on his estate in Hyde Park, NY, to house the papers and collections of his public life that stretched back to 1910, when he was elected to the state Senate of New York.

Roosevelt set a standard for openness, asking his aides and cabinet secretaries to contribute to the collection, and almost every President who followed carried on in the spirit of Roosevelt – also building libraries to house their papers.

But this system was voluntary and began to crumble with the resignation of our 37th President, Richard Nixon.

Nixon had an agreement with the General Services Administration (GSA) which would have allowed him to keep all his records locked away, including the infamous Watergate tapes, and mandated many of them be destroyed.

This put us right back where we started, with a former President choosing what historical records the public was entitled to. Congress passed legislation in 1974 specifically ordering that the federal government take control of Nixon's records and then in 1978 passed legislation declaring that Presidential papers were public property that must be turned over to the National Archives at the end of an Administration and be open to the public after five years.

Systems, however, were put in place to allow a former president to review documents and challenge their release on the grounds of executive privilege. But the presumption was in favor of openness unless the former president could show the court a compelling reason to withhold the documents.

But then, as mentioned, President Bush weakened the law with Executive Order 13233, issued on Nov. 1, 2001. Just to repeat, under this order, not only former presidents and their heirs, but vice presidents and their heirs as well, could withhold the release of documents by claiming executive privilege.

The order also required those challenging claims of executive privilege to prove in court that they have a "demonstrated, specific need" for the documents – an impossibly high standard since only the document's author can know precisely what a document contains.

And since the Executive Order also allowed for an indefinite review period, these records – housed in Presidential libraries maintained by the taxpayers – could be locked away for indefinite periods of time, making them about as useful as the ashes of Lincoln's letters.

In reversing Bush's executive order, President Obama made clear that only the sitting President can claim executive privilege – not their heirs, and not their vice presidents or the vice presidents' heirs.

In signing the new executive order, President Obama said: "Going forward, anytime the American people want to know something that I or a former President wants to withhold, we will have to consult with the Attorney General and the White House Counsel, whose business it is to ensure compliance with the rule of law. Information will not be withheld just because I say so. It will be withheld because a separate authority believes my request is well grounded in the Constitution."

This is wise public policy and should be the law of the land – subject to repeal only by Congress, not by executive order.

When President Roosevelt dedicated his library and began opening up his records and other artifacts to public view, he made it clear that this kind of openness is good for a democracy:

"The dedication of a library," Roosevelt said, "is in itself an act of faith. To bring together the records of the past and to house them in buildings where they will be preserved for the use of men and women in the future, a Nation must believe in three things. It must believe in the past. It must believe in the future. It must, above all, believe in the capacity of its own people so to learn from the past that they can gain in judgment in creating their own future."

This Congress can now reassert Roosevelt's faith in our democracy. That is why I urge my colleague, Sen. Sessions, to release his hold on H.R. 35 so we can pass it, get it to the President and make history now by preserving Presidential history as an open resource for Americans to learn from in the future.

CHAPTER SOURCES

The following chapters have been previously published:

Chapter 1 – This is an edited reformatted and augmented version of a Congressional Research Service publication, report R41513, dated December 1 , 2010.

Chapter 2 – This is an edited reformatted and augmented version of a Congressional Research Service publication, report R40209, dated February 24, 2011.

Chapter 3 – This is an edited reformatted and augmented version of a Congressional Research Service publication, report RS20825, dated August 6, 2009.

Chapter 4 – This is an edited reformatted and augmented version of a Congressional Research Service publication, report R40238, dated February 17, 2009.

Chapter 5 – This is an edited reformatted and augmented version of a United States Government Accountability Office publication, report GAO-11-390, dated February 2011.

Chapter 6 – This is an edited reformatted and augmented version of a National Archives and Records Administration publication, report PL 110-404, dated September 25, 2009.

Chapter 7 – These remarks were delievered as a statement given on June 8, 2010. Senator Libeberman on Presidental records Act.

INDEX

A

Abraham, 5, 29, 39, 69, 104
abuse, 23
access, viii, ix, 5, 12, 18, 19, 32, 40, 43, 44, 45, 47, 49, 58, 65, 67, 70, 72, 73, 77, 78, 79, 80, 81, 83, 84, 85, 86, 89, 91, 92, 93, 95, 100, 101, 102
accessibility, 87, 91
administrative support, 91, 99
adults, 69
advancement, 68
age, 8, 15, 74
agencies, 36, 60, 83
Air Force, 16, 69
Alaska, 97
American History, 23, 95
American Presidency, 23, 69, 84
appetite, 144
appointments, 45, 79
appropriations, 2, 4, 5, 11, 20, 29, 33, 39, 55, 74, 76, 142
Appropriations Act, 33, 37, 38
assassination, 144
assessment, 58, 78
assets, 42, 100
atmosphere, 35
authorities, 9, 72
authority, viii, 2, 5, 8, 12, 17, 18, 19, 22, 38, 40, 43, 44, 45, 46, 48, 49, 59, 61, 68, 71, 73, 79, 86, 87, 90, 142, 145

B

ban, 34
base, 73, 74, 77, 92, 94, 95, 97, 142

benefits, 13, 37, 69, 73, 86, 90, 91, 95, 96, 97, 99, 101
blends, 81
blogs, 41
Bureau of Labor Statistics, 142
bureaucracy, 35
burn, 144

C

Cabinet, 110
cabinets, 67
candidates, 58, 60
capital projects, 74
Capitol Visitors Center, 95
catalyst, 69
Census, 53
challenges, 45, 81, 92
charitable organizations, 64
charities, 23
Chicago, 103, 104
children, 23, 69, 102
CIA, 142
cities, 5, 88
citizens, 59, 69, 72, 100
City, 97
civic life, 69
civil rights, 69
Civil War, 144
clarity, 86
Clinton Administration, ix, 80, 83, 143
Clinton nomination, 28
closure, 80
Cold War, 84
collaboration, 16, 56
College Station, 3, 28, 37, 54, 106
college students, 69

commercial, 45, 52, 58, 60
communication, 45, 81
communities, 68, 69, 85, 88, 90, 91, 96, 101, 102
community, 69, 84, 91, 93, 101, 102, 103, 109
compensation, 60
competition, 23, 85, 96
compilation, 85
complement, 84, 88, 93, 94
complexity, 66, 68, 71, 79, 93
compliance, 39, 64, 74, 145
computing, 23
conditioning, 77
conference, 22, 81, 89
conflict, 19, 60
conflict of interest, 19
congress, 23, 25
Congress, v, vii, viii, 1, 2, 4, 5, 7, 8, 9, 10, 11, 12, 14, 15, 17, 18, 19, 20, 21, 22, 23, 24, 27, 28, 29, 30, 31, 32, 33, 34, 35, 36, 37, 38, 40, 41, 42, 43, 44, 46, 47, 48, 49, 55, 57, 60, 65, 68, 70, 71, 72, 73, 74, 78, 79, 82, 93, 95, 97, 103, 104, 105, 144, 145
conservation, 77, 78
Consolidated Appropriations Act, 33, 37, 38
conspiracy, 144
Constitution, 35, 59, 145
construction, 1, 2, 3, 4, 5, 7, 9, 12, 16, 17, 18, 20, 22, 28, 29, 36, 38, 51, 53, 54, 55, 57, 64, 67, 71, 74, 77, 87, 94, 97, 99, 106, 107, 108, 109, 135, 138, 142
Consumer Price Index, 142
consumption, 75
conversations, 37
coordination, 17, 55, 94
cost, 7, 9, 12, 23, 28, 30, 37, 44, 56, 57, 67, 69, 71, 73, 77, 84, 87, 88, 89, 90, 91, 92, 93, 94, 96, 97, 98, 99, 100, 101, 102, 106, 113, 115, 119, 135, 142
cost benefits, 97
cost saving, 84, 88, 93, 94, 96, 97, 98, 99
critical thinking, 68
cultural heritage, 102
curricula, 102

D

database, 47
DC metropolitan area, 95
democracy, 67, 100, 102, 145
depth, 96
destruction, 18
dignity, 14
directives, 59, 67
directors, 17, 59, 60, 61
disability, 81
disaster, 18
disclosure, 13, 19, 24, 27, 28, 29, 30, 31, 32, 33, 40, 43, 44, 45, 46, 47, 48, 49
dispersion, 8
disposition, 35, 72
District of Columbia, 53
diversity, 66, 88, 93
division of labor, 19
donations, 7, 10, 15, 28, 36, 39, 53, 55, 57, 76
donors, viii, 10, 13, 23, 27, 28, 30, 40, 93
draft, viii, 51, 62, 71

E

earnings, 12, 23, 76
economic downturn, 76
economies of scale, 99
editors, 21
education, 17, 55, 62, 68, 69, 74, 76, 84, 85, 87, 88, 90, 93, 94, 95, 96, 99, 100
educational experience, 100
educational institutions, 69
educational opportunities, 102
educational programs, 56, 62, 69, 84, 86, 90, 92, 102, 107
educational research, 24
educators, 68, 95, 102
election, 7, 36, 59, 69, 90, 115, 116, 117, 118, 122, 123, 124, 125, 126, 127, 128, 129, 130, 131, 132, 133, 134, 135, 136, 137, 138, 139, 140, 141
electronic systems, 81
e-mail, 62
emergency, 36
employees, viii, 39, 51, 52, 53, 55, 58, 59, 60, 64, 102
employment, 59
endowments, 11, 12, 33, 39, 53, 55, 64, 71, 76, 77
energy, 69, 75, 87
energy consumption, 75
enforcement, 46
environment, 88, 89, 93
environmental conditions, 71
equipment, 2, 5, 8, 9, 10, 11, 12, 38, 56, 57, 68, 71, 75
equity, 83
ERA, 83, 84, 96
erosion, 81
ethical standards, 14
ethics, 23, 33, 39, 59, 60
etiquette, 35
Europe, 67
evidence, 22, 53

evolution, 66, 94
executive branch, 44, 46, 49
executive order, viii, ix, 40, 43, 44, 45, 46, 47, 48, 49, 143, 145
Executive Order, 45, 46, 49, 82, 83, 145
executive orders, 49
executive power, 48
exercise, 69
expertise, 85, 93, 102, 103

F

fabrication, 107, 108, 110
faith, 145
families, 35, 37
family members, 29, 39
fear, 15
fears, 23
Federal Election Campaign Act (FECA), vii, 27, 30
federal facilities, 53
federal funds, 12, 29, 53, 92
Federal funds, 75
federal government, vii, viii, 1, 3, 4, 5, 6, 7, 10, 13, 14, 17, 18, 19, 20, 21, 23, 30, 35, 36, 37, 38, 39, 44, 49, 51, 54, 55, 57, 58, 144
Federal Government, ix, 16, 65, 69, 76, 83, 85, 96, 98, 109
federal law, 12, 29, 51, 57
Federal law, vii, 27, 58
Federal Register, 49
films, 22, 77
financial, ix, 17, 18, 30, 32, 45, 56, 65, 76, 85, 86, 96, 97, 101
financial incentives, 85
financial support, 17, 18, 76, 86, 101
financial system, 56
fires, 144
fiscal year 2009, 55, 56
flexibility, 68, 85, 90
flooding, 39
force, 82, 90
Ford, 3, 5, 14, 28, 37, 38, 54, 61, 69, 74, 75, 105, 109, 112
foreign policy, 45, 47, 83
foundations, vii, viii, 2, 4, 5, 11, 12, 13, 14, 15, 16, 17, 18, 19, 20, 23, 25, 28, 29, 30, 32, 33, 51, 52, 53, 56, 57, 59, 60, 61, 63, 64, 68, 84
fragments, 144
freedom, 100
friction, 17, 86
funding, vii, 2, 3, 5, 7, 9, 11, 12, 13, 14, 16, 18, 19, 21, 22, 27, 29, 32, 47, 56, 64, 66, 73, 76, 77, 78, 82, 84, 85, 86, 92, 94, 95, 96, 97, 98, 99, 100, 106, 107, 108, 109, 110, 113
fundraising, vii, 4, 19, 27, 28, 29, 30, 31, 32, 33, 40, 42, 60
funds, viii, 1, 2, 5, 7, 9, 10, 11, 12, 28, 29, 32, 33, 36, 38, 39, 51, 53, 55, 56, 60, 64, 66, 67, 73, 74, 75, 76, 77, 78, 87, 88, 90, 92, 106, 108

G

GAO, viii, 51, 52, 53, 54, 56, 57, 60, 62, 64, 147
General Services Administration's (GSA's) Administrator, vii, 1, 2
Georgia, 3, 28, 105
governments, 53
grades, 69
grants, viii, 40, 43, 46, 47, 58, 68, 92, 101
greed, 11
growth, 15, 71, 80, 96
GSA, vii, 1, 2, 8, 9, 10, 22, 52, 54, 61, 144
guidance, 52, 78
guidelines, 15, 47

H

health, 14, 62, 69
health care, 69
health problems, 14
historical collections, 90, 91
history, vii, ix, 2, 4, 6, 8, 13, 14, 21, 22, 24, 36, 39, 65, 68, 69, 79, 100, 102, 143, 144, 145
homes, 31
Honest Leadership and Open Government Act (HLOGA), vii, 27
host, 60, 85
House, 4, 8, 10, 11, 12, 13, 15, 16, 19, 20, 21, 22, 23, 24, 27, 28, 29, 30, 31, 33, 34, 35, 36, 37, 39, 40, 41, 42, 44, 46, 47, 53, 55, 68, 69, 78, 80, 83, 95, 145
House of Representatives, 53
House Report, 10
housing, 8, 13, 37, 55
human, 24
human right, 24
human rights, 24
humidity, 77

I

identification, 34
identity, 95, 101
illusions, 10

image, 142
images, 68
improvements, ix, 11, 38, 65, 71, 74, 82, 108, 109
income, 11, 13, 16, 29, 39, 56, 57, 71, 76, 77, 88, 99
income tax, 13
Independence, 3, 15, 28, 36, 54, 105
individuals, 13, 15, 39, 57, 66
industry, 14
infancy, 67
inflation, 75, 106, 107, 108, 109, 110, 111, 142
infrastructure, 39, 67, 71, 73, 74, 83, 88, 107, 108, 110
institutions, 16, 63, 68, 69, 94, 100
integration, 69
integrity, 72
interest groups, 30, 101
Internal Revenue Service, viii, 27, 30
intrinsic value, 142
invasions, 69
investments, 77
Iowa, 3, 9, 21, 28, 54, 105
Iran, 14
IRC, 12, 23, 30, 33
issues, ix, 2, 6, 13, 16, 23, 24, 25, 27, 28, 29, 32, 33, 34, 47, 59, 60, 65, 69, 78, 84, 94, 95, 101, 143

J

JFK Library Museum, 14
judiciary, 49
Judiciary Committee, 31, 143

L

land acquisition, 99
law enforcement, 46
laws, viii, 4, 8, 12, 20, 23, 51, 52, 53, 57, 58, 59
laws and regulations, viii, 51, 52, 53, 58
lead, 2, 88, 89, 142
learning, 5, 9, 38
LEED, 142
legal issues, 25
legislation, viii, 4, 6, 7, 10, 11, 19, 21, 23, 28, 29, 31, 32, 35, 36, 37, 40, 43, 47, 48, 68, 70, 71, 72, 97, 143, 144
lending, 16
librarians, 102
library–foundation relationships, viii, 51, 53, 63
life cycle, 94, 97
lifetime, 32
light, 2, 4
literacy, 69, 85

litigation, 80
loans, 16
lobbying, 23, 30, 33
local community, 91
local government, 53
loyalty, 59, 93

M

majority, 18, 80, 82, 85, 92, 100, 142
man, 15
management, 2, 29, 35, 36, 55, 57, 60, 67, 84, 88, 89, 90, 92, 94, 98, 99, 101
mark up, 15
marketing, 101
Maryland, 105
materials, vii, viii, 1, 2, 4, 6, 7, 8, 9, 11, 17, 18, 20, 35, 36, 37, 44, 45, 55, 57, 68, 72, 77, 78, 83, 84, 85, 86, 92, 93, 142
matter, 18, 28, 32, 60, 97
media, 30, 48, 60, 69, 142
medical, 45
memory, 14
messages, 81
mice, 144
military, 6, 49, 69
mission, 17, 60, 62, 64, 67, 68, 72, 75, 84, 85, 96, 100, 101
missions, 19, 28, 64
Missouri, 3, 7, 15, 28, 36, 103, 105
models, ix, 6, 12, 25, 36, 65, 66, 67, 70, 73, 84, 90, 93, 96, 97, 100, 101, 113
modernization, 88
modifications, 4, 110
modules, 84
museums, vii, 1, 13, 16, 19, 25, 28, 32, 55, 66, 84, 90, 92, 93, 95, 96, 101

N

National Archives and Records Administration (NARA), vii, viii, 1, 2, 14, 28, 35, 44, 51, 53
national security, 44, 45, 46, 47, 49, 79
National Security Council, 83
networking, 67
Newseum, 95
nominee, ix, 143
NPS, 107

Index

O

Obama, viii, ix, 24, 30, 33, 39, 40, 43, 44, 46, 47, 48, 67, 69, 71, 97, 98, 143, 145
Obama Administration, ix, 43, 143
Office of Management and Budget, 42, 64
officials, viii, 46, 51, 53, 54, 56, 59, 61, 72
openness, ix, 143, 144, 145
operating costs, 22, 68, 74, 76, 77, 100, 142
operations, ix, 1, 2, 7, 10, 11, 13, 14, 17, 28, 29, 39, 44, 60, 65, 71, 73, 87, 89, 91, 99, 142
opportunities, 69, 71, 74, 91, 95, 102
optimism, 12
outreach, 56, 75, 84, 85, 86
oversight, 9, 14, 29, 39, 99
ownership, 19, 23, 35, 55, 57, 70, 71, 72, 79

P

PACs, 13, 30
paradigm shift, 67
parents, 102
participants, 69
peace, 62
penalties, 23, 31, 33
permit, 48, 72, 77, 79
personality, 15
photographs, 20, 77
playing, 69
policy, 2, 15, 16, 28, 29, 30, 32, 33, 36, 44, 45, 47, 52, 53, 57, 60, 83, 88, 90, 91, 100, 145
policy issues, 28, 29
political action committees (PACs), 13, 30
political party, 59, 60
politics, 24, 35
polling, 59
precedent, 72
preservation, vii, viii, ix, 1, 2, 6, 7, 8, 12, 17, 22, 35, 36, 39, 40, 43, 47, 48, 49, 65, 72, 73, 77, 78, 83, 89, 91, 94, 97, 101, 142
presidency, 14, 17, 18, 23, 47, 48, 49, 67, 113
president, 14, 15, 16, 17, 24, 48, 55, 56, 64, 97, 113, 145
President, vii, viii, ix, 1, 2, 3, 4, 5, 6, 7, 8, 9, 11, 12, 14, 15, 17, 18, 19, 20, 21, 22, 23, 27, 28, 29, 30, 31, 32, 33, 35, 36, 37, 38, 39, 40, 43, 44, 45, 46, 47, 48, 49, 55, 56, 57, 66, 67, 68, 71, 72, 73, 76, 78, 79, 80, 81, 83, 84, 85, 88, 89, 90, 92, 93, 94, 95, 96, 97, 98, 103, 142, 143, 144, 145
President Clinton, 15, 27
President Obama, ix, 40, 43, 44, 46, 47, 48, 67, 97, 98, 143, 145
Presidential Administration, 84, 88
prevention, 23
principal laws, viii, 51, 53
principles, 59, 86
private ownership, 35, 71, 72, 79
privatization, 66
producers, 36
professionals, 95
profit, 28, 52, 58, 60, 86
program staff, 59, 99
programming, 2, 4, 11, 12, 14, 28, 29, 56, 73, 74, 84, 87, 88, 89, 91, 95, 102
project, 6, 7, 37, 59, 61, 73, 78
propaganda, 23
protection, 14, 44, 77
prototype, 6, 36
public affairs, 16
public interest, 22, 58, 86, 101
public life, 144
public policy, 145
public safety, 23
public service, 36, 105, 143
public support, 23
public-private partnerships, 86
publishing, 23

R

recommendations, viii, 51, 72, 99
reform, 38
Reform, 4, 19, 30, 31, 34, 40, 41, 53
regional facilities, 66
regulations, viii, 36, 51, 53, 58, 60, 61, 80, 85, 86, 87
regulatory changes, vii, 27
regulatory requirements, 72, 82
reimburse, 60
relatives, 6
rent, 90
repair, 39, 74, 77, 87, 89, 108, 109
reproduction, 16
requirements, vii, ix, 2, 3, 4, 7, 11, 12, 13, 17, 30, 31, 32, 33, 34, 38, 39, 48, 57, 59, 65, 67, 71, 72, 77, 80, 82, 85, 87, 99
research facilities, 71
researchers, vii, viii, 1, 5, 14, 15, 18, 51, 53, 54, 68, 69, 83, 94, 101
resolution, 47
resource allocation, 55
resources, 5, 17, 18, 56, 67, 69, 72, 76, 81, 85, 93, 95, 96, 101, 102, 142
response, 28, 30, 80, 81, 102
restoration, 39, 55

restrictions, viii, 8, 12, 22, 32, 33, 35, 64, 79, 80, 82, 88
retained earnings, 76
revenue, 14, 16, 17, 53, 56, 68, 76, 85, 101
rights, 8, 24, 51, 57, 69, 72
risk, 77, 78, 89, 90
risk assessment, 78
rodents, 144
role-playing, 69
rule of law, 145
rules, 31, 40, 46, 47, 52, 57, 58

S

safety, 23, 77
savings, 12, 71, 75, 84, 87, 88, 89, 92, 93, 94, 96, 97, 98, 99
scholarship, 13, 44, 48
school, 4, 16, 69, 100, 101, 102
scope, 5, 32, 33, 34, 69, 79
secondary school students, 100
security, 18, 44, 45, 46, 47, 49, 55, 71, 73, 76, 77, 79, 142
security guard, 142
seminars, 60
Senate, 4, 8, 9, 10, 11, 13, 19, 22, 23, 27, 28, 30, 31, 33, 34, 39, 40, 42, 46, 47, 70, 143, 144
services, 18, 60, 113, 142
shape, 8, 14, 62, 100, 102
showing, 113
silver, 75
social network, 67
software, 84
specialists, 55
specifications, 71
spreadsheets, 113
staff members, 102
staffing, 55, 73, 84, 87, 93, 98, 101, 142
stakeholders, 67, 103
state, 6, 9, 35, 38, 49, 53, 61, 68, 85, 91, 93, 142, 144
states, 21, 45, 82
statutes, 17, 36, 37, 57, 60, 61, 70
statutory authority, 71
storage, 15, 25, 67, 71, 74, 87, 88, 89, 91, 93, 94, 96, 106, 107, 108, 142
structure, 81, 85, 110
style, 81
supervision, 4, 5, 37, 38, 39, 44, 59
support staff, 73
Supreme Court, ix, 68, 71, 81, 143
Supreme Court nominee, ix, 143
surplus, 76
surrogates, 67
systematic processing, 81

T

taxpayers, 37, 145
teachers, 84, 102
technical comments, 62
technologies, 67, 92, 101
technology, 18, 67, 84, 91, 142
telephone, 41
telephone numbers, 41
temperature, 77
tension, ix, 13, 14, 15, 32, 65
tenure, 72
testing, 23
textiles, 78
The Presidential Libraries Act, v, vii, 1, 2, 7, 8, 10, 33, 38, 55, 57, 68, 70, 76
The Public Historian, 14, 15, 16, 20, 24, 25, 41, 142
time frame, 48, 113
Title I, 72
Title II, 72
Title V, 23
total costs, 11, 12, 113
tourism, 14, 101
trade, 45, 79, 99
traditions, 4
transactions, 6, 12, 22
transparency, vii, 27, 29, 32, 44
Treasury, 70
treatment, 18, 77, 78
trust fund, 10, 22, 56, 76
Trust Fund, 10, 22, 55, 68, 73, 76, 112

U

U.S. Office of Special Counsel, 52, 58, 64
United States, 1, 2, iii, v, vii, viii, 1, 2, 5, 7, 8, 9, 10, 11, 30, 31, 36, 38, 43, 44, 51, 55, 56, 61, 62, 65, 68, 70, 72, 80, 147
universities, 35, 57, 68, 84, 85, 92
updating, 56, 61, 75
utility costs, 10

V

variations, 55
vehicles, 77
ventilation, 77
venue, 16
Vice President, viii, 40, 43, 44, 45, 46, 47, 48, 49, 78
videos, 69

Index

Vietnam, 68
voicing, 31
vote, 31, 46, 47

W

walking, 13
war, 67
Washington, 5, 18, 20, 21, 22, 23, 24, 25, 33, 34, 37, 41, 42, 48, 49, 69, 72, 78, 83, 85, 88, 90, 91, 92, 94, 95, 97, 102, 103, 106, 142, 143, 144
web, 66, 67, 81, 84, 92, 94, 95, 106
web sites, 106

websites, 41, 100
White House, 12, 16, 35, 36, 37, 55, 68, 69, 78, 80, 83, 95, 145
William J. Clinton Foundation, 24, 28, 33
Wisconsin, 103
withdrawal, 80
World War I, 36
worldwide, 62

Y

Yale University, 103, 104, 105
yield, 77, 88